david hall

In the Company HEROES

An Insider's Guide to Entrepreneurs at Work

KOGAN
PAGE

This book is dedicated to my partner Ellen, for her love, support, friendship and wise counsel.

First published in 1999
Reprinted in 2000

Kogan Page Limited
120 Pentonville Road
London
N1 9JN
UK

Kogan Page Limited
163 Central Avenue, Suite 2
Dover
NH 03820
USA

© David Hall, 1999

British Library Cataloguing in Publication Data

A CIP record for this book is available from the British Library.

ISBN 0 7494 3060 5

Typeset by Kogan Page Limited
Printed and bound by Bell & Bain Ltd, Glasgow

contents

preface

Entrepreneurship *n*   A human creative act requiring vision, passion, sheer guts and determination.

Entrepreneur *n*   A hero/heroine, a warrior, a maverick.

What is this book about?

This book tries to answer the questions most people want to know about starting, building, revitalizing or reinventing a business:

- What preparation do people undertake before embarking on their entrepreneurial career?
- How do they start businesses and sleep easy in their beds?
- How do they grow successful businesses?
- How do they revitalize and reinvent mature businesses?
- How do they keep their organizations entrepreneurial, resisting the temptation to become bureaucratic and over managed?

The book seeks to answer these questions by providing the wisdom from 50 successful entrepreneurs from around the world. In effect a book by entrepreneurs for entrepreneurs. You are invited to join them 'in the company of heroes'.

Entrepreneurs are heroes. They make their contribution by creating successful businesses through their vision, passion and obsessive commitment.

The extraordinary power of the entrepreneurial mind continues to create new exciting businesses across the world. Wherever entrepreneurship is a common occurrence, the economy booms.

Entrepreneurs have been described as 'people who start businesses and make businesses grow', but that's far too narrow a definition. This book is not simply for those of you who would like to start a business of your own. It is also designed for those who work in established companies where the entrepreneurial spark has been extinguished. As companies grow larger and mature they frequently suffer from a creeping paralysis; systems and bureaucratic procedures become more important than ideas or innovation. They become incapable of reacting swiftly to market trends and new consumer preferences. Restoring these essential skills in mature companies is vital to protect jobs and enhance living standards.

In this book we will also meet people who have discovered the secret of revitalizing their companies, reapplying entrepreneurial principles to the mature business and transforming its performance. Entrepreneurs are also people who generate and apply creative ideas to business; they spot an opportunity and find a creative way of meeting it. Risk-taking, believing enough in your idea to gamble your future livelihood on it, is another entrepreneurial trait. But, after years of working as an entrepreneur and working with entrepreneurs I personally prefer this definition:

> An entrepreneur is someone who builds a business of value, often from practically nothing.

Read this book and you will see what I mean.

Without entrepreneurs an economy can run along under its own steam for a while, but in the end it is bound to stagnate and fall behind. The whole community suffers the consequences. That's why entrepreneurs, in my view, are heroes we cannot do without.

While this book celebrates the achievements of up-and-coming entrepreneurs, it also has a practical purpose. Many volumes have been written about the life stories of entrepreneurs in the past, but none have set out to analyze and describe how they actually create valued businesses from nothing. I try to put that right here, by giving you access to the recipes for success used by 50 successful new entrepreneurs, unsung heroes, from around the globe, and my own experiences of working with entrepreneurs and of running a business.

In Britain, the skills of the entrepreneur have been under-valued until very recently. In fact, entrepreneurship has been so undervalued that we have not even bothered to invent a word to describe it. So we borrow the French word *entrepreneur*. If you need any further evidence of the lack of commitment to entrepreneurship in the UK, answer this question – who is the most senior person responsible in the UK government for looking after the interests of entrepreneurs? Don't know? Neither do I. Who looks after the interest of entrepreneurs in the USA? President Bill Clinton, who personally leads the Small Business Administration.

The lack of esteem I found as I visited and interviewed many of our most enterprising business people in my view reflects a deep-seated prejudice in Britain against people who have the guts to set up their own businesses and make a go of it. We can trace it back to the elitist nature of British society a hundred years or so ago, when being in 'trade' was regarded as socially inferior to working in the professions or owning a country estate. Although entrepreneurs may be heroes they are not the ones who get the medals, particularly in the UK.

Although we've made great strides in the UK over the past 10 years to make business attractive to the brightest and best, the stigma still regrettably sticks. Entrepreneurs in Britain are too often equated with racketeers and spivs, epitomized by the British TV character Arthur Daley. Arthur thrives in a world of dodgy deals and hoodwinked customers. I am sure that there is an Arthur Daley equivalent in most countries. As we'll see, the true entrepreneur bears no resemblance to the Arthur Daleys of this world. Stereotyping of this sort is regrettable and needs eradicating. This book I hope will make a contribution to that important task.

But first let me introduce myself; I started my own business 17 years ago, literally on the kitchen table, and built it up to employ over 100 people before selling it to the management three years ago. This business would be described, I suppose, as management consultancy, but the term conjures up so many images of smart inexperienced MBAs going round installing business systems and drawing up elaborate business plans that I never used the term. Instead I saw my company and myself as facilitators, helping our clients to help themselves. In the course of my work I got to know many up-and-coming business people and you'll meet some of them in the pages of this book.

Five years ago, I was asked to make a study of entrepreneurs on behalf of Scottish Enterprise, an agency charged by the UK government with the support and regeneration of the Scottish economy. To start with, I looked into what research there was into the practice of entrepreneurship: amazingly, very little had ever been done in the UK. Feeling like an explorer venturing into unknown territory, I spent many months meeting successful entrepreneurs and gathering information on how they had gone about building up their businesses.

In addition, my quest for knowledge took me to the USA, where I met US entrepreneurs and discovered Babson College near Boston, a college that has specialized in teaching entrepreneurship skills for more than 40 years, putting most of the UK business schools to shame. At Babson they see the successful entrepreneur as the lynchpin in creating the most dynamic and entrepreneurial economy in the world. Armed with the information in this book, I would like to try to help UK businesses to do the same.

Putting together the experience of successful UK entrepreneurs with those in the US, and adding for good measure examples I have come across in South Africa and Western Australia, will, I hope, provide inspiration and practical help to people everywhere who want to make a success of business.

Why was this book written?

Before settling down to read about the entrepreneurs and to absorb the lessons of their success, it's perhaps worth emphasizing why I wrote the book and why I hope you'll find it a refreshing read.

- Entrepreneurship has been called the 'silent revolution'. There is very little written about it compared with, say, the revolution in Information Technology. Yet some people are already predicting it will be the next major wave to transform the economic prospects of many countries. At the same time, surveys show that more people than ever want to work for themselves, and many new university graduates now want to set up their own business in preference to working for larger companies.
- Traditional studies of entrepreneurs do very little to guide people on how to go about becoming an entrepreneur. Instead they have focused on the personalities of a few well-known business people, or tell their life stories. This is of limited value to people wanting to know *how* to become successful entrepreneurs.
- Most business books deal with big business, ignoring the fact that 90% of people are employed in small businesses. As a result, the real driving forces of entrepreneurship, which is a phenomenon often associated with small to medium-sized companies, remains shrouded in mystery and myth.
- Many businesses that were once entrepreneurial have become stale and need to rediscover innovation and entrepreneurship. The experience of entrepreneurs is just as relevant for these companies as for start-up businesses.
- I write as a successful entrepreneur myself, and as one who's been fascinated by the entrepreneurial process since making *Winning*, a television series about creating business success, for the BBC in 1992. Meeting some of the UK's most successful entrepreneurs was a heartening process, and I detected common threads to their stories no matter what the business or where it was. I became convinced we needed to study the recipes used to create business success and pass the knowledge on.

Recipe is a good word. What I have tried to do here is to show that the entrepreneurial business process is as varied and diverse as the work of a master chef. Each business, like each dish, needs its own recipe for success. People who read this book can pick and choose which of the recipes or steps of recipes, provided by practising entrepreneurs, most closely match their own particular circumstances and the sort of problems they have to face.

However, the book does not pretend to suggest that there is one 'right way'. Nothing is the answer to everything. That is why I provide different approaches for you to choose from.

You will also find that the entrepreneurial processes change as the business grows. So, for example, at start-up I present a basic selling process to help those new to selling. Later in growing a business, entrepreneurs need more advanced selling and negotiating processes. Similarly, team building is dealt with differently at three stages of the business's development. This reflects the reality of how entrepreneurs develop their capabilities to match the growth stage of their enterprises.

If, by the time you close the last page, you have not gained some real understanding of what makes entrepreneurs tick and why in the end they succeed, I shall be disappointed.

May the entrepreneurial force be with you.

acknowledgements

Entrepreneurs cannot succeed alone, and neither can writers. My sincere thanks to my colleagues and supporters:

- Andy Forester, who helped me to write the book and contributed much to its flow and to all the entrepreneurs who allowed me to share their stories and wisdom, hopefully for the benefit of others.
- Pat Lomax of Kogan Page, who spotted the opportunity to create *In the Company of Heroes*.
- My friends around the globe, who introduced me to the heroes, including: Helen Jones and Terry Ord in Australia, Hennie Bornman in South Africa and Rich McGourty in the USA.
- The sponsors of my research work, especially Dr Brian McVey of Scottish Enterprise, John Taylor, the former CEO of The Development Board of Rural Wales, and Christopher Duff, CEO of Rotherham Chamber of Commerce, Training and Enterprise.
- Angela Mason, my personal assistant, who typed and checked the manuscript, she says it felt like 500 times!

one

understanding
entrepreneurs

- The dream
- Refugees from large corporations
- Creating value from practically nothing
- Taking the risk
- Beg, borrow, befriend
- Taking the long view
- Spotting an opportunity
- Exploiting an opportunity
- The skills of the entrepreneur
- The rest of the book

Many people who could successfully start up a business are put off by a belief that they are just not cut out for it. 'I have no head for figures', 'I haven't a clue about what's involved in drawing up a business plan', 'I haven't been to business school', and 'I haven't the leadership qualities required'.

But all this is based on a misconception. Namely that the qualities needed to start the business are the ones typically displayed by business executives turned out by the top business schools – the ability to manipulate a balance sheet, to understand economic value-added techniques, or to develop a detailed corporate strategy for the future. Without such training and the right personality to go with it, the conventional wisdom holds, people are condemned to work forever as employees.

This is just not true in real life. Ten years of working with successful entrepreneurs, and observing how they do the business, has convinced me of one thing more than any other.

Successful entrepreneurs think, talk and behave in a completely different way from the way we have been told business people should think, talk and behave.

Few of them have any business school training, and few are people who would stand out in a crowd. What they do share is an inner drive and an ability to spot opportunities that other people might miss. The good news is that such thinking and behaviour is not something you are born with, but like any craft it can be acquired and developed.

In this first chapter I want to introduce you to the factors they have in common, some of which you may find you share.

The dream

Most entrepreneurs start with an idea about how they might change the lives of themselves, their families, and occasionally even the world. They want to be their own boss, to feel that they are in control of their lives. They want to build a better and more secure future for their family. In the long run they want to be rich enough to stop worrying about money, to feel good about themselves, to be free.

Dave Wallinga had the dream. Dave launched DNA Visual Business Solutions Inc. in Chicago in 1994.

They now have a staff of 12 and a turnover of $3 million providing Internet consulting and development services with a special interest in e-business and the management of knowledge. Dave was tired of being a cost centre; he wanted to be the business.

> I wanted to work in a business where what I do is the business.

Many also want to feel they've made some difference to the wider community, to make a mark – no matter how small – on the face of history.

Phil Crane had the dream. Phil started Deep Sea World in Edinburgh in the early 1990s. Built into the natural landscape on the north shore of the Forth Bridge, Sea World is a Disney-style visitor attraction, which employs 80 people in the high season.

> I really enjoy the excitement of building a business and making money. It's great. I always wanted to be financially independent so when I spotted the opportunity to start Deep Sea World I thought this business has legs, it will deliver my dream of doing something that was fun, educational, entertaining and helping the environment.

Refugees from large corporations

However, more than half of the entrepreneurs I've worked with and interviewed were not just driven by the dream. They had often worked for years in larger companies and had become increasingly frustrated at the lost opportunities that their companies had showed little interest in pursuing.

Norman White is a good example. He's a non-executive director of Calluna plc (floated on the USM [Unlisted Securities Market] of the London Stock Exchange in October 1994, joined Official List, December 1996) at Glenrothes in Scotland, a company he co-founded in 1991 as managing director and which now employs over 120 people and exports 90 per cent of its products. He was an academic scientist, researching theoretical physics, who moved into industry in 1975 to expand his horizons. He joined Burroughs, a US-owned multinational specializing in office and computer equipment. His first job was as an engineer working on the design and development of advanced disk drives. Since that time he has been directly involved in co-founding start-up technology companies:

> I enjoyed my time at Burroughs. But the company wasn't organized to take advantage of the enormous pace of change brought about by the microchip revolution. It was clear that computing systems were going to become smaller and more compact. The future lay in exploiting this trend and using new technologies to that end. In my case, I could see how disk drives could be miniaturized but the parent company had too much inertia and was too involved in its existing programmes to take that step, which was quite frustrating.
>
> There were three other senior managers in our plant who felt the same way and we shared a common enthusiasm to do our own thing. We had a vision of how a new company could be very successful. We took our courage in both hands and left as a group to start the company, which we called Rodime (floated [as Rodime plc] on NASDAQ (New York) September 1983. Joined Official List of London Stock Exchange, 1986) to concentrate on this new technology. We never regretted leaving behind the security of the big company. In fact it was an exhilarating time.

In a sense, people like Norman White are refugees from big business. The flight of intellectual capital this involves should worry big businesses, but it apparently rarely does.As the Norman White story suggests, successful entrepreneurs don't see themselves going off to run a one-person show, they set out from the start to create a valued business by exploiting their new business opportunity.

Most entrepreneurs recognize they need help along the way. Being an ideas man or woman doesn't make you a good administrator or a marketing wizard. They have to find competent people with quite different skills to join them along the way.

Take Tom Hunter, one of the great success stories in Scotland. Tom had a bright idea that there was money to be made in selling branded sporting products in an increasingly health-conscious nation.

> I borrowed £10,000 in 1989 and started selling training shoes from the back of a van. I then noticed there was excess space in two of the high street fashion retailers and I suggested I take a corner of their shop and give them a commission, and they took me up on it.

He built up Sports Division, an empire of retail shops employing 7,500 people, which he has just sold for £290 million. He freely admits his success is due to building a strong team. His forte has been in choosing the right people to do the jobs he would just be no good at.

Tom quickly realized that recruiting good people into his team was going to be critical to his growth plan.

> All my key people have come through personal recommendations. My job was to build our team and keep everybody feeling part of it. They needed to feel that there's a role to play, that their voice is heard and they were not just dictated to from the top.

When Tom wanted to expand into England and really grow his business he recognized he needed to find someone with 'big retail experience' to enhance his team's skills, and the rest is history.

The need to build a balanced team to run the business is a theme covered in greater depth in Chapter 7.

Creating value from practically nothing

Everyone imagines that the most successful entrepreneurs need to find large sums of money to get them started. In fact there's a whole government support industry built on that assumption. But in reality most of our entrepreneurs had very little money of their own to begin with. They were not privileged people, neither were they very highly educated.

What they had in common was an ability to spot a business opportunity and pursue it relentlessly.

Take, for example, the case of John Pye of Reflex Systems Ltd, one of Yorkshire's most successful new entrepreneurs. He came from a humble background, left school and became a diesel fitter for a short time. He then trained as a dental technician.

> From being 5 years old I learnt to play the piano, which allowed me to subsidize my income. I earned £45 a week as a trainee dental technician and about £50 a week for doing two 20-minute musical spots.

John felt that there had to be more to life than this, so he took a job with a music retailer. Working behind the counter for a music retailer in Rotherham for very little money, mainly commission based, didn't look like a great start in life until an opportunity unexpectedly came along.

One day his boss announced he was closing the business down. He'd had enough, and John would have to find another job. In an area of high unemployment, finding another job was not going to be easy. John was only 19 and an unlikely businessman, but he had already come to the view that the business had far more potential than the owner realized:

> He had about 2,000 square feet of retail space and a small but loyal customer base, so I thought I could make a go of it.

John's approach was a classic example of how to get going with no cost to himself:

> I negotiated a rent-free period and contacted suppliers; I negotiated a supply on a sale or return basis, with time-scales attached.

All that was needed now was a modest cash reserve to pay for the initial stock and the wages of the staff until the business got going. John reckoned he'd need about £2,500. *With a persistence that is the mark of almost all entrepreneurs* he went knocking on the doors of all the local banks until he found a manager willing to lend him the money without strings, and with no security of any kind to back it up.

'*He just seemed to like my face and recognized my determination,*' says John.

That's how, before he was 20, John found himself unexpectedly running a business. He knew very little about business practice. He just took a common-sense decision to make a go of it and picked up the ropes of running the business as he went along.

He illustrates one of the major themes of this book. Any business skills needed by the entrepreneur can be picked up by almost anybody. A whole support infrastructure already exists in most places to provide these skills. Don't let a lack of such skills put you off.

John Pye now presides over an empire in Yorkshire, which consists of two operating divisions, specializing in the design and installation of commercial audio systems and the design and installation of closed circuit television and associated technologies. The business employs up to 50 people on a direct and non-direct basis and supplies products and services to many household names throughout the leisure, retail and industrial sectors. The two divisions combined produce a substantial turnover with an excellent bottom line profit, whilst John Pye still retains a 99 per cent holding.

Entrepreneurs like John who started with nothing and built up substantial businesses are not the exception. Even in industries usually regarded as high entry cost businesses, where investment in research and development is required, I've come across extraordinary success stories

Robert Webster who runs Ztagg is a good example. In 1994 Robert was walking along a Gold Coast Beach in Australia with some friends, discussing the problems of glare that they all faced as surfers. Whilst they all wore sunglasses on the beach, they took them off when they hit the water. They recognized that the sun reflecting off the water and particularly the white foam of the breakers had the potential to cause severe eye damage, including skin cancer.

> The glare is so bright that it can actually be painful to open your eyes, and there have been times when my mates and I have actually been temporarily blinded. The crazy thing is that every time I would get out of the water I would be reminded of this problem. But really this has existed for as long as people have been surfing, yet none, not even the massive, multinational sunglasses companies have tackled this.

So he started to explore the possibilities for eyewear that were comfortable, would stay on the wearer's head, not fog up and not get mangled after the surfer gets dumped by tons of water. Apart from these practical issues, any design would also have to accommodate the aesthetic demands of the surfers to look good.

After months of research, development and testing, a new eyewear combination was completed and formal application made for a provisional patent and design registration.

Since initiating his patent and design registrations in Australia, Robert has applied for patent protection in other countries. This is a complex and time-consuming process; however, eventually these applications should give Robert and his company a monopoly in several trade mark classes, including eyewear, clothing, footwear and headgear.

At this stage the research, development and intellectual property rights expenses exceed sales.

As Robert said:

> The future looks less bright!

Taking the risk

However many safety nets entrepreneurs seek to construct beneath themselves, at some point they have still have to risk everything in the pursuit of their dream.

This is what makes them different from every other profession and in my view is another reason why they are heroes.

There is no other club in the world that when you join you put everything on the line, including your personal assets, reputation, ego, sanity and sometimes your personal relationships.

The upside is that there are few better ways to have as much fun, or feel as fulfilled, as being an entrepreneur.

Beg, borrow, befriend

If there is a good business opportunity to be seized, the successful entrepreneur does not allow a lack of money to stand in the way. This is one of the most striking conclusions to be drawn from my research. John Pye and Tom Hunter are good examples. It all runs counter to the received wisdom, which tells us that entrepreneurs need to go out and raise large sums in venture capital if they are to succeed. Turn to a government support agency such as Business Link in the UK and you'll be advised to draw up a business plan (with help from their team of advisers) containing projections of how the company will develop and how much working capital is required to get it there. Banks respect this sort of grand plan, and are prepared to lend to support it, although they generally want to secure the loan against the assets of the would-be businessperson. As a result some businesses get off to a bad start, being saddled with debt from day one.

The experiences of John Pye and Tom Hunter suggest this is not the way to build a sound business. Few would-be entrepreneurs have all the resources they need. But instead of borrowing money on a grand scale, they turn instead to family and friends to get them started. They literally 'beg, borrow, and befriend' to get the required resources.

To give you an example, take a look at Neil Gibson – now Managing Director of the JHB Group in Scotland, one of Scotland's new entrepreneurial companies. In 1987 Neil was working in Glasgow for JHB, a company that provided a painting and protective coating service to the gas industry. It had been taken over and sold several times over, and the frequent changes in ownership unsettled the whole business. Neil organized a management buy-out at a knock-down price and set about running the business himself. Many people in Neil's position would have been tempted to borrow money to equip an office to replace the antiquated oak-panelled cupboard the former MD had used and take on a secretary to give him the status an MD is entitled to. Neil did neither of these things. Instead:

> I got a carpenter friend to convert my attic so that I could use it as an office. I installed a telephone extension from the household line. Then I

persuaded my sister to do any typing I required during her lunch hour. This was my base for the next two years, by which time I had got the business off the ground.

David Latham runs the high-tech Labtech Limited in Presteigne, Mid-Wales, which supplies microwave technology to the electronics industry, and he knows all about beg, borrow, befriend.

When Dave wanted to open a new factory he begged, borrowed and befriended people to the extent that he marshalled £3 million of high-tech electronic kits for the princely sum of £120,000.

We bought second hand and did deals all over the place in order to equip our new facility.

Far from being a disadvantage, a lack of resources seems to spur entrepreneurs to make things happen. It provides drive and commitment. Conversely, access to unlimited resources can have the opposite effect and might explain why large companies with big budgets often struggle to be entrepreneurial. That's one reason why 95 per cent of all radical innovations in the 20th century, be it in the field of cars, computers, photocopiers, even X-ray equipment, have come from companies employing fewer than 20 people.

In fact, having too much cash can actually dampen the entrepreneurial spirit. Most business growth is funded from retained profits rather than from borrowing against future profits. The best entrepreneurs seem to realize this truth instinctively.

Taking the long view

One of the most prevailing myths about these enterprising people is that they have a 'get rich quick' mentality – a sort of 'here today, gone tomorrow' attitude to business. It is enshrined in the common perception of entrepreneurs as 'smart operators' or even 'racketeers' in the Arthur Daley mould.

In fact successful entrepreneurs aren't like that. Yes, they want to be rich – but they also want to build a business that will last, often something that can be passed on to the family. They exhibit a patient determination in the face of the inevitable setbacks, they persist, and they generally get there in the end. They also are often public-spirited, getting real satisfaction in building something of lasting value to the community.

A good example would be Terry Bramall, now Chairman of Keepmoat plc, a fast-expanding Yorkshire building firm. Terry's father started his building business 70 years ago. Now Keepmoat is one of Britain's top companies.

> We may have started in a small way in a joiner's yard in Wath-Upon-Dearne but we always wanted to become a substantial employer in an area where coal-mines were being closed and men thrown on to the street. We put that aim in our mission statement. The road to success has been long and hard. There have been quite a few bumps along the way – but in the end we've achieved our goal. We've now have a business employing a thousand people and a turnover of £100 million a year. And, yes, after 20 years, I am delighted with our success.

Terry Bramall remains a modest and private man. He doesn't fit that other popular image of the entrepreneur, the flamboyant and publicity-conscious style of business leader better described as a tycoon. Richard Branson in Britain would be a good example of someone who fits this popular image, but he is very much the exception. Most entrepreneurs are ordinary people like you and me: it just so happens they do extraordinary things – that is what makes them heroes.

A glossary of terms

Just to be sure we grasp the notion of what being an entrepreneur is all about, and to dispel any misconceptions and confusions you might have, let's turn to the entrepreneur's dictionary for help:

Lifestyle business *n*	Self-employed person not seeking to employ people or grow a business.
Wheeler dealer *n*	Only interested in making a fast buck. Typified by Arthur Daley or that other TV character, Del Boy. A real-life example would be a racketeer like Robert Maxwell. Confused in the UK with entrepreneurs.
Tycoon *n*	Entrepreneurs who have become very big, very rich and very famous. Typified in the UK by Richard Branson and Anita Roddick. Most books about them project them as typical entrepreneurs, when they are very much the exception.
Entrepreneur *n*	Somebody who starts and builds something of long-term value, often from practically nothing. Usually an unsung hero.

Spotting an opportunity

The one common feature that distinguishes all entrepreneurs is their ability to spot a business opportunity and to react quickly to take advantage of it.

We've seen it already in the cases we have looked at:

- Norman White saw that the trend to miniaturization created new opportunities for a business that could produce the specialized hardware that was needed.
- John Pye saw there was an opportunity to provide for the growing need for good sound systems.
- Tom Hunter became aware that there was a untapped demand for fashionable sportswear in Scotland.

But opportunities can present themselves almost anywhere.

John Noble of Loch Fyne Oysters Limited is unlike the other entrepreneurs we've met so far in coming from a family with money. His father owned a 12,000-hectare estate on the shores of Loch Fyne in the Scottish Highlands. The problem John faced was finding cash to pay substantial 'death duties' when his father died and left him the estate.

> We had some forestry and sheep-farming on the estate. But they didn't make much money, not enough to settle the debts or even make a profit. There was tourism but it was pretty seasonal. Then it suddenly struck us. Loch Fyne is a beautiful sea loch with exceptionally clear water. Why not grow oysters? I mean, if Brittany can do it why can't we? I was joined in the venture by Andrew Lane, who became managing director of the business.

This was the origin of what is now a highly profitable business that continues to grow and diversify. It required only a small labour force, and the product was of high enough value for it to be flown to the dinner tables of London, Paris and elsewhere. The opportunity had been there for years, but it took a crisis in the family finances to give birth to the idea.

Can we do anything to sharpen our awareness of the opportunities that exist out there? Clearly necessity, if not the mother of invention, at least acts as an efficient midwife. But in fact we can train ourselves to spot such opportunities, as we'll see in Chapter 3.

Exploiting an opportunity

Entrepreneurs, however, not only spot opportunities; they exploit and use them to build a successful, profitable business.

John Noble shows how that can be done.

First of all he needed to develop the skills required to run an oyster farm. Nobody in Scotland had experience of commercially producing shellfish. But the French had been doing it for years.

'I thought,' John relates, '*why not ask the French oyster-growers to show us the ropes?*'

As often happens in cases like these, John got in touch with some Brittany oyster producers and was surprised to find how willing they were to let them into the secrets of the trade:

> Andrew, my manager, who spoke some French, went to Brittany and spent six weeks there as observer and unpaid helper. He made a careful note of all that was going on, and received a lot of useful hints. He was also given access to quite a stock of written procedures. When he came back we felt ready to have a go ourselves.

So the trip to France helped Loch Fyne Oysters to start to build the capability to grow oysters.

But the firm also needed to marshal the *resources* needed to get the enterprise up and running. Seed oysters cost money, so do the platforms they're grown on, and it takes a year for the young oysters to mature. Funds were needed to pay for this investment.

> Our major resource problem was a lack of cash, although the lack of it gave us a discipline we might otherwise not have had. We had a precious breathing space because the payment of death duties didn't have to be immediate. Since we were a Highland company, we approached the Highlands and Islands Development Board for help, and after a bit of arm-twisting, persuaded them to give us a grant to cover about 50 per cent of the cost. The rest we got from the bank.

In this way John and Andrew found the cash to get the enterprise under way. That only left the problem of finding customers. They were, after all, 500 miles from London and nobody had ever heard of Loch Fyne Oysters. He could have spent a lot on advertising, but he realized that he could achieve just as much without spending a penny, using cheap PR – magazine articles, little pieces in gossip columns, and photographs of lovely Loch Fyne and its oyster beds all duly turned up:

> We rented out some cottages to summer visitors and some of them turned out to be journalists and photographers. When I showed them what we were doing they were fascinated. They did the rest.

John and Andrew's business has gone from strength to strength:

> We started a smokehouse in 1979 and also started dealing in west coast shells. We then set up three oyster houses in England and one at Loch Fyne.

Fifty per cent of their £5 million sales are now in export markets.

So even a man of some standing in the local community was not too proud to apply the maxim 'beg, borrow and befriend' to good account.

The entrepreneurial process we have been examining so far can be summarized by the simple model shown in Figure 1.1.

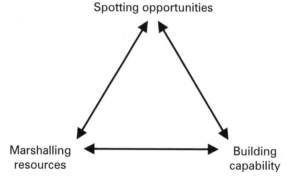

Figure 1.1   *The entrepreneurial process*

The three tasks of entrepreneurship are:

1. Spotting, creating or seizing opportunities: where others often see only chaos or confusion.
2. Marshalling the resources: which others may own, in order to take up the opportunity.
3. Building the capability: within the business to translate the opportunity into something of value.

So if you want to become an entrepreneur then you need to learn to think and act like one.

Some of the skills entrepreneurs use in *spotting opportunities* are listening and learning. They ask the questions other people miss and are really inquisitive, thirsting for knowledge and learning.

In order *to marshal resources* they are often good resource investigators, knowing who to ask, and most importantly they are good negotiators. All entrepreneurship starts with a deal, so they learn how to get resources, often on the cheap.

Finally they *build the capabilities* needed to develop their business. This might be their own learning or picking the people with the skills required to move the business forward. They learn how to network and build alliances and partnerships to get the capabilities they require. We will be examining these skills and processes in detail throughout this book.

But you do not have to start with spotting an opportunity:

- John Pye started with the *capability* to market and sell sound systems, which allowed him to *spot the opportunity* to set up his own business. In order to do this he needed to get his *resources* on the cheap.
- John Noble had the *resources*, a loch to *create the opportunity* of an oyster business. He needed to build his *capability* to grow oysters.
- Robert Webster did start with *spotting an opportunity* to reduce the risk of eye cancer for surfers. He needed to build the *capability* to develop and market the product with limited *resources*.

So the lesson from entrepreneurs is that it does not matter where you start on the entrepreneurial triangle: *opportunities, resources* or *capabilities*. The critical factor is that you create an *opportunity* by solving customer problems.

The central premise of this book is that it is both possible and highly desirable to try to remain entrepreneurial throughout the life cycle of a business, not just during the exciting times of start-up and growth. We will see how it is possible to be entrepreneurial and revitalize your business even at the survival stage. We will see how entrepreneurs spot opportunities internally to revitalize their business, making them more efficient by reducing *resources*. They spot *opportunities*, even in businesses that are struggling to compete on price, to recreate competitive advantage by spotting new *opportunities* or building new *capabilities*. As the dog analogy goes, entrepreneurship is for life, not just for start-up! Staying entrepreneurial throughout the life cycle of the business is the central message of this book and it provides hope and opportunity for all businesses. Entrepreneurial skills are also vital for large businesses, quangos and even the civil service, in fact anywhere where people need to create value from nothing.

The skills of the entrepreneur

By this time you should be getting some feel of what it is like to be an entrepreneur. You might even have come to the view that being an entrepreneur can be exciting and rewarding.

So where do you start if you want to learn how to do the job?

In Britain there is a network of business support centres that provide help for start-up businesses. However, it is fair to say that most successful entrepreneurs have not found them much use in helping them develop their real entrepreneurial skills.

The problem is that the traditional business support system sees businesses in terms of systems, procedures and specific skills, such as book-keeping or time management. Much of this is left brain stuff, ie rational and logical. So they will provide help in producing a business plan or a marketing strategy, they will offer training in filling in VAT forms and export procedures, and so on. But if that is all there is to creating a successful business we would all be living in Hawaii!

Working with entrepreneurs has convinced me that entrepreneurs have very little use for formal bureaucratic systems and don't operate according to traditional business rules. Entrepreneurship is much more of a craft than a science.

Entrepreneurs are mainly right-brain thinkers, employing much more of their creative and imaginative faculties in their business, yet business is taught as a left-brain rational planning activity.

But it goes further than that – the techniques used by entrepreneurs are not described in business books *because we lack a vocabulary to describe what they do.*

As part of the research programme I brought a whole group of entrepreneurs together. They generally did not know each other and had never met as a group before. Yet they all agreed that they operate in very similar ways. In discussion, we were able to create a new vocabulary, which conveyed for them what entrepreneurship was all about. Here are some examples; there are many more throughout this book.

Spotting an opportunity

Entrepreneurs do not sit down and work out a marketing strategy. They spot opportunities (as we have seen) which drive the business forward. At a later stage some traditional marketing may be required – see under 'Backfilling'.

Roughing it at the start

Entrepreneurs do not waste their energies working out elaborate business plans to convince a bank they are worthy of a loan. Instead, they agreed, they preferred not to burden themselves with debt but to cut out all necessary expenditure and marshal as much free help as they could get. This meant there was no spending on flash cars or plush offices but just on the absolute essentials. Nor was there any notion of paying out fat salaries from what was essentially borrowed money. As for ways of getting started with few or no resources, we've already seen examples of *'beg, borrow and befriend'* in action.

Backfilling

Backfilling is a term for a key growth process. Entrepreneurs do not grow by grand plans or strategies. They spot an opportunity and turn it into a personal crusade or project. They then often take their eye off the core business. This may start to falter so they are forced to return to their core business and backfill (the metaphor is of someone digging a trench and then filling it in behind them afterwards). They do this by appointing people, providing training, or putting simple systems in place.

System slippage

Entrepreneurs revitalize mature businesses by identifying which of their systems, formal and informal, are not being used effectively. They calculate the costs of the 'slippage' and take action to restore the system or process. This normally boosts efficiency and improves profits.

Just doing it

Entrepreneurs learn by doing. When they run up against a problem they find ways to go around, over or through the problem. This 'can do' mentality provides the energy and commitment to remove blockages to progress and solve problems. In the entrepreneurial way, problem solving = learning and by this definition entrepreneurs are excellent learners.

But they don't solve problems by breaking them down and analyzing them in the way recommended in business books. Instead they use an intuitive approach employing trial and error, trying out hunches, discarding solutions that do not work until they find one that does. They often learn from the experiences of their peers.

Networking

Networking is of course not a new term, but entrepreneurs use it in a specific way. They learn by talking with other successful entrepreneurs (peers). They value the wisdom of those who have 'been there and done it'.

This explains why many read the biographies of successful entrepreneurs or will attend events at which their heroes – successful entrepreneurs – share their wisdom. *Entrepreneurs are generally good at synthesizing informa-*

tion from a range of sources they learn to value. Hence the potential value of the entrepreneurial stories in this book.

Problem seeking problem solving

The way entrepreneurial businesses create new opportunities with no track record is by problem seeking problem solving. They seek the real problems that potential customers are currently facing and offer to provide solutions.

Dewhirst's, who make shirts amongst other things, once helped Marks & Spencer through a difficult period in the early 1920s by extending their credit terms from 60 to 120 days. Marks & Spencer survived and said they would always buy shirts from Dewhirst and they still do today, 60 years later.

Creating marketing space

Many businesses often start off with some competitive advantage but this gets eroded over time and the business ends up competing on price. Entrepreneurs re-create competitive advantage and improve their profits in distinctive ways, as we shall see later.

Reinventing the business

Businesses that started off with the entrepreneurial spirit often become over-managed, in a bureaucratic sense, as they grow. Entrepreneurs who transform their business normally follow a similar pattern of behaviour in order to revive their business fortunes.

Comparing the ways entrepreneurs prefer to learn with the current offerings by business support agencies is very revealing:

The entrepreneurial way of learning	*Traditional business support offerings*
Personal problem solving	Training courses
Successful peers	Textbooks
Family and friends	Consultants and trainers
Informal social contacts	Business advisers

So you can begin to understand why entrepreneurs avoid business books and 'experts'; they much prefer to learn from their own social networks and personal contacts.

The rest of the book

From here on the book is for you to pick and choose from. Chapters 1–4 will appeal particularly to people who have never run a business but are thinking of starting one. Chapters 5–8 will be of special value for those who are starting or in the early stages of running their own businesses, while Chapters 9–14 provide a guide to growing a business and restoring entrepreneurial skills in mature businesses. Whatever your personal position, however, each chapter offers its own surprising insights into just why entrepreneurial behaviour matters so much.

The recipes provide you with lots of ideas to get you started and then your own natural problem-solving skills will take over.

Entrepreneurial skills, you will see, can be learnt and applied, and the more that master the art the better off we will be.

> Entrepreneurship and innovation are central to the creative process in the economy and to promoting growth, increasing productivity, and creating jobs…. (We need) more risk-takers who can rapidly turn ideas into products and businesses.
>
> (UK White Paper on Competitiveness, November 1998)

Could you be a successful entrepreneur?

Recognizing entrepreneurial behaviour in yourself

Think for a moment, about the last time you made something happen, which gave you personal satisfaction:

- Did you take on something other people were wary of?
- Did you spot an opportunity to make a difference?
- Was there a difficult problem that you resolved?
- Did you have to be really creative to get the resources needed, maybe on the cheap?
- Did you find yourself talking with a whole range of people who could help you?
- Did you find you became obsessed with achieving success?
- Did setbacks increase your determination to achieve success?
- Did you have to personally learn some new tricks to get the job done?

So why were you pleased with yourself?

Probably because you made something happen that became important to you with limited resources and against the odds.

You found a real fire in yourself and a determination to succeed. You were prepared to do almost anything in your power to achieve success. You kept going when logic perhaps said stop.

You created something of value to you from practically nothing.

You were entrepreneurial.

serving **the**
apprenticeship

- The three key areas in which to gain experience
- Planning your apprenticeship
- Twelve ways to serve your apprenticeship

In the old days people learnt a trade by serving an apprenticeship – a period in which, working with master craftsmen, they could pick up the ropes and begin to understand the secrets of the trade. Although a lot of time might be wasted by asking the apprentice to do all sorts of jobs unrelated to the craft, such as making cups of tea, apprentices had the good solid value of learning in a hands-on way.

Every aspiring entrepreneur should try if possible to serve an apprenticeship that prepares him or her for starting a business. For entrepreneurship is a craft and just like any other craft, and an apprenticeship needs to be served. How is that to be done? Actually it is not so difficult. Most of my successful entrepreneurs had such training, although they may not have recognized it as such at the time.

Some, like Clive Skelton, certainly see it all clearly now. Clive is the Managing Director following an MBO of a company that cold rolls steel plate and sections into circles and part segments for various markets. Quite shrewdly his business is called T.H.E. Section Bending Company.

Before this, he worked for 17 years with a multinational company making mild steel wire. Those years were a wonderful training for his future success, as he told me:

> I started in transport. This was great because you learnt about the customer base and the products. Two years later I went into production control, which helped me further to know the rest of the company. Then I moved into sales. I enjoyed talking to customers, finding out what they wanted. I was there for eight years. So when the opportunity came along to run T.H.E Section Bending Company I had a good

> grounding in business; customers, products, the industry network and
> what made it tick.

Most successful entrepreneurs echo Clive's experiences. Studies show that 90
per cent of them start their businesses in the same sector as the one they had
worked in for at least 10 years. In the process they gather 'chunks of experiences' which prove invaluable in helping them develop their own business.

There are a number of key areas where the apprenticeship needs to be
served.

The key areas can be broken down into three broad categories:

- Experience of the industry: including the products and customers, how
  to do the business in the industry.
- Business skills and knowledge: running meetings, interpersonal skills,
  problem-solving skills, decision making etc. The traditional personal
  business skills and experiences.
- Personal skills: development of the personal skills and attitudes
  required to run a successful entrepreneurial business.

Experience of the industry

Most successful entrepreneurs have a good grounding in the industry in
which they set up their own business. However, it is difficult for one person
to develop all the experiences required. Therefore many entrepreneurs
start or build with a team of people with complementary experiences.

These experiences break down into four broad tasks.

Driving

This is done by the lead entrepreneur who provides the energy and takes
responsibility of the business overall.

> A few of us, managers at Burroughs at the time, felt why don't we try
> and control our destiny a bit more? We have the talent, we understand
> the technology and the business. So we decided to do something on
> our own. My role was technical director of Rodime and I established a
> product profile for the whole operation.
>
> (Norman White, Calluna Technology)

Doing

This is the technical operation or productive role. This task is to produce
the goods or service to the standards and costs required in an innovative
manner.

An innovation by the Eagle Boys pizza store in Albury, New South Wales, Australia is a good example. This resulted in the development of the two-tiered box, which came from the recognition that the majority of telephone orders were for two pizzas:

> At one time, our goal was simply to get two pizzas into one box without the pizzas and the box turning to mush. But this innovation has saved us 20 per cent on our box expenses. The heat generated from the two pizzas keeps them piping hot. We are using less materials for each box, and the strength is augmented by recycled paper stock, so it is an environmentally friendly move.
>
> (Tom Potter, Eagle Boys Pizza Store)

Selling

This is the customer contact task. The business winners and networkers.

> My role is to develop exports. I spend three months abroad a year covering the Far East, Japan and Eastern Europe. I will go to Japan three times this year because it is a major market for us. We need to be in constant dialogue with our customers and that's my job.
>
> (Richard McDonald, Carpenter and Patterson, a
> pipe support manufacturer from Welshpool)

Controlling

Keeping control of the key aspects of the business, particularly finance, is the fourth key task.

> When I joined Campbells and we decided to buy the company I was able to go completely through the company and tidy up the balance sheet finding out everything which needed to be written off. The company was really on the slide and had an accountant who was really just very much under the control of the managing director. So we got the whole balance sheet tidied out and the assets we did buy were good assets. We bought the assets and liabilities. Everything was written off that wasn't a good asset. We closed down a lot of business the company was doing which wasn't profitable before we started, so we started off with the business we wanted. We started making money right away. We cut back on stocks, debtors and we were able to pay our borrowings off in no time at all. It was all done on overdraft and term loan. We have no outside shareholders. Just the five of us, so things went from strength to strength. We obviously knew it was a learning

curve, we had ideas, the business didn't have a quality image. We right away started to change that and it's now paying dividends.
(John Ferguson, Campbell Brothers,
a meat and poultry supplier in Midlothian)

It is obviously rare for a single entrepreneur to get full in-depth experience in the four areas. This is the reason why so few single entrepreneurial businesses develop sales over £1 million.

Budding entrepreneurs therefore should try to maximize their experiences in the areas where they excel and to find partners or key people to cover the other areas.

If you intend to start a business then make sure you get these four key tasks covered by competent people.

Business skills and knowledge

Basic business skills can be developed before starting your own business.

This book is not about traditional basic business skills. They are well covered by courses, books and development opportunities with employers.

Personal skills

The development of the key personal skills and attitudes required to start and build a successful business can be developed as part of the apprenticeship. Some can only be developed by 'doing it' once the business starts.

The key skills we identified with our entrepreneurs were:

- taking responsibility: taking responsibility for the business;
- being persistent: keeping going, often in the face of adversity;
- seeking help: proactively seeking help from people who can help the business;
- obsessive commitment: becoming obsessed and working hard focusing on those issues that add real value to the business;
- coping with ambiguity, uncertainty and risk: dealing with uncertainty in a positive manner;
- building a network: building and maintaining a network of key contacts critical for the business success;
- providing leadership: providing the inspiration and a role model for how the business should operate.

Many studies particularly, in the USA, confirm the need to develop these personal skills and attitudes, if the enterprise is to be successful.

The entrepreneurial apprenticeship

A self-assessment

In order to take stock of where you are currently with serving your entrepreneurial apprenticeship, answer these questions as honestly as possible. Try talking them through with people who will be honest with you to get a more reliable score.

Strongly
disagree
1 2 3

Strongly
agree
4 5

		1	2	3	4	5
1.	I have had enough experience to lead and drive a business venture.	1	2	3	4	5
2.	I am good at planning, coordinating and controlling a business venture.	1	2	3	4	5
3.	I have a clear vision of where I want to take my business.	1	2	3	4	5
4.	I have all the technical skills to support the business.	1	2	3	4	5
5.	I know how to produce quality, products/services to deadlines within cost limits.	1	2	3	4	5
6.	I know the customers and their needs.	1	2	3	4	5
7.	I am an excellent networker and know the movers and shakers in our industry.	1	2	3	4	5
8.	I know how to delight the customers.	1	2	3	4	5
9.	I am ready to take personal responsibility for my business.	1	2	3	4	5
10.	I can provide the leadership required by my business.	1	2	3	4	5
11.	I am obsessively committed to my business.	1	2	3	4	5
12.	I know who to talk to, to get help when required.	1	2	3	4	5
13.	I am good at controlling all aspects of a business.	1	2	3	4	5
14.	I understand how to control the key financial measures, profits, cash flow, debtors and creditors.	1	2	3	4	5
15.	I know how to do business in our industry.	1	2	3	4	5
16.	I am able to cope with uncertainty and risks.	1	2	3	4	5
17.	I have learnt how to be persistent, particularly during adversity.	1	2	3	4	5
18.	I am good at problem solving.	1	2	3	4	5

19. I have the skills and experience to make good decisions.		1	2	3	4	5
20. I am ready to start a business.		1	2	3	4	5

Total score _____ %

If you score 80+ on this questionnaire then you are ready to take over from Richard Branson!

Do not be discouraged by low scores. These are areas where you need to ensure you work on your business. It does not have to be done by you personally. Richard Branson once said 'I can't read a balance sheet but I know somebody who can.'

This quick assessment might also give you some clues about where you need to plan to get experiences before you start your business. Broadly, scores of 1 and 2 are areas to develop or delegate and 4 and 5 are strengths.

Twelve ways of serving the apprenticeship needed to start and build a successful enterprise

These tips come directly from our entrepreneurs' experiences:

- *Volunteer for projects:* Get yourself onto project teams that will provide you with the kind of experiences you lack.
- *Learn from good role models:* Find out who is good at what you need to learn to do well to become really successful. Talk with them and ask lots of questions. Watch how they operate. I deliberately got myself alongside some very good operators when I was serving my apprenticeship.
- *Mix with the right people:* Join clubs or groups where entrepreneurs meet and discuss their businesses. Being in the right groups is very helpful because entrepreneurial spirit is infectious. If you do not personally find them interesting then consider doing something else!
- *Read biographies of entrepreneurs:* Read the biographies of successful entrepreneurs. You will discover it's not what they do, it's the way that they do it – the entrepreneurial way.
- *The day job and night job:* Experiment with your new business whilst still in employment. I practised as a consultant at night and at weekends before launching my own business.
- *Build your contacts:* Build up your personal network of contacts before starting your business. Who can help you? Who can provide you with information, contacts and intelligence? Ask what can you do for them. (Remember, networking is a two-way street.)

- *Become a customer:* Try to become a customer for the products and services you intend to offer before you start. Many business start-ups are by buyers who recognize they could do better than their suppliers.
- *Get your resources in place:* Investigate suppliers and potential employees. Picking the right people is crucial. Do it before you start in order to hit the deck running.
- *Gaining your spurs:* Deliberately put yourself into situations to gain the experience you need. If you have never sold anything, spend time at a car boot sale and sell things. Get rid of your inhibitions before starting....
- *Talk to people:* Talk your ideas through with trusted confidantes. Ask for feedback. Check our your assumptions. One word of warning: some people are particularly free with their advice on how you should spend your money. A useful test question is to ask 'what would you really do if it was your money?' You often get a different response.
- *Get out of your box:* Deliberately do things you do not do normally. Dealing with uncertainty and building your resistance to stressful situations will prove invaluable.
- *Avoid 'Nay sayers' and experts:* Some business 'experts' believe their role is to save you from yourself. 'Watch out for the VAT man.' 'The bank manager will interrogate you.' 'You need 54 NVQs in business before you start.' Talk to people who are positive and encourage you, not the negatives.

Your business recipe

Entrepreneurs produce business plans for banks, they rarely use them to run their business. In case you misread that last sentence: *Entrepreneurs do not run the business by using long detailed business plans.*

They actually think through all the issues and build a business recipe. This is an in-head mental rehearsal of how they want their business to be. Sometimes they do some research but this normally is talking to potential customers and people, not desk research in libraries.

The business recipe would cover issues such as:

- Spotting opportunities
  - Who really are my customers?
  - What problems do they have?
  - What price do they say they will pay?
  - How much will I make?
- Building capabilities
  - What do they say I need to do to get their business?

- What do I really need to do to make this work?
- What new skills do I need to learn?
- Marshalling resources
  - Where can I get good reliable suppliers?
  - Who can help me?
  - Where can I beg, borrow or befriend people to get resources on the cheap?

The purpose of outlining a business recipe at this early stage is to try to provide a focus for serving your apprenticeship. These are the key questions you will have to answer when designing and forming your business. Try to ensure your apprenticeship produces the kind of experiences that will help you answer these types of questions. In other words, serve an apprenticeship with a purpose.

Finally, there is another reason for serving the apprenticeship. That is to raise cash to start your business. Most business starts are self-funded, so building up cash reserves before you start is another good tip from our entrepreneurs.

The business recipe is the bridge that brings together all your experiences to help you start your business. If old habits die hard and you feel compelled to write your recipe down, try to get it on one page of A4 paper. This is also a good discipline for providing focus and prioritizing.

In serving your apprenticeship you may have spotted a business opportunity. The next chapter will help you shape it up.

three

spotting
opportunities

- Ideas vs opportunities
- The markets to go for
- The niche market
- New markets
- A big fish in a small pond
- A small fish in a big pond
- A unique product or service
- An eye for profitability
- Bring out the best ideas
- A practical approach to opportunity creation
- The role of creative thinking
- Change creates opportunities
- Test your entrepreneurial skills

Opportunities are the spark that ignites the entrepreneurial flame. We've already seen how important it is for entrepreneurs to recognize a good business opportunity when they see it. If you don't think you have the gift of seeing the world entrepreneurially, think again. Because the ability to recognize an opportunity grows with experience and the development of a positive attitude. Entrepreneurs see the cup half-full, not half-empty. In this chapter we are going to look at ways of developing an eye for opportunity.

The first thing to establish is that spotting a business opportunity is not the same as having a business idea. Some ideas lead on to opportunity, many just don't make business sense.

Consider the case of the British ideas man, Sir Clive Sinclair. He had the great idea of producing a cheap electric runabout vehicle, the C5, with the admirable objective of cutting air pollution in cities and making motorized transport affordable to all at the same time. There was loads of advance publicity as the public waited for this exciting concept to be unveiled. Sir Clive personally launched it with great enthusiasm.

The C5 turned out to be a huge flop, in a business sense at least. It turned out to be very small, very low on the road, and open to the weather. The public didn't take to it – a few photographs showing the vehicle dwarfed by lorries and buses on crowded city streets carried a powerful message. It was not safe. That perception was enough to kill off the whole idea as a business proposition.

Sir Clive now makes bicycles with little electric motors attached. They do not seem to have been a great commercial hit. While Sir Clive may consider himself to be an entrepreneur, I would class him as something quite different – an inventor.

Inventors have ideas and often make the most remarkable technical breakthroughs, but that doesn't make them successful business people. Entrepreneurs, on the other hand, may invent nothing themselves. Those who do, like James Dyson who has revolutionized the technology of vacuum cleaners, would never dream of launching it on the public without testing the waters.

Whether an entrepreneur has the idea for a new product or a new service, it doesn't become an opportunity until it has been tried out on the potential customer.

'I have this really great idea which I have spent ages thinking about' – how often have we heard this from budding entrepreneurs? But it is no good creating an idea in the mind, however passionately: it has to match a market, or potential market, need.

In Silicon Valley in California 60 new entrepreneurial millionaires are created every day. In this hotbed of entrepreneurship the venture capitalists who provide most of their funds say the key question they have learnt to ask is: Does this opportunity solve a real problem or add value for a customer? If it does they investigate further. They know that entrepreneurship is a market-driven activity.

So in the entrepreneur's dictionary:

Idea:	Something I am personally passionate about.
Opportunity:	Something which solves a real problem or adds value for a customer.

When entrepreneurs consider new business ideas, they discriminate by asking the same question: Does the idea solve a real problem for customers or have the potential to add value to their lives? If the answer is positive, they then set about marshalling the resources needed to turn the idea into business reality. This is what they bring to the party and makes them different from inventors.

You don't have to go to the United States to find examples of creative entrepreneurs at work.

Consider the case of Phil Crane. In the 1980s he spotted the potential in lifestyle change in the spread of cheap video recorders and TV sets. Families were no longer forced to share a single TV set and tastes within one family were startlingly diverse. Phil's chain of video stores in the 1980s solved a problem for many families by bringing cinema entertainment into the home. He's moved on since then.

In the 1980s he spent some time in New Zealand and saw the popularity of a large undersea aquarium, where you could see sharks and other exotic fish at close quarters. In 1990 he got a chance to bring this concept to Scotland:

> I heard that a guy that had built one of these aquariums was in Europe looking for sites. I also knew that his aquarium in New Zealand became the number one attraction overnight, and has remained so ever since. I went out to meet him in New Zealand, and offered him a deal. I came back, talked to the local council and had some very good feedback from them. So we were off and running.

The result was Scotland's first underwater theme park – Deep Sea World situated on the Firth of Forth at North Quay close to Edinburgh, a major centre for tourism, and no more than an hour away from three-quarters of Scotland's population.

Phil seized the opportunity because years of experiences in entrepreneurship taught him it was a good commercial idea. But not before he had followed that hunch up with some research of his own:

> I looked around America, looked in Australia where this concept came from originally and at a couple of instances where this particular concept worked really well. I asked lots of questions, tapping into the wisdom of successful people.
>
> A lot of people say: 'That sounds like a great idea', and I tend to go on a gut feel – but then you have got to do quite a bit of analysis and you look at the market. You have to judge it on that; is the market there?

It has paid off handsomely as he has seen his business become a main feature of Scottish leisure. Last year the theme park welcomed 400,000 visitors and its turnover reached £2.4 million.

In July 1998 a second aquarium opened, The Blue Planet at Ellesmere Port, Cheshire. Both attendance and turnover look to be double that of North Quay. Phil floated his company on the AIM in 1996.

Plans are now well advanced to open aquariums in Madrid, Seville, Utrecht and North America.

In Phil's case the customer was the general public and he clearly added something to people's enjoyment of life.

But many of our entrepreneurs serve the needs not of the public direct but those of big companies. The same entrepreneurial principles apply.

Let's take the case of Labtech, a fast-growing success story in Mid Wales. The lead entrepreneur here was David Latham. The big opportunity he spotted was the growing importance of microwave technology in electronics.

David is another one of those entrepreneurs who began his career working for a big company, in his case the British-based computer and systems manufacturer ICL. A trained scientist, David was engaged in research work on advanced printed circuits.

> ICL was an excellent company to work for, very structured, very high tech, there was an unlimited amount of money thrown at us to develop new products.

Unfortunately, after a couple of years working there, ICL decided to close the facility down and David was one of hundreds made redundant.

> I had been helping a small company in Herefordshire to set up making prototype printed circuits. I use to spend the odd weekend and holidays sorting out technical problems. I never got paid for this work, but it was a lovely part of the country to visit and I was pleased to see the company grow slowly. When I was made redundant they offered me a job as technical manager and I jumped at the chance.

David learnt people management skills, visited customers, and became involved in sales. The company prospered but the major shareholder was not a very pleasant person and rode roughshod over the other three directors, taking away the profits to set up other companies that failed.

> After seven years I was fed up working for this guy. I didn't have any future in the business, and I had had a major illness. I had no life insurance, and no relative who owned a house; nobody was going to leave me anything, so it was down to me: I could either rob Barclays or start my own business.

However, David could thank the company for preparing the way for his success in business:

> I had gone there as a scientist, and learned about customers, employees, legislation and all the other things you need to know to start on your own. I told the owner, when I left, that the most important lesson I

had learned from him was how not to run a company; he subsequently went bust!

David started Labtech in 1983 with the help of just £25,000 capital (an overdraft facility from a local bank) and a subsidized factory unit in Presteigne, Mid Wales, then a local unemployment black spot. Labtech had its eye on the military market, where microwaves were increasingly used in radar installations and in satellites. The firm manufactured the circuitry the technology demanded.

David already had a network to help him get orders. He had made several valuable contacts in firms such as Marconi, British Aerospace, Plessey and Racal, while working for his previous company. He could go to them, demonstrate how microwave technology could help them with the problems they faced, and then take it from there. It wasn't long before contractors were coming to him at an early stage in their development programme to test out ideas.

> We didn't worry if a customer came to see us, if he was designing a circuit and didn't know whether something was possible. We had a history and a showcase, we would say 'OK you want a hole that is half a millimetre in diameter in the circuit board and you're worried about it? Here's one we did for someone else, with holes half that size and far more technically difficult.' Working with them in this way meant our technology was built into the designs from the start.

But David Latham illustrates a second lesson. Entrepreneurs can't rest on their laurels. They sometimes have to find solutions to their own business problems if the market suddenly changes.

In 1989 the end of the Cold War brought the 'peace dividend' in its aftermath. Defence orders began to be cut back. What was Labtech to do?

> We had two options, we could either go into decline like a lot of the big defence-oriented companies did, or look for opportunities. There was a growing consumer market for microwave technology, but we knew there were a finite number of customers in the UK. We decided to cast our net wider and go global.

Of course Labtech didn't have sale agents overseas and no contacts to speak of in Europe, other than in the military market. So how were the new customers to be found? David tried what others in the company considered a long shot: he placed an advertisement in a specialist microwave user magazine distributed across Europe, and gambled a bit of money on making sure it extolled the virtues of their capabilities, doing all the photographs and text himself:

> My colleagues thought that I had gone crazy because it cost £1,500. But the week after it came out I had a phone call from Sweden and this guy said, 'Can you really make these kind of circuits?' I said yes.

David didn't know it but he was about to break into one of the world's fastest-growing markets – the manufacture of base stations for mobile phones. Production of these symbols of the new age of telecommunication has soared since 1990 as user charges have fallen and people increasingly have come to see them as something as essential to living as bread or bagels.

It wasn't just a matter of luck either. They would never have won that first European contract had they not offered their new customers the sort of help that had become their hallmark:

> The phone call was from Ericsson, the big Swedish mobile communications firm. It turned out they had major problems which we could help them with, through our technology. We asked them exactly what the problem was and then came out with a solution. That was how we got started with Ericsson.

Labtech now exports two-thirds of its production all over the word and is growing at a rate of knots – 25 per cent on average every year. David finds his company riding on a wave. But he still retains his entrepreneurial inclinations:

> The company fax machine is still situated outside my office and nothing upsets me more than seeing an enquiry come in and being ignored. I personally want to pick it up and telephone the guy and thank him for his enquiry. I don't think I can ever change that.

'Superior opportunities'

We can become successful entrepreneurs by learning from examples like these. Phil Crane and David Latham ultimately spotted not just opportunities but 'superior opportunities' – ones that have led on to real growth.

So how can we go about spotting these special opportunities? When I analyzed the history of my group of successful new business people a clear pattern emerged.

The markets to go for

You don't have to be an Einstein to see that some markets are more difficult than others for any new company to break into, never mind how enterprising and creative. Microsoft is going to be very difficult to topple from its perch as the top supplier of computer software, while in Britain it would be very difficult to challenge any of the supermarket giants who take an increasing share of the domestic food market. Mainstream markets are difficult for new companies to make much impression on.

The niche market

Instead entrepreneurs need to turn their sights mostly on what are known as niche markets – non-mainstream markets catering for specialist needs. Body Shop began in this way, offering cosmetics and body care products made without using animal products or manufactured chemicals. They were appealing to a small but growing segment of the population, not taking Boots or the supermarkets head-on.

Halo Foods of Tywyn in southern Snowdonia, one of the companies that was part of my research project, learned that lesson almost by chance. It is run by Peter Saunders, who worked for BP as a chemical engineer before being gripped by the idea of starting his own business. He chose to go into food, and makes snack bars and specialist food products now for some of Britain's best-known food companies and retailers. What Peter didn't anticipate was that one of his early products had a special quality that appealed to another market.

> Some of our healthy eating bars were low calorie, but we never thought of them as that. Then in the mid-1980s, we had an enquiry about slimming snacks. It was from an international food company.

Peter was astute enough to see the opportunity afforded by switching the emphasis into low calorie snacks.

> We switched to making slimming snacks and complete meal replacements. The latter were very carefully balanced nutritionally, and fortified with vitamins and minerals. We had to develop what for us was new technology. The production lines though could easily be adapted to produce this new range of products.

Peter now turns over £13 million and employs more than 200 people in the

Snowdonia National Park, because he spotted a superior opportunity.

Among entrepreneurs we have already encountered we can see the same principle in action. John Ferguson of Campbell Brothers in Midlothian decided not to try to compete in the mainstream food market, but went instead for the quality food segment.

If niche markets produce superior opportunities we can go further and say that the really superior opportunities occur in such markets when there is the prospect of exceptionally large benefits for the customers.

To illustrate what I'm talking about here, let's look at the example of Aber Instruments, based in Aberystwyth in West Wales.

Aber is one of those firms spun off from university research – in this case work on fermentation. They employ 18 staff with a turnover of £900,000. Beer making is an ancient craft, centuries old. But until recently it was as much an art as a science. The sampling of products as they matured was a rough and ready business using a hydrometer and random sampling from the vat. There was inevitably a lot of waste.

Aber's answer was to design and produce a set of sophisticated instruments which would keep the brewer precisely informed about what was going on in the brewing vat all through the process. Managing Director Barry Wise told me:

> It gives our customers tremendous benefits. We help them measure the quantity of live yeast, which enters the brewing vessel. It is at this point of entry into the fermentation vessel that our equipment is very useful.

Aber's instruments and controls make the production of consistently good beer possible and big brewers from all over the world now beat a path to their door. This one small company now exports 80 per cent of its product to countries as diverse as Canada, Israel and China.

New markets

One lesson is that even mature markets like beer production still have niches capable of being filled by enterprising companies.

Nonetheless the greatest opportunities are obviously likely to lie in expanding new markets. The sharpest entrepreneurs see the emerging trends early and move in before the competition has arrived.

Tom Hunter's a good example of this. You'll remember he set up a big chain of specialist sports clothing shops, Sports Division, across Scotland, the UK and Ireland and has just sold it for £290 million. That proved to be a very superior opportunity. But how did he spot it? He's quite modest about it:

I started in 1984. I had been to University, graduated in Marketing and Economics. I couldn't find a job. My father was involved with a company, which I wasn't involved in. I was still staying at home, and I noticed that branded trainers were a big part of the turnover and wondered how I could get that product on to the High Street without being able to afford a shop. I came up with the idea of taking space in someone else's store. I made up a letter head, told a pack of lies that it was a fast-expanding company, wrote to two companies and one of them gave me a chance, and that is how it started.

Look at most success stories in new business and you find similar examples of sudden insights like this on the part of entrepreneurs – people who caught the tide of change and took advantage of a new trend or fashion.

Being first to spot these trends is of course an advantage. But you do not have to be first to do well.

I have a rule of thumb: find any market growing at 25 per cent a year or more and you can be sure there are many new niche markets continuously being created, markets whose needs you can aim to satisfy.

Mobile telecommunications is a classic example at the moment and we have seen how that created a superior opportunity for Labtech.

'*Our technology is based deep inside every cellular telephone so every time anybody switches on they are using our equipment,*' he told me.

That's good news for David and his team at Labtech. There were 4 million new mobile phone subscribers in the first three months of 1999 alone!

But as well as niches in mobile phone production, sales, and services, there is also an explosion in land-line telephone services and a big expansion in the number of major companies in the market, all of whom offer niche opportunities.

E-commerce (business via the Internet) if anything is moving ahead at an even faster pace and thousands of companies are piling into what is seen as the marketing method of the future. So many indeed that the attrition rate of new businesses is likely to be akin to that of the poor infantry in the 1914–18 War. But, as we'll see later, there are ways of approaching these burgeoning new markets to maximize your chances of success.

A big fish in a small pond

Still, unless you have a strong nerve and exceptional energy you might be better advised to steer clear of some of these over-crowded marketplaces. There are, on the evidence available, easier and more predictable pickings to be made elsewhere.

Jim's Mowers based in Melbourne is a classic example. Jim Penham spotted the opportunity to set up a business mowing people's lawns. Jim expanded his business by offering to franchise the sale of lawn mowing rounds to people. He is now the largest lawn mowing business in Australia with over 1,400 franchises in all the major towns.

Jim has now set up a dog wash franchise and a rubbish franchise.

Still the company is worth just $5–6 million. A big fish in a small pond.

If there *is* a lesson here, it is that *new businesses can quickly establish themselves as big fishes in relatively limited ponds*. Be in a position to set the industry standard when it comes to prices and in attracting new customers: if a firm can win 20 per cent of that market it can be a market leader, and enjoy the advantages normally associated with much larger companies.

A small fish in a big pond

Being the big fish in a small pond is one formula for success. But so too can be small fishes if the pond is big enough. When the market is so big, gaining only a small market share can be very profitable and provide plenty of scope for growth, especially if you have your own niche in it.

Dave Wallinga spent the early part of his career as part of an internal communications group in Ameritech, a regional US telecommunications firm. He could have stayed with Ameritech and done very well within the structure of that $10 billion dollar company. But, Dave found that his role had one major, built-in drawback – he was and always would be a cost, a support function.

In 1989 Dave left Ameritech to join CRD – Communications, Research and Development – a small consulting firm focused on business communications. This was a first step towards entrepreneurship. It was a position from which he could better gauge the marketplace and the demands of entrepreneurship. It was during Dave's time with CRD that the Internet-led communications explosion occurred.

Dave and a friend (Andy) made their move and launched DNA (Dave and Andy) in 1994. Even in the short time since beginning their business, it has shifted from being an integrated business communications company – providing services ranging from traditional print to interactive media – to what they are now, a provider of Internet consulting and development services with a special interest in e-business and the management of knowledge.

The business continues to evolve – it is now DNA Visual Business Solutions Inc. Once they had two offices, a staff of 60 and revenues of $6 million. An opportune sale of one office and a part of the business now leaves them with one office, a staff of 12, and revenues of $3 million. Most importantly, though, underneath these numbers is the promise of development and a talent for entrepreneurial adaptation to the needs of the marketplace and changing technology.

A unique product or service

Very occasionally an entrepreneur may come across an 'extra superior opportunity'. This happens, typically, when a company has made some technical breakthrough protected by patent, remembering, of course, that the technical breakthrough needs to offer benefit to the customer.

Jim Frazier illustrates what can happen. Jim was a cameraman who until the late 1980s worked on wildlife documentaries for David Attenborough, and was continually frustrated by the limitations which traditional camera lenses placed on his art.

In the late 1970s, when he approached a physicist about the prospect of developing a versatile lens that would enable him to take shots rapidly as well as in focus, Jim was told what he wanted was impossible.

Over the next 10 years Jim kept rebuilding the lens and, with much trial and effort, formulated a new lens with three revolutionary features:

- a 'set and forget' focus which holds everything, from front of lens to infinity, in focus;
- a swivel tip so that without moving the camera you can swivel the lens in any direction, completing a sphere if need be;
- a built-in image rotator that allows the image to be rotated inside the lens without spinning the camera.

Jim had struck a deal where Panavision, the lens manufacturer, agreed to patent the device at their cost, whilst Jim's company, Mantis Wildlife Films, would own the patent. In addition Mantis gets a set fee for every lens made, plus, when Panavision rents them out, a percentage of all lens rental.

Although Panavision's patent costs exceeded $1 million, the return on their investment has been enormous. Apart from the image quality produced by the new lens, it has also dramatically reduced production costs. For example, what used to be a three-day shoot now takes one day.

An eye for profitability

So far we've seen how entrepreneurs look out for opportunities (problems faced by potential customers for which they can provide solutions), and considered where such opportunities are most likely to be found. The smart entrepreneurs ask themselves a further question: Where are profit margins likely to be highest?

Hi-tech entrepreneurial companies on the Cambridge Science Park enjoy high profit margins of at least 80 per cent.

These are often state-of-the-art technology companies. It is possible to develop good profit margins in low-tech businesses providing they provide real benefits for which their customers are prepared to pay.

Ann Adlington of Triple 'A' Ranch charges 40 per cent more than her competitors because of they way she delights the dog owners who entrust their pets to her when they go on holiday. High profits are Ann's reward for doing that bit extra for customers; service beyond expectations. We discover a lot more about Ann in Chapter 6.

So entrepreneurs do not find high profit opportunities, they create them. Success is often in the detail, making sure the customer gets good products and real satisfaction. As the management guru Tom Peters once said, 'If you give a customer something worth paying for, they will pay for it.'

If a customer can turn to the Yellow Pages and get another 20 suppliers just like you, why should they pay you any extra? So another cardinal rule is Bigger Customer Benefits = Bigger Profits for you.

We have to add a rider to this. Clearly entrepreneurs will find it difficult to break into business areas where they have no direct experience of their own to fall back on. A company with expertise in computer software would find it difficult to suddenly become an advertising agency.

But every type of commercial activity offers higher margins in some areas than it will in others. It is important to find out where the higher margins lie in the business area most suited to your experience.

Bringing out the best ideas

Crisis plays a part in producing solid commercial ideas to judge by the stories the entrepreneurs told me. Phil Crane, for instance, had some very bad experiences with earlier businesses, but the trauma sharpened his awareness of possible ways forward. The crisis caused by death duties played a part in stimulating John Noble to come up with Loch Fyne Oysters.

But the job people were engaged in, at the time they spotted the opportunity, seems to play an even bigger part.

Dave Wallinga's experiences with CRD research gave him invaluable insights into the marketplace for the Internet explosion. Jim Frazier's experiences filming with David Attenborough allowed him to see the need for a better camera lens. Norman White and David Latham developed their ideas in a work situation.

This more or less corresponds with an in-depth study of where new business opportunities came from, detailed by Norman Case in his article 'The origins of entrepreneurship'.

He found the sources of opportunities could be broken down into categories:

Source of opportunities	Percentage of companies
Working in someone else's business	47
Improving an existing product/service	15
Identifying an unfilled niche	11
Other sources	16

So almost 50 per cent of all new business opportunities were spotted whilst working for someone else's business and many others from some indirect link with such work.

This is not really surprising since you need to be close to the action to spot opportunities. One of the great myths of entrepreneurship is that entrepreneurs have sudden flashes of inspiration and just see the opportunity. Usually the idea grows and gets kicked around among friends and colleagues before it emerges as a commercial proposition.

A practical approach to opportunity creation

Remember the principle that an opportunity is created when you solve a customer's problem. So if you are in employment and come into contact with customers, you can start generating opportunities by asking the right questions, focusing on areas where customers are experiencing pain or frustration in their own businesses.

Here are some to try, courtesy of the entrepreneurs we meet in this book:

- Start by asking the customers what is it about suppliers that gives them the greatest grief.
- Try to get the customer to be honest – many are too polite or too afraid of giving offence to tell you the honest truth straight away.
- What differences are there between what is really happening and what is supposed to happen, when it comes to these supply problems?
- How does your company fail to deliver on its promises to customers?
- What disappoints customers about the present service? What should your company be doing to improve things for customers such as him or her?

▩ Are there any particular problems in supply that need to be solved?
▩ What will he or she want as a customer three years from now?
▩ Is there any big need that at present isn't being met?
▩ What challenges should suppliers respond to?
▩ What opportunities should you be creating?
▩ What do your customers/employees say about your business?

Most customers are never asked for their opinions in this way. The very fact that such matters are being discussed means that they gain new insight into their own businesses and by doing so create new opportunities for an entrepreneur to fill the gap in the present provision.

Discussions of this sort are obviously much easier in practice for salespeople than for those who have no direct contact with customers. This explains why it is important to get yourself in front of real live customers. It is far too important to leave to the sales team!

Remember the entrepreneur's cardinal principle:

opportunity = solving customers' problems

The role of creative thinking

No amount of discussion with customers will allow you to spot the opportunity unless you apply some creative thought to the process. But we can *channel that creativity* in ways that are more likely to bring positive results.

Start by considering the idea that there are at least seven basic ways to improve a product or service.

You can make things:

▩ higher quality;
▩ smaller;
▩ faster;
▩ easier;
▩ cheaper;
▩ more attractive;
▩ work better;

or a combination of these.

Here are some examples from our entrepreneurs:

▩ Jim Frazier of Mantis Wildlife Films introduced a lens that makes it *easier* to film wildlife as well as reducing production costs.
▩ Kevin Smith of Act Controls improves the process control of engineer-

ing equipment. It reduced the cycle time in an engineering process from 23 hours to 16 hours. It made it *faster*.

- David Latham's products perform *better* in extremely high temperatures than conventional circuit boards. Temperatures range from –40 °C to 200 °C.
- Tom Hunter, Sports Division, combines 'branded products', ie *quality* at the 'right prices', ie *cheaper*.
- Tom Potter of Eagle Boys Pizza Stores introduced new pizza boxes that made it *cheaper* to package pizzas.
- Anne-Marie Jackson of Handcast Design designs gifts for ladies, which are of *higher quality* and *more attractive* than many of their competitors.
- Barry Wise of Aber Instruments makes it *easier* to control the quality and quantity of the brewing process.

So how can your product or service improve things for your customers?

Change creates opportunities

We live in a world that seems to change ever faster. Fifty years ago the high streets were dominated by just a few big shops and each sector of manufacturing industry by a few large firms, who had apparently been around a long time. Consumers seemed happy with little choice. Families changed clothes with the seasons, had one holiday a year, and happily ate the same round of meals week in week out.

Now firms rise and fall at a frightening speed and consumer tastes have expanded and become subject to an ever faster rate of 'churn'. While many people see only chaos, and long-established firms struggle to survive, the good news is that change is the friend of the entrepreneur: the faster it is the greater the opportunity.

In these circumstances big firms find it hard to keep up with the pace of change. This gives an enormous advantage to the new small firm who can spot the gaps in the market and the new trends. *Opportunities can be seized quickly while their larger competitors study them, or conduct feasibility studies or write business plans.* It can take a large corporation five years or more to change its strategy or at least six months to get a capital application accepted. *In contrast, entrepreneurs can nimbly move in to grasp opportunities.*

To take but one example, this is how two young Australian designers, Tony Di Donato and Peter Asprey, described how they moved in and took business from under the noses of their competitors. They started in a Melbourne design studio in 1993. Asprey Di Donato Design have built an impressive blue chip client list, including Peters Ice Cream, Kraft, Herbert Adams, Edgells and the Victorian Government:

We are beating the big boys because we are fast and flexible.

This is the *competitive edge* entrepreneurial businesses have over their more bureaucratic blue chip competitors.

So where in the fast-changing marketplace out there can entrepreneurs expect to find good opportunities? We haven't got a crystal ball but there are some signposts that can be read from what's happened here in Britain in the past 10 years.

The deregulation of state-regulated industries has provided one rich source of opportunities. The ending of monopoly or near monopoly has led to an explosive growth in both telecommunications and air travel. We have seen the rise of new buccaneering airlines like EasyJet and RyanAir, and new mobile phone operators like Orange and One 2 One. These new companies require suppliers, business allies to help them compete effectively.

There's also been a huge growth in the service economy, from restaurants and coffee bars through the whole gamut of fitness-related industries, garden centres, DIY shops, theme parks, to animal care services and nannies. Firms come and go, but some like Kwik Fit (just taken over by Ford) and Pizza Express seem here to stay.

For example, one cardinal fact to mull over is that in these industries customer service is a critical factor. Seventy per cent of customers leave on average every year on account of poor customer service. This represents a real opportunity for firms who can make efficient and friendly service a feature of their business.

Providing not 'customer service' but 'customer delight' – the art of exceeding customer expectations – is one way to pull in the customers and keep them coming back.

The changes in the way that big companies and many public institutions organize their activities create a further zone where entrepreneurs can find the chance to do well. Once big companies wanted to keep as many as possible of the operations that made up the business in-house, so-called vertical integration.

Now they have been influenced by the view that companies should 'stick with the knitting'. They concentrate on their main or 'core' business where they have special expertise to offer. There has been a trend for companies to hive off non-core activities to outside suppliers. 'Outsourcing' is a policy that applies to everything from component production in manufacturing to stationery supply and cleaning services in any sector of the economy. Labtech, for instance, is one company that has prospered in supplying something as specialized as microwave circuitry to world-leading companies.

The scale of 'outsourcing' is likely to be increased by the coming of electronic commerce, or e-commerce.

Trade through the Internet was worth $12 billion worldwide in 1998. By 2002 it is forecast to reach $500 billion, a growth of over 4,000 per cent. At present 80 per cent of all e-commerce is business to business. A recent British report summed up the prospects for business this way:

> business-to-business trade will be revolutionized – accelerating the shift away from vertical integration towards structures based on contracting out, joint venturing, and other forms of partnership.

So e-commerce represents a major opportunity for creative entrepreneurs, especially if they can build joint ventures or partnerships with other companies. This was the opportunity spotted by Dave Wallinga of DNA.

Finding likeminded partners where 1+1=5 represents a new way of business development for smaller firms that may have special expertise and competence but lack financial resources.

Tom Hunter forms a model of one kind of partnership. He offered something to the big retailers when he suggested he be given space on their floor to sell his sports shoes. He was good at that, and supplied many more customers than he could ever have found had he opened a small shop in a side street in Glasgow. He's now a very rich man.

By this time you should have begun to appreciate where to look for opportunities, superior ones if possible. Can we make the search for ideas any easier? Perhaps you have thought of looking up as much market research as you can find in the area where you think you have the necessary expertise. Let me give you a warning: *the information available about market characteristics and trends is inversely related to the real potential of the opportunity*. In other words, if the data is published in books, even if it shows great potential, then competitors will very likely have already been there and the opportunity will have diminished.

The good news, however, is that *most published information is often incomplete and contradictory. Entrepreneurs make sense of incomplete information;* they see possibilities where others only see chaos.

Labtech saw that the defence business was facing decline. Most big companies in defence cut back on their workforces to stay profitable as orders fell. Labtech made the imaginative leap, as David Latham told me:

> Our business was for military radar. There was no immediate prospect of future expansion there, quite the reverse. We saw that microwaves were coming into their own in many civilian products. So we made the switch into mobile phones.

Labtech showed the nimbleness that gives small enterprises their competitive advantage, and the ability to react fast to changing market conditions. In later chapters we will see how to go about organizing your company to keep that entrepreneurial flair alive.

Luck creates opportunities

Undoubtedly luck can play a big part in spotting and creating opportunities and this is obviously difficult to plan. Being in the right place at the right time enabled Bill Gates to persuade 'IBM to leave the software to Microsoft whilst IBM concentrated on the important stuff – the hardware'. He would have needed help from above (God) to see that this would make him worth $100 billion in 20 years!

However, you can't get lucky sat in your office writing marketing plans. You do need to be out in the marketplace talking with customers.

As David Latham told me:

> The more time we spend with customers the luckier we seem to get.

A final word of warning...

Maybe you already have your eyes on a business opportunity, or you'll come up with one when you do the exercise below. Be careful about who you talk to you about your opportunity. Racketeers make a virtue of stealing other people's opportunities.

If possible, try to get it patented or take advice from lawyers about your intellectual property rights. I once formed a limited company, The Learning Organization, to prevent competitors stealing the brand name. Think about putting copyright © on all documents and if necessary, insist people sign secrecy agreements. This is not paranoia, it is just good commercial sense – the entrepreneurial way.

Test your entrepreneurial skill

Do you want to test how creative you are in spotting opportunities? Think about the areas covered in this chapter. Concentrate on your field of interest and get a few friends and colleagues to brainstorm ideas for making a product or service quicker, easier, smaller, better, cheaper, or more attractive.

How many new ideas did you come up with? Pick one of these and test it against the assessment questionnaire below. This will help you assess how superior your opportunity is, against the well-established entrepreneurial criteria.

Totally disagree			Totally agree	
1	2	3	4	5

1. The opportunity exists in a market niche where we can provide real benefits to customers. 1 2 3 4 5

2. The market is growing between 10 and 30 per cent per annum. 1 2 3 4 5

3. It is a relatively new but developing market. 1 2 3 4 5

4. We can capture at least 20 per cent of the market **or** in a large market we can gain a significant and attractive market share. 1 2 3 4 5

5. We can create a real defensible competitive advantage. 1 2 3 4 5

6. High and durable profits are available (50–80 per cent gross margins) 1 2 3 4 5

7. The opportunity really fits with our vision. 1 2 3 4 5

8. The opportunity provides an acceptable balance between risks and rewards. 1 2 3 4 5

9. We already have the management capability to take up this opportunity. 1 2 3 4 5

10. We have served our apprenticeship in the market and products which will help us take this opportunity. 1 2 3 4 5

Score _____

$\times 2 =$ _____ per cent

This is a tough questionnaire. Remember it assesses whether you really do have a superior opportunity.

Do not be put off by low scores. You have identified areas to focus on, which will help you plan how to get further experience.

Really low scores probably represent weak opportunities, not that you can never become an entrepreneur. Take heart. Keep looking!

The more high scores your opportunity matches, the more attractive and superior it becomes.

To this data you can add personal criteria to match your circumstances. For example, one of our entrepreneurs wanted to find opportunities in Australia so that he could spend time with relatives who had emigrated.

designing **your**
business

- Building a vision
- Building your jigsaw
- Finding your first customers
- Producing a business case
- Creating your recipe for success
- Ten myths about entrepreneurs

It is often about this point in the development of a new business that the entrepreneur starts to get really excited.

You have served your apprenticeship, and spotted a trend or a customer problem.

Now you need to test the idea with real people, your potential customers. How do you do it?

Robert Webster of Ztagg in Australia spent months researching, developing and testing his new eyewear glasses for surfers. He took pains, however, to test it with real surfers on what he calls the back beaches.

He wanted real customers to test his new products and give him feedback.

Other successful entrepreneurs test the market less scientifically; they just know from meeting people that they can offer a service people are willing to pay for.

Phil Crane just knew the people of Edinburgh would love his sea world spectacular, and they did.

'Some things you don't need the market research statistics to tell you it will be interesting to people,' he said.

We've already seen that others, like Phil Crane, saw that there was already a market for new services and products in other countries. He could see no reason why the same idea wouldn't be successful in Britain. Even so, Phil looked into the financial record of similar theme parks in the USA before he went ahead with Deep Sea World, while Peter Saunders made personal visits to the USA to test the market before launching Halo Foods in the USA. They took a sensible and pragmatic approach.

Norman White of Calluna Technology worked in the business of disk drives before setting up Calluna. He found there was a market for his product because he had many years' experience as an employee with someone else.

All of these methods of establishing whether you have a genuine business opportunity are valid. The question is, once you've gone through that process, what should the next step be?

Conventional wisdom tells us that we need to begin with a business plan. These plans are based on business school models and are essentially analytical. They break the business down in a mechanical way, set targets for growth, and predict cash flow. In my experience they miss out the most important factor making for business success – the obsessive commitment, passion and vision of the founder.

All the successful entrepreneurs I have worked with, or researched, shared a real passion for what they were trying to achieve. They drove the business forward, and the very fact that they had set their sights on a specific goal seemed to galvanize people within the organization.

We are not talking about some wild unrealistic dream, but challenging, achievable goals that provide the energy to go forward. Let me illustrate what I mean.

Peter Keary, who owns the Elton Hotel near Rotherham, had the goal of owning his own hotel.

> I had been managing hotels for many years for other people and in 1984 decided to go on my own. I had always dreamt of being my own boss and doing my own thing. When, in 1984, the chance came along I grabbed it.

Peter Saunders set up Halo Foods first and foremost because of his entrepreneurial instincts and his belief that the food sector offered lots of interesting opportunities.

Another entrepreneur, Laurence Young, had a vision of passing his successful business, The Lodge on the Loch, on to his family:

> My father ran a hotel at Onich (in the West Highlands) so it was in the blood. My aim has been to build a business around it to leave something worthwhile for the family when I retire.

Driven by this vision, Laurence Young now owns three hotels in the area and has developed a 'visitor attraction' at Ballachulish. The business is now worth 10 times as much in real terms, no mean achievement for 10 years' work.

The point about having this sort of vision is that it chimes in with the way successful entrepreneurs work. They don't work in a cold analytical fashion but are involved in a creative process by which they fit the pieces of their businesses together, more like assembling a jigsaw than erecting a building.

Building a vision

Visioning is a very powerful entrepreneurial process. It provides energy and creates obsessive commitment to build a successful business.

Here is how to do it in a practical way.

Think about your opportunity:

- What will it look like when you are successful?
- Who will your customers be?
- How big will your business have become?
- What will people be saying about you?
- What sales will you have?
- Who will be proud of you?

This next bit is going to sound really wimpy. I promise you this is how really successful sports people, business people, pop idols and others design success. Write down your answers to these questions on a card or a private journal.

Do not go flashing them round at the pub because this will give the pessimists a chance to laugh at you.

Write down your vision in as much detail as possible.

Each day reread your vision and imagine what it will be like when you achieve it.

Keeping the end game in sight is the way to stay focused and committed, particularly when the going gets a bit tough.

My first vision

When I started my business in 1988 my 10-year vision was: 1) to build a business to £5 million sales; and 2) to write a business book.

I wrote these down on postcards and carried them everywhere. I read the vision in the morning and when times got hard it helped me stay focused and to see the big picture. My partner reminds me about it today because I had realized all of this vision by 1994. This initial success and growing confidence encouraged me to lift my vision to include:

- to write and present a TV series;
- to use my business as an opportunity to travel the world;
- to create a business not dependent on my personal fee-earning capacity but one with a steady income flow from other sources;
- to work with people I really liked and trusted;
- to continue to learn, grow and enjoy what I was doing.

Once this vision had been realized I felt the need to move on and that my existing business might be holding me back.

So my vision in 1996 became to:

- exit the business by selling it to my colleagues;
- concentrate on my personal consulting practice;
- to write another business book about entrepreneurs which summarized my work over the last five years and allowed me to move onto something else.

So the visioning is a continuous development process. The vision changes as confidence grows and aspirations are realized. Vision is a journey, not a destination. (Yes, I know it sounds a bit naff but that's what it really feels like.)

Don't worry if your vision does not come to you straight away. It will emerge at some point during the development of your business. In my case it came almost two years after starting out when I started to think about making a change – 'growing my business'.

Visioning is a powerful driver. Psychologists tell us that visioning allows the unconscious mind to work on the vision, creating new ideas to help you achieve it. Some of my sporting and business heroes used these techniques to attain their goals. I simply thought, if this is working for them then it's good enough for me. Give it a go. You might surprise yourself.

Building your jigsaw

Now that you have begun to develop your vision it is time to consider the resources you will need to bring together to make a success of it.

When I ask entrepreneurs how they learn the craft of running their businesses, I find that they are an eclectic bunch – they behave like magpies, picking up attractive ideas wherever they can find them.

So in drawing up your overall business design you should go out to meet successful entrepreneurs because we know that entrepreneurs learn from each other. One of their favourite design methods is deliberately to involve themselves in a variety of experiences, picking up and integrating the bits they want into the design of their business.

They often find that 1+1+1 can make 5.

John Noble sent his right-hand man to learn how to farm oysters from the French. Tom Hunter recruited a retailer with blue chip experience to bring the wisdom of large companies to help him grow his business. Learning from others is the entrepreneur's favoured way of learning.

The trick is to learn from good role models, not poor ones.

You'll remember that any successful business needs four elements if it is to succeed and grow: *driving, doing, selling* and *controlling*.

The *drive* comes from the lead entrepreneur and if you are not the sort of person to find visions compelling and worth striving for, you will be in trouble. But the very fact that you are reading this book suggests that you probably have that approach to life.

Your 'apprenticeship' as an entrepreneur should have taught you something about *doing* – giving you an understanding of how the technical side of your chosen business works. If you haven't got that basic knowledge you can follow the example of John Noble and find people who can give you the skills you lack. But it is far better to build up your business in an area of operation you are already familiar with.

Selling is a capability you will need, but it is a specialist skill that otherwise capable entrepreneurs don't always possess. What can you do about it?

Finding your first customers

Often selling depends on having done some 'networking' and made the contacts. People like to do business with people they already know.

People who have served their 'apprenticeship' often have a formidable network at their fingertips before they launch themselves into the world of business. They 'hit the ground running'.

David Latham of Labtech, the firm making microwave circuits, had a large network of contacts in Britain's big defence companies from the years he had spent working in research and development at ICL.

> The radar business was a small world and over the years I had met most of the key people at conferences or in committees at the MoD. Now that I was in business for myself I found I could phone in, make an appointment, and discuss their technical problems with them. I was pushing at an open door.

Neil Gibson of the JHB Group, based in Glasgow, had a very similar experience. He took the step of talking to potential customers for his specialist paints before he launched his new company:

> When I had the idea of taking over JHB – I talked to all my customers and told them what I was contemplating doing. They all said they would give me a chance and that is all you can ask for.
>
> The great advantage was I knew a lot of these customers from my days at the old JHB and it was not a matter of being put on a list of potential suppliers – often that leads nowhere. In this industry you can't just walk up and knock on the door. Because they had known me over a long period of time they were prepared to meet me and discuss business.

If there is a lesson it is that successful entrepreneurs don't just sit in the office and expect business to come to them. They go out and actively seek it.

However, in the early days, firms with no particular expertise in selling or without established networks may be able to find the sort of help they need by hiring in the expertise.

I am thinking of the service offered by an agent like Suzanne Tomblin of Lincoln who will organize a mail-shot, a telephone follow-up and even personal visits by agents to help the sales effort. Companies like this offer a ready-made 'virtual sales force' and all for a modest fee that helps keep scarce cash resources within the company.

Bethan Jones of the Export Association in Mid Wales runs a 'shared export salesmen scheme' for small companies who cannot afford full time export salespeople so they join together to employ a salesperson. They share the costs and the salespeople bring in the new business.

Then there's the Internet, which offers a low-cost way of selling across national borders. If you think your business could benefit from the growing fashion for e-commerce, again there are firms who will help you design your Web page and make sure the payment system is foolproof.

Joe Mogodi of Mogodi Memorials always had a dream of working for himself. However, he joined Nissan and was sent to Japan for training. He discovered, through a friend, a small factory that was manufacturing tombstones from granite chips. This is what Joe had been looking for all his life. Unfortunately Joe faced a major problem back home. His target market, mainly black people, did not believe that a fellow black person could manufacture tombstones of quality. Joe persisted and when a prominent black businessman bought a stone from him his business took off.

Joe is now the biggest tombstone manufacture in Northern Province and the third largest in South Africa.

Joe took an approach that can be best described as 'standing in the customer's shoes'. What would customers for a tombstone expect their supplier to look like? How would they behave? Joe designed his business to meet the customers' expectations. He got the details right from the start.

When Daewoo, the Korean company, started in the UK car market four years ago, they had no reputation or track record, so they decided to design their sales operation 'stood in their customers' shoes'.

They placed adverts in the media: Tell us what is wrong with car dealerships? What do you dislike about buying cars from dealers in the UK? They expected 10,000 replies, but received 250,000 responses. They had a list of 250,000 potential customers and the 12 reasons why people disliked car dealerships became their sales offering.

For example, people told them they disliked pushy salesmen on commission and price lists with 'extras'. So they did away with salespeople and had a one-price all-inclusive offer. By standing in their customers' shoes they were able to design their business based on 'real' customer feedback. They doubled their market share targets in three years!

Attention to detail is something all entrepreneurs should try to cultivate. James Dyson saw that his company had to be designed to complement his revolutionary vacuum cleaner, a product that was redesigned more than 500 times before he was finally happy with it. The cleaner emerged with distinctive colouring and clean lines, and it was super-efficient. He has described how he and his team designed the business in the same image, not just in areas like packaging and user literature, but down to detailing how the telephones were to be answered and how the customers were to be dealt with.

That sort of designing amounts to a form of *control*. I need to sound a note of warning here. Trying to control and supervise every aspect of the business is natural in the early stages. But as the business matures, so does the need to make sure that the people who work for the business are involved in the design process. They have got to feel they have ownership of it. We have all had experience of the parroted 'How may I help you?' insincere telephone manner.

Control in the sense of financial control is often the one area most entrepreneurs have little or no expertise in when they start out. And mistakes made in the early months can destroy the business. Borrowing too much money, spending money on symbols like flashy cars and plush offices, lashing out on expensive advertising, these are pitfalls successful entrepreneurs learn to avoid. As we have seen, they *'rough it at the start'* and *'beg, borrow and befriend'*.

But experience suggests there has to be something more – even if you can avoid turning to banks and lending institutions you still need to prepare a *business case* to help think through objectively the business prospects for the new company.

Producing a business case

A business case differs from a business plan in that it is concerned only with answering the question: Do I have a viable business here? It will determine whether the business opportunity you have spotted can really be turned into a sustainable business.

So far, if you have followed the entrepreneurial way, you will have gathered lots of ideas and a store of useful information about your business. But does your vision, the opportunity, and prospects for sales all hang together? In short, do you have a viable business? It is worth recalling the entrepreneurial model we looked at earlier with the key elements needed for business success (Figure 4.1).

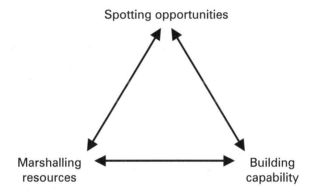

Figure 4.1 *The entrepreneurial process*

Overall you need to know:

- Will customers pay for my product/service?
- Is it a real opportunity or just an idea?
- How will I get the resources to take up this opportunity?
- Can I get them cheaply enough?
- What will we have to learn to do well to take up this opportunity?
- What capabilities do we need to build?

This is where we test the dreams in reality. This process is really not linear, it is much more like creating a patchwork quilt.

You have already come across the sort of questions you need to ask in the chapter on 'apprenticeship' (Chapter 2). Only this time you need facts, not assumptions.

Who really are my customers?

In the case of Phil Crane the answer would be families and young people living within an hour's journey of North Queensferry (where Deep Sea World has been built) plus tourist visitors to Edinburgh.

In other cases the answer may not be so straightforward. If your business is to be making TV programmes, who are the customers? The viewers or British broadcasting company executives? If you produce oysters, are your customers the fish wholesalers, the restaurateurs or the people who like eating oysters and are prepared to pay highly for the pleasure?

How do I reach potential customers?

Answering the first question helps provide answers to this question. John Noble realized his primary customers were the restaurateurs and they were strictly finite in number and could be reached by mail-shot, telephone, and by personal calling. Joe Mogodi used a prominent figure to engage others to buy.

Peter Keary of the Elton Hotel sends out regular mail-shots. As with much in business, there is no one 'right' way, it depends on your product and your customers.

What do they tell me they want?

During your apprenticeship years you will have gathered intelligence to help you answer this question. But now you need to listen more carefully to see how they react to your idea.

Phil Crane's customers told him they wanted entertaining and educating but above all to have fun.

John Ferguson's hotel customers wanted the very best quality meat products.

What price do they say they will pay?

If you give customers what they want they will pay you for it. It is possible to be too cheap as well as too expensive; you would not expect to pay a Mini price for a Rolls-Royce or vice versa.

John Noble discovered that his overseas customers were prepared to pay premium prices for his oysters and salmon.

What do I need to do to get their business?

David Latham needed to respond quickly to customer requests:

> We had an exhibition in June in San Francisco, and a guy said to me, 'Why should I buy from you, you are thousands of miles away?' He was based in New York, and I said 'If you can send me the data on Sunday, we will ship your stuff on a Wednesday by UPS and it will be in your office on Thursday. Can you get that kind of service in the States?' and the answer was no.

How do I create a competitive advantage?

A competitive advantage gives you the edge on your competitors by creating a unique point of difference and it might enable you to get higher prices for your products. Sources of competitive advantage include quality, customer service, technology and even relationships with key people. You should try to avoid 'being the cheapest' as your competitive advantage, because you may well enjoy lots of sales but make little profit.

David Latham has a technical edge. Neil Gibson has a very strong network of customer contacts and key influencers. John Ferguson provides the best meat available that his customers can order 24 hours a day.

Competitive advantage is created, not bestowed on you by customers.

Clearly there may be other important questions you need to ask, dependent on your business:

- Where can I get good reliable suppliers?
- Who can I trust to help me?
- Where can I get resources on the cheap?
- Who will give me money?
- What do I need to do to survive short term?

You should write out in detail the answers to these questions. If you have any gaps or questions you cannot answer, then it's back to the drawing board. Make a list of any assumptions you make that may need to be tested.

Let's assume you have been able to find answers to all the questions. We can now start to draw up the business case.

Drawing up the business case

The business case starts with the most basic building block – *a reliable sales forecast*.

It is probably best to take an example to see how you can work the forecast out (see box).

An example of Deep Sea World

In 1990 Phil Crane ploughed his profits from his video business into establishing Deep Sea World on the Firth of Forth. How did he calculate his sales for year one?

> I had gathered in a lot of research about this sort of attraction from looking at the annual reports of similar operations in the USA and New Zealand. I reckoned I could handle a maximum of 4,000 visitors a day and that I should aim at 3,000 as an acceptable figure for year 1. The site was next to a motorway, within 15 miles of Edinburgh and I reckoned this was realistic.

But a sales forecast does not only involve the number of customers but how much each is willing to pay. How did he estimate that figure?

> There were other attractions already up and running – Edinburgh Zoo, Stirling Castle, Falkland Palace. The Zoo was the nearest equivalent. They charged £5.00 an adult and £3.00 a child. Because I had a new-style attraction, I reckoned £5.00 and £3.00 was about right. I reckoned there would be two kids for every 1 adult – so in a typical day based on my research I'd have 1,000 adults and 2,000 kids.

This gave him a sales forecast of 360 days @ £11,000 a day or £3,960,000 pounds a year.

This figure of nearly £4 million was clearly optimistic.

> You have to allow for the fact that this is a seasonal trade and that there are peaks and troughs even in a typical summer week. I reckoned, based on New Zealand experience, that this would reduce the total numbers by about a third, so that £2,640,000 would be more realistic.

So there should be an estimate of seasonality included in the business case wherever it is a factor.

The next stage in preparing the business case is to calculate the projected profit, by subtracting the anticipated costs from the forecast sales.

After this we need to work out the *break-even point*.

To do this you must take the overall predicted costs and work out on a weekly or monthly basis how much income from sales is needed to match those costs. You can calculate the break-even point by taking total sales less variable costs (those which vary with sales, ie materials and labour) which leaves an amount to pay for your overheads; the break-even point is a point when you can pay all overheads. Knowing the break-even point is a critical way of monitoring the progress of the business. If sales fall below the forecast level, speedy action can be taken to cut costs accordingly; being aware of using this approach has saved many businesses.

A record of how many firm orders you have received for your product or service at the outset of trading should also be part of the *business case*.

It needs to be completed by working out *cash-flow projections*. This is a chart showing just when cash is expected to flow into and out of the business – something which many start-up businesses ignore at their peril, especially if they have no credit facilities capable of dealing with such factors as time-delays on payments coming in.

Along with this should be forecasts of just how much the business will owe at any one time and how much will be owed to it – a *creditors and debtors forecast*.

It may sound a complicated business but, once you have the information, a day spent with a qualified accountant is usually enough to put these figures and forecasts in place.

This process helps you focus on your business objectives and check your progress towards them; be warned, it is no guarantee that you won't be faced by unpleasant surprises or difficult moments. The box below describes a hard business lesson.

A hard business lesson

Despite all the care Phil Crane put into drawing up his plan, the whole operation got off to a very bad start:

> Two weeks after we opened we were told that there was a £1.5 million overspend on the construction work – I had never faced that before in my life. It could almost have been a knock-out blow, but we had to fight it. We had to restructure the company financially. That was a huge learning process that should stand me in good stead for the next 60 years!

> Phil, like all good entrepreneurs, had the tenacity and the flexibility to make adjustments to his plans and see off the crisis. But it is worth adding a few tips to everyone drawing up a *business case*.

Some useful tips and lessons for entrepreneurs

- Get professional help on producing the numbers.
- People generally over-estimate sales and underestimate start-up costs.
- They assume positive cash flows too quickly.
- Some customers who said they were interested at the research stage change their minds.
- It can take longer to make sales than anticipated.
- Produce a survival budget and stick to it.

There are hundreds of books and guides from banks and Business Links on how to produce a basic business case. So I don't intend to cover here what is well covered by most traditional business texts. Don't be afraid to take advice and seek help when you feel you need it.

Creating your recipe for success

Let's assume you have now drawn up your business case. It's a building block that puts a solid foundation under your business.

But beware. The metaphor of putting up a building might lead you to think that constructing a successful business is an ordered process that proceeds logically from one floor to the next. This is an assumption made by many business authors who write guides describing business building as a step-by-step process, a linear process.

In fact the entrepreneurs I have met and studied have not behaved in this way and don't see business building in those terms. The jigsaw or the patchwork quilt provides better metaphors. There's an element of creative imagination involved and the order you put the pieces together is not predetermined but depends on the circumstances, and on the style of the entrepreneur.

Another useful metaphor is that of the chef in his kitchen. The chef puts together a list of the ingredients and quantities required in great detail. Some of the most successful of all the entrepreneurs I have met use exactly this approach to running a business. They create a recipe.

Your recipe

After the business case it can be really helpful to develop your own recipe. A detailed recipe will enable you to do business in a consistent manner and helps you build a strong company culture right from the start of trading.

We have already seen something of this approach in the example of Joe Mogodi and his effort to 'stand in the shoes of the customer'.

However, a more comprehensive company recipe has been developed by Keepmoat plc, an outstanding example of a successful entrepreneurial-driven company. Keepmoat, a Doncaster-based building firm, has grown from nothing to a turnover of £100 million a year in just 20 years and in 1994 was named the 11th most successful private firm in the UK (Jordan Market Survey).

Terry Bramall of Keepmoat has been in charge from the start and has developed the recipe that has become known as *'The Keepmoat Way'*.

Terry told me:

> This is not a useless piece of bureaucratic jargon. It's a statement in plain English of Keepmoat's objectives, and its guiding principles. Because we have written them down, talk about them regularly and use them to help make decisions, everybody appreciates what makes the company tick, what its values are. It also keeps us focused on the issues we as a company see as essential to our future.

But can you write a recipe like this before you have built the business up? Or has it grown with time?

> You can certainly start with your strategy, particularly mission, vision and values and with a definition of how everyone in the company is expected to behave in relation to absolutely central concerns like customer relations. Obviously with time you may want to add or subtract from the recipe and everybody at Keepmoat is encouraged to raise issues they think should be added or taken away. It is not cast in concrete.

The present recipe used at Keepmoat is shown in the box below.

The Keepmoat Way

- Focus on regeneration of homes and building new starter homes.
- Build partnerships with local authorities.

- Delight customers.
- Complete all jobs within cost and time deadlines.
- Manage the milestones (key points on all contracts).
- Induct people in the Keepmoat Way.
- Use established processes to make good decisions and protect plans.
- Treat each other with dignity and respect.
- Encourage team working; particularly cross-team.
- Support managers through difficult trading times.

Notice that competent successful entrepreneurs are quite open about and are willing to share their recipes. They know it took them 20 years to develop and it would probably take at least as long for a competitor to copy.

When I built a business we established our recipe (see box).

The David Hall Partnership Way

- Seek to delight customers at every opportunity.
- Stick to the products and markets we know.
- Develop competent confident people.
- Maintain the highest quality standard.
- Provide innovative solutions to customer problems.
- No surprises for the shareholders.

We did not always manage to live up to these principles, but they did serve as a useful way of describing how we wanted to try to do business and what made us different.

An overall design for your business

So, in summary, designing the business involves:

1. assessing your opportunity;
2. creating the capability;
3. finding the resources;
4. preparing a business case; and
5. devising a recipe.

One more thing, creating the company identity by which it will be known to the outside world. To help you in that task I end with another list, which you can use to check off your own progress. It is not exclusive but it can get your new company off to a good start. Virtually all aspects of your business can be designed. Successful entrepreneurs do not leave these things to chance.

We are now ready to get motoring. The box below contains a design checklist.

Design checklist

Business name
Logo
Products/service
Customer service
Sales methods
Literature
Customer incentives
Induction
Training
Dress
Offices
Culture – the way you do things
Team working
Communication methods
Letterheads
Web site
How you work together
Partnerships and alliances
Job titles

To enable you to start your business in the right frame of mind here are 10 myths about entrepreneurs, which hopefully by now you recognize as being false. They also serve as a summary of some of the key points covered so far in this book.

Ten myths about entrepreneurs

Myth 1   Entrepreneurs are dodgy business people who are only interested in making a fast buck for themselves.

Reality   There is confusion in the UK, between entrepreneurs who seek to create value, and racketeers who are only interested in making money for themselves.

Entrepreneurship can happen in schools, churches, hospitals, the public sector, in fact, anywhere where people create value from nothing.

Myth 2   Entrepreneurs use formal traditional business approaches to create success.

Reality   Entrepreneurs spot opportunities, get resources on the cheap and build their skills in order to create valued businesses.

Myth 3   Entrepreneurs are risk takers.

Reality   Entrepreneurs do take carefully calculated risks. They then spend a great deal of time and energy in doing all they can to minimize those risks.

Myth 4   Entrepreneurs are born not made.

Reality   Entrepreneurs serve an apprenticeship acquiring skills, contacts and experiences often over a long period to enable them to start their business. This includes large doses of personal development.

Myth 5   Money from a bank is the biggest blockage to starting a business.

Reality   Cash is not normally a real blockage. Eighty per cent of start-up capital is from personal savings, 30 per cent from family and friends and only 15 per cent from the banks. Note: More than one source is used in most cases.

However, raising money can be a problem for high-tech start-ups that require large investments up-front.

Myth 6   If an entrepreneur has sufficient capital he or she cannot go wrong.

Reality   The opposite is true. Too much money can encourage a lack of discipline that can lead to impulsive spending which normally creates problems.

Myth 7   Any really good idea can be turned into a successful business.

Reality   Entrepreneurs understand the difference between an idea and an opportunity.

An idea is something they are personally passionate about. An opportunity normally solves a customer's problem.

The Sinclair C5 is a classic example of an idea that was not an opportunity.

Myth 8   Large companies need to create a culture of entrepreneurship and innovation in order to continually develop.

Reality   Large companies need to encourage enterprising individuals, providing them with the space and support to experiment and be entrepreneurial.

Myth 9   Entrepreneurs are egotistical, independent and are their own masters.

Reality   Entrepreneurs are egotistical and independent but they actually can choose to serve many masters, including employees, shareholders, customers, creditors and their own families. It is also extremely rare to develop a business to more than £1 million single-handedly.

Myth 10   Starting an entrepreneurial business is risky and often ends in failure.

Reality   Most businesses that end cease trading, they do not fail. Less than 2 per cent actually go bankrupt. Businesses fail, entrepreneurs do not.

starting **your business**

- Safe starts
- Roughing it at the start
- Selecting and creating new customers
- What customers expect
- Winning new customers
- The principle of customer delight
- Picking the right people
- Finding help
- Experimenting and learning
- Getting paid on time

The more I have worked with entrepreneurs and researched the way they started and run their businesses the more I have realized why entrepreneurs don't read traditional business books. Academics and journalists write most business books. Most have never run a business of their own, and have never been in the shoes of the entrepreneur. From the point of view of the entrepreneur they compound this lack of experience by trying to analyze and categorize business behaviour. Entrepreneurs don't sit analyzing their businesses, they get on with the job and come up with solutions to problems as they arrive. Most, like Phil Crane, learn from practical experience.

But if I believed entrepreneurs learned only from their own experience there would be no point in writing this book. There is a very steep learning curve for entrepreneurs at start-up, and this book aims to help you to avoid some of the pitfalls. Many of the successful role models we've been looking at admit that there is one group they are willing to take lessons from – other entrepreneurs who have perhaps faced similar problems and challenges and come up with practical solutions. When I brought a number of them together they soon found they had much to talk about and much to learn from each other.

Richard Holt, who runs a successful IT consultancy in Chester, was a founder member of the group who wanted to do business in Belgium.

> The cost of an airfare, £300 return, was just prohibitive; a colleague in the group told me about a specialist travel company based in Manchester, that organized business flights to Belgium for £175. That one bit of information saved me a least £10k a year and more importantly allowed me to expand my business. The group of fellow entrepreneurs is an invaluable way of sharing experiences with each other.

Tom Hunter also values the support of fellow entrepreneurs:

> The network is very, very important. I have been involved with a few organizations with similar-minded people so we get together and thrash things about, and that's very important. It's a group of entrepreneurs and some pretty high-powered people. If somebody comes up with a bright business idea and it needs financing they can go and finance it. It is just a whole network of ideas. It's very helpful because we are all entrepreneurs working together.

It is precisely because entrepreneurs are prepared to listen and learn from others like them that the experiences of the successful entrepreneurs brought to you in this book should be of such value to people wanting to emulate them in building a growing and profitable business.

By now you should have begun to create the vision that will drive your new business, and have judged just what sort of business your experience of life and work has best prepared you for. You may perhaps have already spotted an opportunity, preferably a 'superior' opportunity. You are ready to start on the road to fortune.

In this section of the book, we'll be considering how to get the business up and running, and how to build it up into a profitable company with a bright future. The vision for many entrepreneurs at start-up is summarized by Kevin Smith of ACT Controls in one word: Survival. So before you spend a penny of your hard-earned savings, or go rushing off to try to raise cash, let's take some sound advice from people who have been there and survived successfully.

A safe start – minimizing cash flow problems

Most successful entrepreneurs, as we saw, served an apprenticeship of around 10 years with an employer before eventually launching their own company. However, they were able to think about their new business, and test out ideas, while they still had the benefit of a salary.

When the time came to take the plunge and launch themselves into their new venture, many found ways to cushion the shock of transition. They opted for what I call a *safe start*. They chose not to begin full-time, but to overlap working for themselves with part-time working at their old job. This is what I've described as having a 'day job' and a 'night job'.

Phil Crane knows all about safe starts:

> I spent almost a year in India, South America and Australia. I came back to the UK to go to medical school. I started studying for that in the mornings and I was running a garage, owned by my brother, in the afternoons. I had a night job as well. I didn't have any money whatsoever, but I got the merchant bug. I bought a car for £30 and sold it for £70, and I thought 'This is amazing.' I got a real buzz out of that, so I started my own car business; each car paid for the new one. I then got a chance to get a franchise, and ended up with two franchises, and I bought my own garage; that was largely off the winnings from the Grand National.

The great advantage of starting off your business in this way, working on it in the evening and weekends, is that it creates a financial resource you can draw on to ease you through difficulties which often arise in the early days of trading.

Another option is to negotiate a deal with your employer, allowing you to go part-time while you start your business. This is how I started my business. I negotiated a three-year deal under which I worked for 100 days a year for my then employer. The 100 days paid the mortgage and gave me a small guaranteed income while I devoted the bulk of my energies to setting up my own business.

The income from the 100 days had another benefit, which I hadn't foreseen at the time. When you start up you find you have to spend money, if only to buy office stationery, computers, and have a letterhead designed. No matter how effective your efforts have been in drumming up advance business or in winning orders when you start, you will find there is lag before income from sales starts to come in. This is the 'hockey stick' effect – the cash-flow graph looks like a hockey stick with a steep plunge in the cash reserve before income gradually builds up – and often forces new business into debt right from the start. Many never get themselves out of hock.

So take a tip from successful entrepreneurs: be creative in considering how you can engineer a safe way to get started.

Roughing it at the start – conserving your cash in order to survive

We have already seen that successful entrepreneurs had found there was much to be said for 'roughing it at the start'.

Peter Keary, who runs the Elton Hotel, described a very typical caution when it comes to spending money:

> It would have been very nice to have a plush office with a brass plate on the door but we borrowed a lot of money to buy the hotel, so we had very little spare initially.
>
> I did several jobs in the hotel, often working 16-hour days, to save costs on recruiting new staff. If the chef was off, I filled in. We could not afford to advertise and had to ban any non-essential expenditure. We just had to get on with it.

As it happened, Peter's 'roughing it at the start' policy paid off and now he has doubled the turnover and has a really strong business. But whatever the circumstances, the principle of roughing it as far as you can is one you should adopt.

The effect of keeping expenditure to a minimum is to conserve any capital you may have in as liquid a form as possible. It may be needed if anything goes wrong, and it almost certainly will.

The adage – a fool and his cash are soon parted – is one that start-up entrepreneurs need to take very seriously. Plenty of people will flock to your door when the business first gets started, and their priorities are not the same as yours. Watch out particularly for photocopier salespeople, stationery reps, those who offer 'the best pension deal this century', and insurance salesmen. Their job is to part you from your money; yours is to be like Scrooge and hold on to every penny you can.

'Roughing it' means spreading payments when you can, doing without an office until you really need it and then negotiating short, easy get out leases. Forget the Porsche – hire a van instead. Put a sign on your desk: *How can I get it for nothing?* You will find that your Scrooge-like resolve means you can negotiate better deals – take a leaf out of John Pye's book: '*I had to learn to negotiate for everything; when you have few resources you have little option.*'

Roughing it and beg, borrow and befriend go hand in hand.

Because in Britain we have few positive images of successful entrepreneurs available to us, successful entrepreneurs are too often seen as big spenders with extravagant lifestyles. They own flash cars, live in big houses, and spend long holidays in exotic foreign places, often with a yacht as a floating hotel. It may be unfair to someone like Richard Branson (the owner of Virgin Airways among other things) but that is how he tends to be seen – as a millionaire dilettante with time to spare. Real-life new entrepreneurs are in my experience quite the opposite.

They are scavengers who dislike waste. Many get their relatives to do the secretarial work for free. They are more likely to get their office furniture from a second-hand shop than from Harrods, drive vans rather than flash sports cars and get their products delivered by a helpful relative rather than by Federal Express or DHL. It's all about conserving cash by getting the job done cost-effectively.

A Scottish friend of mine who runs a watersports centre is typical, a master at begging, borrowing, and befriending people to get the resources he needed to build his business. He wants to remain nameless in case his story confirms the English prejudices about the Scots' spending habits!

This is how he started his restaurant:

> We started doing bacon rolls out of a caravan, which someone had given me in order to get it off their hands. I put a hole in the side and put a flap on it and a gas ring. My wife's sister ran it. She was an academic during the winter months and it became a family joke.

Now the restaurant employs five people and has seating for 60. Again a miracle of parsimonious ingenuity:

> My wife bought the restaurant chairs when the RAF (the Air Force had a base nearby) was having a clear out. They cost us £3 apiece. They were also throwing out old foam and I'd got a friend staying who was a soft furnisher. So I took 40 pieces of foam and he reupholstered the seats for free. We ended up with 60 new chairs at a cost of about £200. Had we bought them new we would be looking at spending thousands of pounds.

His sailing instruction business was equally started on a shoestring:

> When I started I bought my first sailing boat second hand. I then persuaded my friend's housekeeper to buy a boat and lease it to me. Then we had a stroke of good fortune. Some friends tipped me off that a sailing centre up the road was getting rid of some sailing boats and we picked three up for free. I swapped these three Wayfarers, which were big boats, for nine new canoes and we brought them back here for our canoeing courses. I've still got one, which I've had for 20 years. I got all my resources for nothing.

This even applies to his house, an attractive log cabin:

> One day they were taking down the telegraph poles. I stopped the car and said to the foreman: Can I buy them? How much? He said 50p each. Over the next four years I bought 100. We have just finished building the house. So I suppose frugality is the name of the game.

Frugal, frugal, frugal is the message from my Scottish friend. Although he's an extreme example of a low-spending entrepreneur, the others I met – almost without exception – had got where they had by carefully watching their pennies. And it has made the difference in the end between success and failure.

The habits of entrepreneurs

The best-selling US book, *The Millionaires Next Door*, about entrepreneurs who become millionaires, reveals their surprising habits:

> They live well below their means. They buy cheap cars and suits off the peg. They build up investments but live in modest houses. They do invest in the best tax assessment and investment advice. They believe financial independence is more important than displaying high social status. They also ask for discounts and buy well. In Texas they call people who have flash lifestyles beyond their means as Big Hats No Cattle.

If you want to calculate what you should be worth right now, a simple rule of thumb in the 'Millionaires Next Door' book might help:

Multiply your age by your pre-tax income from all sources except inheritance. Divide by 10. This, less any inherited wealth, is what your net worth should be.

For example: Mr 'X' has a pre-tax income of 50k. He is 50 years old.

$$\frac{50 \times 50}{10} = 250k$$

This is the benchmark achieved by the 'Millionaires Next Door'. Learn the lesson from them. Do the calculation yourself and see if you are ahead or behind where you should be at this stage of your life. If it is less than your benchmark criteria, then it's back to living within your means.

When people do create valued businesses they can enjoy the trappings of success a little more if they choose to.

Tom Hunter survived with help from a kind benefactor:

> My major customer wanted me to expand through their stores, which I did. However, the Chairman who had befriended me took me into his office and said he was changing the way they paid me; instead of them taking all the money and paying me 6–8 weeks later, I was to bank the takings and pay them. At this point they owed me £30,000. Six weeks later they went bust owing me just £146.00. That was a real turning point for the business because I would have gone down with them.

So the key questions to ask every time you are tempted to spend your hard-earned cash on resources is:

- Do I really need this resource, can I do without?
- Where can I get this for free?
- Who do I know who could do this for me on the cheap?
- Do I know somebody who can get me this if I can do something for them in return?

It can become a real personal challenge and good fun to get resources cheaply.

Have you noticed how some people seem to pay much less for their cars, holidays or even getting their homes decorated? They have the entrepreneurial knack of finding resources when they need them, and the skill of negotiating with the dash of chutzpah it needs to ask for a special deal. So here is another key element in the entrepreneurial way – *most entrepreneurship starts with a deal of some kind.* Entrepreneurs are deal makers.

You can train yourself to think and act in this entrepreneurial way. Imprint '*Everything is negotiable*' on your mind. It pays to remember that for every £100 you save on resources you can afford to achieve £2,000 less in sales (if your profit margin is 5 per cent) and still make the same profit!

The entrepreneur's shopping list

Item	Entrepreneur	'Blue chip' business executive
Office	Spare bedroom	New business park
Car	Small second-hand car	Jaguar
Suit	Marks & Spencer	Georgio Armani
Lunch	Cheese sandwich	Conran Restaurant
Drinks	Tea and coffee	Fine wines
Filing System	Cardboard boxes	Designer briefcase by Mulberry

Obviously the shopping list is a bit of fun but it serves to make the point about how entrepreneurs behave to in order to conserve cash to survive.

Another trick employed by the entrepreneurs who really make a go of it is to set out to *control* resources as opposed to *owning* them. In that way they can turn them on and off as required.

Here's an example of what I mean:

Jill Macdonald runs Cutting and Wear with her brother in Rotherham. The company originally manufactured Tungsten Carbide hardfacing rod for the gas drilling industry. The discovery of North Sea oil just off Aberdeen provided a real boost so they decided to go into the manufacture of drilling tools, in particular stabilizers.

> We used local suppliers where heat treatment, forging and the engineering skills were readily available. We could use them as and when we needed and frankly we could not have developed this new product without being able to tap into high quality local resources.

When entrepreneurs behave like this, switching off expenditure when the business can't afford it and on again when the resources are needed, they give themselves the protection enjoyed by the double-skinned boat. They can occasionally run onto rocks without sinking the ship. In the early stages of a business this can make all the difference between survival and going down.

As my Scottish friend shows, the customers you deal with need never know your business is lean and sparse in terms of the resources it uses. You can arrange things to give quite the contrary impression.

A virtual office

When I started up my business my wife answered the telephone, my son typed the invoices, and to provide the training I offered companies, I employed staff by the day on a subcontract basis. My sales calls were done by an agency at an hourly charge, I hired a car on a daily basis when I needed one, and an office in London by the hour. My accounts clerk worked half a day a week as and when I needed him.

When I wanted to impress customers I met them in a friend's posh office at Wadworth Hall, a fine mansion house in its own grounds.

On reflection, everything was virtual. I owned nothing, yet customers seemed to think I had a large business!

The principle of controlling, not owning, resources is still a very good one. It is smart not to tie up valuable cash resources in fixed assets, particularly at start-up.

And more resources than ever can now be purchased by the hour. For instance, even today when I meet customers in London, I hire an office by the hour with the full support of telephone, fax, e-mail and secretarial service.

Entrepreneur Mark Dixon has actually created a business by becoming an international provider of serviced offices. Regus is expanding at two new service offices per week and currently has 232 centres worldwide, even though during 1999 the company is still sustaining operating losses reflecting the start-up costs of rapid global expansion. *The Financial Times* reported on 28 May 1999 that the business will be floated at £1 billion, nearly four times its value, in August 1999.

Selecting and creating new customers – focus on targeted customers

Most of us think of customers as people who come to us, and over whom we have little choice. It's a mental picture that comes from the shopping analogy. Some 'customers' in big stores never actually buy anything; they are window shoppers who come just to look, or to keep out of the cold.

But to be a successful entrepreneur you need to put that image out of your mind. Smart entrepreneurs create a profile of the type of customers they would prefer to do business with and then set out to get them.

Customers are of course essential to any commercial enterprise. Until you *create* some customers all you have are costs. But you first have to decide what kind of customer you want. You must *select* them.

When young designers Tony Di Donato and Peter Asprey of Asprey Di Donato Design opened their Melbourne studio in the early 1990s, they admit that they did not appreciate the value of professional management practices. Their youth coupled with the excitement of starting up blinded them to sound business decisions.

To begin with, they put all of their efforts into chasing small accounts without working towards winning a big one.

In 1993, they eventually won their first large account and learned an even more poignant lesson. On the strength of a handshake agreement, the company undertook work worth A$100,000 for a large investment company. Although the completed work was well received, the investment company refused to pay, and Asprey and Di Donato had no legal redress.

> We learnt to always have our terms of trade agreement signed before beginning any project.

Since that time, the company has learnt its lessons and expanded its client base, focusing on the companies it wants to do business with. It has achieved the distinction of beating around 7,000 entries to win the prestigious Chicago Athenaeum, an international good design award, in 1997.

In the financial year 1997–98, the company increased its staff to nine and lifted turnover from A$1.6 million to A$2.2 million. Di Donato says:

> We're not only growing in dollar terms, but also in the type of projects we are taking on, from creating exhibition work, signage and architectural commissions to three-dimensional and interior work.

This is a good example of how companies can both create and select their customers.

Tony and Peter learnt from their early experiences that the best customers for Asprey Di Donato Design would be well-established, large companies, highly rated on the stock market – the sort commonly referred to as 'blue chip' companies. They appreciated that there were many advantages for any small company in targeting this sort of customer:

- Having a blue chip customer gives credibility to the company; this in turn makes it easier to expand the customer base.
- Blue chip companies pay their bills – usually in good time, providing you agree terms and conditions of payment!
- Once such a customer is secured there is likely to be repeat business over the long term.
- Blue chip companies can offer large contracts, transforming the financial prospects for the new company.
- Blue chip companies may well grow. If they do, there is an opportunity to 'piggy back' on their success.
- Work for one part of a blue chip company can lead on to work in their other divisions.
- They generally treat suppliers fairly. (Let me know those that don't – we will start a national black list).

Of course, the sort of business you want to develop may not be suited to supplying that sort of company. But the point is that, as a small business, you should have a policy about the sort of customers you want to work with and target them.

Laurence Young of the Lodge on the Loch Hotel discovered that targeting customers can bring significant benefits:

> One key source market to us is the overseas group market (coach tour operators). This was a market that I knew nothing about. My hotel background hadn't given me any feeling for it. I suppose, being British, I associated it with grannies and grandpas and buckets and spades. We soon came to realize that out there, there is the international market, where there is money and the clients are desperate for quality hotels. We actually target and focus on this market now.

The services I personally offer, advising and helping companies to improve the way they operate, could be of value to a wide range of companies. But which ones should I concentrate on? Personally I target the chief executives of companies in sectors experiencing high levels of change: they tend to need and value my services most.

Just selling to anybody is not good business practice. You can do without bad payers or 'toxic' customers, the sort who give you lots of problems. Remember there are two decisions to be made: does this customer want to buy from us and do we want to work with them? Once you have made your selection they need to be created in a proactive way. It is no good sitting in the office waiting for the customers to come to you.

Obviously you will get enquiries from customers outside these criteria and you will do business with them; it happens to all businesses. However, your criteria for selection provide ideal targets, saving time and energy when you are proactively seeking to create the customers your business needs.

What customers expect from you

In Britain we are not generally good at dealing with customers. If you want to run a business successfully you have to adopt some of the US way.

Archie Norman, the chairman of Asda, tells a story of going 'on a pilgrimage' to Walmart, the US discount retailer.

> I picked out a checkout operator at random and asked what it was she liked about working for Walmart. She said it was the best company in America, her shares were worth $4,500 and she told me she knew the names of all her regular customers.

It obviously had a big impact on Mr Norman:

> This is the attitude to customers we aspired to at Asda.

Walmart must have thought he did a good job because they bought Asda for £6.7 billion in June 1999.

The first secret of creating customers is that customers want their suppliers to be warm and friendly human beings who take an interest in them and their company and not simply in what they are trying to sell. They also like people who appear to be passionate about what they are offering. In this regard, small companies generally have an advantage over bigger concerns. (Why this should be we'll see later in Chapter 9.)

Here, for example, is what David Latham says about the way he wins and keeps customers:

> I read, every week, 20 or 30 journals relating to our industry. Somewhere in these there is a tiny snippet of information; even looking down the job columns, if you see that a company like GEC are advertising for microwave designers and engineers, you know that that is a potential market. If I read in the Sunday Times that GEC had an ad that said 'Microwave engineers required', I'd come into the office on that Sunday and send a fax: 'I have seen your advert in the paper looking for an engineer. We manufacture these kinds of products and if we can be of any assistance to you in the future'… and it was amazing the power of the fax on their desk on Monday morning. Once we get them we really try very hard to keep them by building strong personal relationships.

But being warm and friendly and passionate is not enough, you need to be able to sell effectively.

Winning new customers

If you have never had to sell then these tips from my friend Adrian Norton will get you started. He built two multi-million pound businesses from a telephone and a Yellow Pages Directory. He was an ace salesman.

1. *Get the right attitude to sell.* Customers are not doing you any favours giving you business. Your product/service will solve their problem and make their life easier. Be assertive and confident and proud of your product. If you are not, how can you expect a customer to pay you good money for it?
2. *Qualify a prospect.* Find out the name and job title of the person you want to sell to. If you are doing this by telephone, say to the secretary/receptionist: 'I have been asked to send some information to the person responsible for (buying your product); who should I send it to?' (Nobody has asked me in 20 years who asked me to send the information.)
3. *Get to see prospects face to face.* If a prospect says on the telephone, when you are trying to get an appointment, 'Send me some information in the post, you say, 'I would, but I have lots of information, and I would prefer to make sure you get precisely what you need. So can I call to see you for a few minutes next week?'
4. *Get out of the customer's reception area and into his or her office.* When a customer greets you in his or her reception area and wants to keep you

there (nobody ever sold anybody anything in reception), say 'I have got some information here (briefcase), some of it is confidential. Is there anywhere we can go that is a little more private?'

5. *Understand your products/services.* Make sure you really understand your products and services by completing a features and benefits analysis.

Feature (Describes your product)	*Benefit* (What it will do for the customer)
Gift wrapped	Can buy everything from one shop, including present, paper, card and gift tag. Makes it easy and probably looks better.
24-hour ordering system	Easy to place orders, particularly on a night shift.
Car parking available	Easy, quick, safe and cheap to park. Means I can shop in my lunch hour.

Tip: Make sure your features are really worthwhile, not like those shown in the box below.

Not unique features and benefits

'Free quotations'	Do you know anybody who charges for quotes?
'Value for money'	From whose perspective?
'Family business'	Do they mean the Borgias or the Waltons?
'Part central heating' (in a hotel)	I hope I get in the part with the central heating.
'Traditional family cooking'	Ours was lumpy gravy, overboiled sprouts and rock-hard potatoes!

---

6. *Opening a sales interview with a new customer.* You need to get them talking (who are the interesting people at parties, people who talk about themselves or those that show interest in you?). You show interest by listening, not talking:

Q1. Mr Customer, so that we can get the most out of this meeting, do you mind if I ask you a few questions?

Q2. Can you tell me something about your business? (Most people love talking about their business; after themselves!)

7. *Ask good questions to establish a customer's buying criteria:*

   Q.   What do you look for in a supplier?
   Q.   What disappoints you about suppliers?

   A good question to test the customer's buying system (am I talking to the right person?):

   Q.   Mr Customer, just suppose at the end of this discussion we decide we could do business together. What would I need to do to become a supplier? (They then tell you their system.)

8. *Ask for the order.* Do not be afraid to ask for the business. 'Can we do business together?'
9. *Demonstrate your commitment.* Promise to do something for your potential customer and make sure you deliver it ahead of time. Surprise them with your commitment, 'I will bring a sample round, probably next Tuesday', and deliver it next day.

This may seem very basic, but it will get you started; you can develop your personal preferred style of selling from here.

Customers also want suppliers know what they are talking about. You can't deliver this quality with a sales team that's not properly trained. Recruitment of staff for this role is something you should not leave to chance, and once recruited, make sure they are kept up to date.

David Latham again:

> One of our challenges is to continually develop our sales team. What I've been doing for the last couple of years is that when I go out to visit a customer I take some of our engineers with me and it allows some of my technical and sales skills to rub off. So much depends on seeing the guy in front of you. You can't do it by fax, you can't do it by phone, you've really got to go and sit in front of your customer and get their reaction, more so with customers abroad. Ours is a technical sell to engineers and technical sales forces need to develop these skills.

However, if a business is going to grow and prosper it has to more than make a good impression on the customer – long-term success depends on repeat business. The customer has to come back for more. That means the new business has to be both competent at what it does and keep any promises it makes. Which takes us back to the issue of capability.

Lastly, and probably the most important factor of all, customers need to receive a better service or a better product than they expected.

The principle of customer delight

When I did my first big research project in 1990–91 (the conclusions from which were published in my first book, *The Hallmarks for Successful Business*), I found that customer delight was a crucial factor in retaining and generating business; word-of-mouth soon carried the good news to others, and led to larger profit margins, because customers were willing to pay a higher price.

One outstanding illustration of the power of customer delight can be seen in the case of the Triple A Ranch Hotel near Washington, Tyne and Wear.

Triple A is no ordinary ranch, but a pets' home. While rivals charge £70 a week to house a pet, Triple A charges between £120 and £250, and it is completely booked up.

How does Ann Adlington, the Managing Director, explain it?

> We had the idea of giving each dog a personal carer who has responsibility for the pet for the whole time it stays with us. We recruit young people who genuinely love pets and give them that extra bit of loving care. They make sure the pets are well fed and groomed and exercised everyday. The pets thrive on it and when the owner comes back they are genuinely over the moon about the way they look.

But that's not the full story. The kennels are kept scrupulously fresh and clean, more like a hotel than a dog kennel. That perhaps gave Ann the idea of calling it an animal hotel. In marketing jargon, the pets' ranch has been repositioned to a more expensive market.

At the top end, £250 per week, the pets get a bed, settee and a TV, plus full-time companionship from someone who loves pets.

Dogs can have up to eight walks a day with the option of the agility course – the dog equivalent of an Outward Bound circuit. Optional extras include aerobics for cats. All this might explain why 53 per cent of Ann's customers travel more than 50 miles and she is now looking to franchise the operation nationally.

What tickled me most was the rather cute idea of sending post-cards to their owners' home. When they came back from holiday, there was a card from Rover saying that he was having a wonderful time!

Customer delight means working hard to do more than is expected, that bit extra for your customers. Triple A has won several national awards for outstanding customer service and Ann's business enjoys the benefits of customer (and pet) delight (see box).

Pet delight at Triple A

- Eighty-seven per cent of pets revisit, sometimes without their owners! (only joking).
- Fifty per cent of new business comes directly from recommendations from satisfied clients.
- Ann charges 100% more than her competitors.

Remember: The best way to sell your business to new customers is by exceeding expectations: delighted customers will help you build your business. The box below gives some tips for delighting your customers.

Building your business by delighting customers

Here are some tips from our entrepreneurs to help you create customers:

- Keep a record of where your new customers actually come from. Did they hear about you from an existing customer or did they see you at an exhibition? This is vital information in helping you build your business. It helps you focus your resources on communication channels that work for you.
- Experiment with low-cost ways of creating customers, eg attending exhibitions as a visitor, not an exhibitioner, press releases, mail-shots, etc. Find the ways that work for your business. Generally the most direct methods are the most effective in creating customers, eg direct telephone calls rather than a Yellow Pages advert.
- Use your existing customers to help you create new ones. Ask for a reference or a personal recommendation.
- Be passionate about your business. Customers like passion and energy.
- Show real interest in potential customer businesses. Ask problem-seeking questions. Demonstrating genuine interest in a customer's business is very persuasive and attractive. A common complaint from the customers of service providers is that 'they do not show any real interest in our business'.
- Find out something about potential customers beforehand and appear informed.
- Be persistent when chasing customers. Remember buyers expect to be courted and often make you work to get their business.

Entrepreneurs create customers in a whole variety of ways. At some point, whether you like it or not, someone is going to have to sell your business to customers. Entrepreneurs have firstly got to sell themselves and then their business. People buy people, not products. So copy how the experts charm their way to success in seven easy steps (see box below).

Seven easy steps to charm customers

Pay attention. Consider the person you're with as the only one in the universe that matters.

Don't talk – listen. It's better to laugh at someone else's funny story than tell your own.

Empathize. Watch body language to assess how the other person is feeling. Try to match those feelings.

Be enthusiastic. Use your face and body to convey emotion. If you don't show you're interested, people feel as if they're talking to a brick wall.

Be gentle. Be approachable and non-aggressive. People who intimidate may get respect but they never win other people over.

Be authentic. Be honest and straightforward with people at all times. Honesty builds trust, trust creates customers.

Appear self-confident. A frightened or worried person wins sympathy but is rarely beguiling.

Picking the right people – selecting people to complement the skills of the entrepreneur

As your business gets established, you'll find that creating customer delight is something you cannot do without employing and, if need be, training the right people to deliver it. This brings me on to one of the greatest challenges facing any new entrepreneur – how can I be sure of recruiting people who will help deliver my vision of the future?

Many enterprises get off on the wrong foot from the start with the partnership conundrum. Starting up your own business can be a lonely affair if you haven't got a strong team around you, and partnerships are appealing for that reason alone. But rushing into a partnership is something most new entrepreneurs live to regret, as Norman White can testify from his first business venture:

> Rodime was extremely successful for five or six years. However, in the mid-eighties, it began to go downhill, because it diversified, left its

> Scottish base and tried to expand abroad. One of the founders, the Chairman and Managing Director, was an American. He wanted to re-focus Rodime from Scotland and transplant it into Florida. The company lost its technical edge and its product focus at a time when its competitors were moving production from the US to the Far East. Rodime lost money and eventually ceased operations in 1991.

The company still exists, licensing the valuable intellectual property that was developed during the early years. Norman learnt these lessons in time to start his second business, Calluna Technology, successfully.

The fact is that just because you get along well with someone, or share a vision for the new company, it doesn't guarantee business success, or even amicable working relationships in the long term. Be particularly careful about giving shares in your business away to partners; they may eventually become a real problem if you grow apart or, worse still, fall out. If you are thinking of going into business with a partner, remember our tendency is to recruit people who are like us, having similar likes and styles, *yet we often need people who are different to us in temperament and approach.*

Businesses grow by developing teams of people with different but complementary skills, and learning to tolerate diversity and difference is a key element in running any business.

This is, of course, just as true when it comes to recruiting people to work in the business. For instance, I like to think of myself as an ideas person whose forte is creating a vision for the company and thinking up new opportunities. Dealing with detail and routine, on the other hand, is not my strongest suit. When I recruited my first accountant and he insisted that my expense forms should be filled in correctly, I got very hot under the collar. Then it occurred to me, this was precisely why I had recruited him, to keep me under control and get the details right. If the company was filled with people like me there would be anarchy, but too many like him and we would suffer from bureaucratic paralysis. We needed both sets of skills to make the business work.

But once you have grasped that essential truth there remains the problem of finding the people you can work with and who are needed to make your business a success.

When I first started my business I used every 'approved' device in helping me choose people. I was using psychometric tests, taking up references and utilizing all the recognized selection processes possible. Yet with 'hindsight' my success rate was no more than 1 in 3.

So why is selecting people such a problem?

Partly because it takes more time than most people realistically allow for. In a small company it is almost like taking someone into the family, except more difficult, since you don't select family members on their ability to do a specific job.

Horror stories are common, even among people who have come through the trials and tribulations successfully.

An entrepreneurial team I was working with was very effective and they seemed to get on well together at a personal level. They recruited a new team member to boost the marketing, and within one month she transformed the team into a battlefield, and their performance declined dramatically. The managing director told me:

> We have gone from an open positive team atmosphere to one that is very toxic. I am amazed at the negative effect one person can have on a business.

It can help to get the team involved in the selection process if you want your team to be more like the Waltons than the Borgias!

Sometimes people just turn out to be hopeless at the job, particularly if they are selected for the wrong reason, such as they are 'family'.

An MD of a computer company in the Midlands was a very devoted family man, to the extent that he employed most of them in his business, even though they were unqualified. They all had company cars and appeared to come and go as they pleased.

Imagine the impact of this nepotism and incest on the non-family members of the business.

Sometimes applicants simply tell lies at an interview. I once recruited a temporary secretary who told me she was proficient at Microsoft Word and could take dictation at 60 words per minute. It turned out she had never seen the Microsoft software and her dictation speed was 15 wpm.

The point of this book is not to go into detail about the techniques of interviewing and selection. Bookshops are crammed with books that aim to train managers in these skills, while recruitment agencies who can offer help are not difficult to find. Instead I want to look at the experience (often bitter) of our successful entrepreneurs, and draw out a few of the lessons. These are the pieces of the jigsaw the textbooks don't include.

New financial penalties for getting it wrong

New legislation in the UK introduced in 1999 increases the penalties for unfair dismissal from £12,000 to £50,000 per person. Clearly this increases the pressure on entrepreneurs to pick the right people in the first instance. Three cases in one year will now set you back £150k!

Also, there are a number of 'stress at work' cases simmering at the moment in some large businesses. Watch out for some expensive precedents being created. This whole area of employment claims is being driven by both new legislation and some very litigious lawyers who have learnt from their US counterparts on how to get rich quick.

Word of warning: Make sure your employment practices and processes are 100 per cent watertight; you can't afford to take chances because it can now cost you big bucks! Be warned.

Balancing the team's skills

We've already seen how Norman White learned from his first experience of company formation that partnerships were fraught with danger. Ideas people need to draw in, as partners, people with complementary skills.

Remembering that there are four basic building blocks (*driving, doing, selling, controlling*), you need a strategy that provides all four.

If you are thinking of forming a partnership, consider whether the partners complement each other's skills in these vital departments. If not, it is far better to look for ones that do, or to recruit someone with the necessary skills.

There is also the question of fit. Will the new person fit into the existing team? Some entrepreneurs encourage their team to get involved in the selection process to ensure that the new person fits in.

Entrepreneurs need to play to their strengths and recruit other people to cover their weaknesses.

The recruitment process

Peter Saunders of Halo Foods always had the ambition to attack the export market. His approach to finding the right people to help break into the market is textbook stuff. He took no chances:

> I have always been very clear that if you want the best company then you have got to have the best people. Sometimes this requires a strong nerve because you have to invest in the best people before you can become the best company.
>
> I felt sure there were good opportunities in export, especially in the USA. I recognized also that I was a novice as far as export is concerned. I therefore set out to find somebody with the right skills and experiences.

So here are some tips from the entrepreneurs to increase your chances of picking the right people:

- Have two people at the interview.
- Ask criterion-based questions – these are questions that test the candidates' experience against your specific requirements.

- If the job is important enough, ask people they will be working with to interview them or at least to meet them.
- If the job is a key role, ask candidates to come to a second interview and to provide a five-minute presentation on, for example, 'how they will improve the business in the first six months'.
- You might consider psychometric tests. These can be conducted with a detailed report for around £200 per person. Tests tell you things you just cannot glean at an interview. However, tests are only one piece of the jigsaw; never make a selection decision on test results alone.

Criterion-based questions – an example

Suppose managing a salesperson is part of the job vacancy you wish to fill.

It would be helpful to ask:

- When managing a sales force, exactly how did you do it?
- Give me three examples where you personally improved the performance of your salespeople.
- Exactly what was your role in that process?
- Tell me, what lessons did you learn from that?

This process homes in on the key tasks you need your new recruit to do well. It seeks factual evidence and examples that the candidate has done them successfully in the past. You should seek to get 2–3 believable examples for each key part of their job.

The principle is that the best predictor of future performance is past performance.

'How will you improve the business in the next 6 months?'

Asking applicants to answer this question using a short presentation has three business benefits:

- It let's you see the quality of their thinking and how keen they are to get the job.
- You see their communication skills at first hand.
- You might get some good new ideas for free!

Be wise to references

Always ask for and take up three references. Make sure you get their last two employers. Call them personally on the telephone, check out their details and listen carefully for what is not said as much as what is. Be cautious about really glowing references – you might be doing them a favour by taking a loser off their hands!

An alternative approach

Some of our entrepreneurs preferred to use recruitment agencies to increase their chances of success and reduce the burden on them, especially when the job entailed specialist skills. Peter Saunders of Halo Foods did this to find the sales director he needed:

> We chose a top recruitment firm and we sat down with them and worked out a specification of the person we wanted. Experience in exporting was obviously a key element. If anything, I wanted someone who was over-qualified. In my experience, having someone who has that something 'extra' really pays dividends.

Peter and the recruitment agency also discussed the personal qualities required. Armed with this remit they came up with David Pearce, who was able to shoulder the burden and let Peter concentrate on other aspects of the business.

> David put together a deal with my target US customers very quickly and all I had to do was to travel out and tidy up the details.

A few final thoughts on recruitment...

Not all new businesses can afford to employ recruitment agencies, and if they are not properly briefed they may bring in the wrong sort of person.

Somebody from a big company background, for instance, could present problems you would rather do without.

Working with new and growing companies over the past 20 years, I have seen the consequences again and again. Such recruits haven't got the entrepreneurial skills required. In large companies, when they get problems they call in an expert or put in a capital application. They can end up spending your cash like confetti.

Another painful confession: I once recruited an MD for one of my companies to build a new business. He had worked in a blue chip company and was full of ideas at the interview.

He then spent the first six months acquiring a flash car, putting in new high-tech office equipment, and spending £10,000 on market research we didn't need. Ironically, he did not bring in a single new customer, the job he was hired to do! What made it doubly painful was that I had misguidedly agreed to match his blue chip salary and benefits.

In the final analysis, it is not big-company experience but passion that is the important predictor of success. Pick people who are really passionate about your technology or kind of business. Richard Branson puts part of the success of his music business down to the hiring policy. His competitor, EMI, recruited graduates with MBAs while Branson chose people who were really passionate and interested in music. His business was significantly more profitable.

Finding help – getting support from people who can help

Entrepreneurs starting out in business need to find people who can help them solve their business problems. Most governments now recognize that promoting entrepreneurship is the key to future growth of the economy and a source of new jobs. Under pressure from above, banks declare their willingness to lend funds, while in Britain at least there's now a network of publicly funded agencies offering their services to new businesses. These are not always appropriate, and seem to be constantly being reorganized, ie Business Links, Chambers, RDAs, and the rest.

You'll find that what can be most useful is to find which agencies have the committed and competent individuals working for them. Again, networking with other entrepreneurs in your area will give you a head start in finding these individuals.

One example of how the grapevine approach to business information works can be found in what was once the cutlery capital of the world – Sheffield. Sheffield Business Club has built a regional reputation for being really helpful to local entrepreneurs, so you'll find people from other nearby towns and cities joining the club to plug into the benefits.

Robin Howard of Howard Design and Print has found it invaluable:

> Sheffield Business Club membership has given me valuable support and encouragement and the opportunity to do business in a friendly environment. It is outstanding value for money and there is no reason not

> to join. From the first event at the Arena I immediately saw the benefits and have gained many orders.

As a business person you need to build up your own personal network of helpers, a supporters book of people who can help guide you through any crisis that arises, and open the way to new business.

Not everybody would want to create a 'supporters club' but the principle is valid for all new entrepreneurs. The entrepreneurial way is to establish a network of helpful contacts you value and can work with. Building and maintaining personal relationships can open doors to business in the most unexpected of ways.

Some questions to be answered by your local network

- Which local bank manager is really helpful?
- Who sorts out problems quickly at the Business Link (the UK business support network)?
- Who of the Chamber of Commerce really makes things happen?
- Which local person is an invaluable source for information?
- Which local journalist is really interested in promoting small businesses?
- Which business club really helps local businesses?

High-tech start-ups – companies that require large up-front investments

Perhaps, like Norman White, founder of Calluna Technology, you see an opportunity at the high-tech end of the manufacturing sector. You face an obvious headache. High-tech start-ups inevitably consume large amounts of cash, and it is normally required front-end loaded up-front. This is not only the investment cost of expensive equipment and premises, but also the longer time lag between launch and putting the products on the market. This means raising, at the very least, adequate bridging finance.

Unfortunately banks in Britain seem to have a problem in assessing the prospects for high-tech industry and in understanding what it requires in the way of capital. This was Norman White's experience:

> You can't start up a company like Calluna with two or three people and grow to four people in two years. You have to go in very quickly, so you

need initial start-up finance. That was a massive headache. Over a 10-month period I approached 90 financial institutions or companies of one kind or another, and was turned away every time.

We had raised an initial half a million pounds – £350,000 from Japanese investors I knew and the rest from the six founding partners.

Half a million pounds wouldn't take us very far: it secured our future for six months. We hoped by then to have secured extra funding here in Britain. It didn't come. We just held on by the skin of our teeth. All employees took salary cuts and some of us took no salaries at all.

In the end we secured about £2 million from a syndicate of venture capitalists, which allowed us to go ahead and build the manufacturing plant. Then the venture capitalists started to fight among themselves. Had we not eventually found a sponsoring company in Birmingham with access to private funds and willing to come in on the deal, we could have folded.

I found the process wearing. When fund-raising occupies 90 per cent of your time it distracts you from the real task in hand.

Norman White displayed real persistence at the critical times for his business and has now successfully floated the company. But how many start-up businessmen would have given up the fight?

There has been a slight easing of attitudes over the past three years according to 3I, the British funding agency. Figures from the British Venture Capital Association show that money invested in start-up business rose by 91 per cent in 1998 to £111 million and the average size of the investment doubled. This still, however, remains a drop in the ocean compared to the £2.13 billion invested in management buy-outs. Several successful role models, such as Autonomy and Oxford Asymmetry, have educated venture capitalists that hi-tech starts do lose money for the first few years and need to be funded through this period. While such investments can be expensive and high risk, they also offer high returns, as Autonomy, the £180 million Internet company started by former lecturer Dr Mike Lynch, whose 22 per cent stake is now worth £40 million, clearly demonstrates.

A study in the United States suggests that finding support for high-tech projects is not easy there either. In Silicon Valley about 300 venture capitalists see on average 3,000 opportunities a year from high-tech start-up businesses. On average they lend to 10 only. Four of the 10 become real successes, four or five just stumble along and one or two fail.

So this is a different business from typical low-tech start-ups. The entrepreneurial skills will also be different, with raising finance at decent rates being a real challenge.

So how can you judge what your chances might be? In practice I've found that venture capitalists have two criteria by which they judge any proposal. They ask whether the proposition solves a real customer problem, and they check out the quality and track record of the lead entrepreneur and his or her team.

They are testing *two* elements of the entrepreneurial model:

- Is this a *superior opportunity*?
- Does the team have the *capability*?

before they will provide the *third* element:

- the *financial resources*.

Ask your local business network for advice on finding sources of venture capital.

Experimenting and learning – trying out new ideas in a low-cost way and learning

Capital is difficult to raise and small companies often can't afford to do the in-depth market research that the larger company might consider essential before launching a new product or service. But our entrepreneurs have found a way of doing something similar on the cheap – with low-cost experiments.

Here is an example from Phil Crane:

> I had already been dealing in bits and pieces, so I decided to open a discount store that was actually in the garage. I got stuck into that and bought all sorts of things. We sold everything from digital watches, blankets, clocks, and even squeaky toys. I just experimented to see what worked and dropped it if it didn't, but it led to other things and so I started doing party plans, one thing seemed to lead to another. I was learning the business all the time, because I knew absolutely nothing.

Experimenting to find things that work is one key to the secret of business development. There are no magic answers available in textbooks, meaning that entrepreneurs have to discover what works for them in the context of their business and the situation on the ground.

Time and time again our entrepreneurs have demonstrated that the excitement of starting the business provides energy and commitment and this in turn helps sort out difficulties. The recognition that they are the best experts for their business is a truth that dawns slowly on some entrepreneurs.

Peter Saunders again:

> I felt sure that there were opportunities that needed exploring in America, but how on earth was I to do it? I remained convinced there was a market for us and then leapt at the opportunity of joining an export mission sponsored by the Welsh Office to New York and San Francisco. I came back convinced my hunch was right.

Entrepreneurs need to learn to trust their own judgement and use their intuition and common sense to become their own business gurus. Entrepreneurs like Tony Di Donato and John Pye recall in these early days how they metaphorically came to 'lose their virginity' by becoming attuned to the workings of the commercial business world, as Mary Conneely also discovered:

> You have to deal with outside agencies in business and I discovered you need to scrutinize them very carefully because the success of any business I think is based on trust. You can't trust people who believe that a woman starting up a business has disadvantages, they think that females don't make good managers, women can't succeed in business, but they can. At times I have been too trusting of people.

To be successful, entrepreneurs do not need a business school training, although it can help, but they do need the personal qualities of being persistent, being obsessively committed to the business, and being prepared to cope with uncertainty and ambiguity. These personal traits may be there all along, but the experience of our entrepreneurs suggests that they often acquired such qualities along the way. Similarly, being able to build helpful networks and to seek help from people who can make things happen is a skill many of them have acquired rather than been born with.

How to make sure you get paid on time

Cash-flow problems have been the downfall of many new businesses. One major contributing factor is the failure of new businesses to establish clear terms of trade. In the commercial world this allows creditors to take advantage by not paying you quickly – just when you really need the cash.

Some business books encourage this practice giving advice like: *'Use your creditors to manage your cash flow.' 'Do not pay them until you have to.'*

You need to make sure you don't let your customers take this liberty with your money. A valuable lesson for most entrepreneurs is to set out clearly your terms of trade and ensure you and your customers stick to them.

This might be, for example:

- payment in 30 days;
- strictly net – no discounts;
- interest may be charged on all outstanding debts at bank rate plus 5 per cent on all orders and invoices.

Some businesses send customers a contract setting out all payment conditions.

You should also establish a credit control system, which again is ruthlessly enforced, with no exception.

Your system will probably be something like:

- non-payment after seven days gets a letter – statement;
- 14 days later – a letter and telephone call;
- 30 days later – seven-day letter warning of court action;
- any further slips, court action taken.

Remember some companies employ credit control people whose job is to maximize their cash flow by minimizing yours.

Don't let them do it to you. Take action, otherwise they will try it on. Remember, businesses that fail normally run out of cash. Some people take a lack of action on your part as a sign of weakness, so they exploit it.

In practice, I find a firm friendly telephone call directly to my personal contact, not their credit control department, works in most cases.

The box sets out my terms of trade.

Example terms of trade

Here are my terms of trade:

1. The following charge rates apply up to 31 March 1999, and are reviewed annually.

    1.1 Consultancy rate – (per day)   £
        including problem analysis, facilitation,
        training and field research

    1.2 Expenses
        – Road   p per mile
        – Rail   First Class at cost
        – Air   Business Class at cost

    1.3 Accommodation   Hotel bills to client account direct
                             or recharged at cost.

1.4 Payment
- Invoices are raised on completion of short one-off events.
- Invoices are raised at 14 day intervals on extended assignments to control cash flow for both client and consultant.
- Payment terms are 14 days net.

We reserve the right to charge interest on unpaid bills from one month after delivery of our invoice.

2. Cancellation and postponement fees

– More than six weeks' notice	= no charge
– Between four and six weeks' notice	= 25% of fee
– Between two and four weeks' notice	= 50% of fee
– Between one and two weeks' notice	= 75% of fee
– Less than one week	= full charge

3. All rates listed are exclusive of VAT.

4. Work will commence on receipt of signed terms and conditions from client.

Using this system I have not had one really bad debt in 20 years.

In summary, the good news is that start-up is a great time for most. People recall being frightened, and stressed, but at the same time excited by the high levels of personal challenge, and the commitment and pride they found within themselves. Many of them plan never to retire, unlike the typical manager in the large corporation. They seem to love the 'entrepreneurial life' for its own sake.

controlling **your business**

You'll remember every business needs to have four key capabilities if it is to succeed, *driving*, *doing*, *selling* and *controlling*.

When we looked at control in Chapter 5 we considered it largely as the ability to keep control of costs and to be aware of how exactly your company is faring at any moment in time. But there is another side to control – the ability to control risks. In this chapter we will be looking at how to manage risk in the business, and how to build the sort of information system you will need to make risk control easier, to enable you to sleep easy in your bed. We'll also be letting you into the secret of how to make the most of your bank manager.

Avoiding everyday risks

Successful entrepreneurs take risks, but they are always calculated risks. They also follow the general principle that where possible risks should be minimized. They take the obvious precautions to avoid unnecessary risks, for example:

▦ not using unlicensed computer software (Bill Gates is watching!);

- ensuring proper secure systems are in place for storing important information;
- ensuring their people behave in a proper professional commercial manner at all times;
- keeping accurate accounting records;
- getting tax and VAT returns in on time;

and the many other precautions that are needed to exercise control in any commercial enterprise.

Controlling the basics

Entrepreneurs exercise control over their businesses by establishing simple standards, systems and routines that control the key elements of their recipe for success. They also control the basics by encouraging their managers and supervisors to manage people and ensure that they stick to agreed standards, systems and routines.

This combination of simple systems and standards with the supervision of the people using them enables entrepreneurs to control the basics of their businesses. Examples of some of the basic standards and systems entrepreneurs have established include:

- Recording the source of new business enquiries.
- Sales conversion rates.
- Monitoring cash flow daily.
- Customer feedback processes.
- Complaints procedures.
- Wastage rates.
- Level of cross-selling.
- Customer service standards.

...and many others.

Each business is different, it has its own unique recipe, so consequently standards and systems will differ.

One of the observations from managing directors of companies with operations across Europe is that British workers often dislike sticking to systems and standards – they want to do their own thing.

So although the business might have developed its way of doing things, this can become compromised, leading to service levels and performance suffering, if individuals prefer to do things 'their way'. If this is not corrected, by definition it is condoned and will continue off track.

Entrepreneurs and their managers also need to use basic people management skills in order to maintain standards and consistency. Here is the process:

Step 1   Agree the standard, objectives or process with individuals.
Step 2   Make them accountable for maintaining the standards.
Step 3   Check whether they are complying with the standard, insist they stick to it, keep them on track and don't allow slippages.
Step 4   Celebrate success or learn the lessons.

Too often managers miss steps 3–4 because they are too busy or lack the assertiveness and confidence to confront people.

In Chapter 11 we look at how entrepreneurs can revitalize their business by preventing system slippage.

Control by wandering around

Control of your business should also be exercised by using informal personal approaches.

Tom Peters championed management by walking around (MBWA) and talking with your people. What's really going on in sales? What's happening in the admin team? Somebody suggested that 80 per cent of the information in businesses happens through the grapevine, 75 per cent of which turns out to be correct. What are the jungle drums beating to in your business?

The workers at Swan Hunter Shipyard on the Tyne told me that the company was bust two years before the management seemed to notice. How did they know? They were not doing any welding!

Fred Buijs, the Factory Manager for Nestlé in East London, South Africa, wanders around his production lines and shows three cards, red, yellow and green, to his factory workers. He asks them to select the one that best reflects their performance that day (red for poor, yellow for OK, and green for good).

People select one and he then asks what actions they will take to improve for the rest of the day; everybody has a good laugh but he makes a point in a very subtle way.

Wandering around outside the business also helps to control your business. Dave Osmond of CompuAdd Computers believes that all managing directors or CEOs should spend at least 50 per cent of their time visiting customers:

> This way you control your business by nipping potential problems in the bud – you also pick up new opportunities.

There are other categories of risk that can be insured against, should things go badly wrong. Entrepreneurs need to find out about those available to cover their area of business. While they should take advice from an insurance expert on what to look for and where, they still need to shop around for the best deal.

Avoiding financial risk

While wandering around and insurance can reduce operational risk, one of the most notorious forms of risk facing entrepreneurs is in raising money to get the business started – one reason why successful entrepreneurs adopt the principle of *'beg, borrow* and *befriend'*. Some formal borrowing, however, may still be necessary, as people like John Pye found out:

> I had nothing to start with so I needed to borrow £2,500 just to get going.

Very often it is this initial start-up capital that seems to be a blockage.

So maybe you too will be forced to consider borrowing start-up capital from a bank. Some businesses fail because they are just under capitalized right from start-up. Banks are not really into taking risks themselves, so they will certainly try to shift all risk on to your shoulders, and ask you to sign a personal guarantee, which means you will have to find cash to pay off the debt if the company fails. That could mean selling your house. Alternatively they may ask you to put up personal assets as collateral to be held against the loan, which amounts to the same thing for most people – you will have to deposit the deeds of your house with the bank as security. I have had personal experience of both types of loan and you should resist any such suggestion from a bank if you can.

Once you have signed a personal guarantee, banks may be reluctant to hand it back even when you have repaid the loan. This happened to me, even after I had successfully sold my business. Banks have no sense of humour on these matters. The other day I noticed that the bank profits had taken a dive so I wrote to my bank manager: 'I see your bank's in trouble and as I have some money deposited with you, could I have the deeds to your house?'! He has yet to reply....

Easier said than done perhaps, since bank head offices have laid down formulae for lending to new businesses which limits the discretion of bank managers. Limits do not entirely eliminate, that's the point. The first reaction of any local branch manager will be to pull out the standard form, have you fill it in, and then assess your credit-worthiness (more about this later) and the prospects for the business. The bank won't consider lending you money at all unless you pass these tests. So when the bank offers you a loan you have already passed an important test. Naturally the bank will try to get you to sign a personal guarantee or provide collateral, but you need to realize that this is not generally a 'take it or leave it' affair. Banks are generally as keen to lend to you as you are to borrow, since that is how they make money. They need your business. What's more, there are other banks in the high street that are also looking for business.

So my advice is to treat banks as you would any other supplier and shop around to find the best deal. When the bank manager realizes he (it is usually a he) will have to work for your business, that you have options available, he will be inclined to exercise any discretion he has and offer you a better deal. Instead of signing personal guarantees or handing your property deeds over, you should negotiate, negotiate, negotiate.

Of course, at this stage some would-be entrepreneurs imagine that signing a personal guarantee is no big deal since their company has 'limited liability' status. Don't make this mistake: the personal guarantee still stands and the heavy mob can still be sent to get your house keys!

Given the risk-aversion displayed by banks, if you can find an alternative source of finance you should consider taking it. Sometimes there are government-sponsored support agencies that might offer help in the form of grants, or you might look for a 'business angel', a rich investor prepared to put money into your business in return for a shareholding. Of course, you have to be sure you can work with such a person.

It is only common sense to take good legal and financial advice from experienced and qualified professionals before you take out a loan or enter into an ownership-sharing deal. This is one area where frugality is out of the window; pay for the best advice you can afford. To illustrate just what you can face as an innocent abroad in the dangerous waters of corporate finance, here is what happened to one entrepreneur:

> I was asked to invest in a new business and it seemed quite an attractive proposition. So good that I was inclined to borrow up to the hilt to get a share of the action. Then one Saturday morning two accountants turned up at my house unannounced, with several legal documents to sign. They told me the deal couldn't go through unless I signed on the dotted line there and then. I couldn't get legal advice at short-notice on a Saturday morning and they knew it. Fortunately so did I. I refused to sign and pulled out of the deal.

The entrepreneur in this case was me! As it happened the business folded soon after, heavily in debt, but I kept my shirt.

Minority shareholders in a business can be placed under similar pressure to sign up to a bank loan with a personal guarantee thrown in. This you must never do. Think about it: you are probably at equal risk with the majority shareholders, but with potentially much less in the way of return. The lesson here must be – *match risks against rewards.*

Managing banks and other investors

Bank managers are an easy target for entrepreneurs' ridicule and abuse. They get blamed for not understanding entrepreneurs, being unsympathetic and even putting obstacles in the way.

Remember the experience of Phil Crane in his early days as an entrepreneur:

> I found banks useless, absolutely useless. It's like everything else. Once you've been a success it is easy. Banks aren't there to be entrepreneurial. What they want is entrepreneurs willing to take risks but they don't take many risks themselves. The shareholders don't pay them to take big risks.

But like it or not, entrepreneurs will have to deal with them and build a relationship if they can. So it is worth sitting back and looking at the world from their point of view. Doing this certainly changed the view of Neil Gibson, the man who bought out the JHB Group.

> We tended to see the banks as just being a problem and as people who are unhelpful and unsupportive. Until our own bank, the Bank of Scotland, held a short seminar called 'Managing your bank manager' and invited us along. It was very illuminating. We looked at things from our perspective and had been keeping the bank in the dark, quite unintentionally. We knew when money was due, and we knew we had the wherewithal to pay bills, but the bank manger didn't. What they said was, give us your information, come in and talk to us. Tell us what you are doing and tell us what you need and we will tell you how we can help you.
>
> Since then we have taken them at their word and we haven't had too many problems with them. In fact I would have to say our bank is absolutely fabulous and have given us terrific support over the years.

The fact is that many new businesses haven't learned that lesson and don't know how to deal with banks. Remember I am on the side of the entrepreneur, but I can see and understand the bank point of view as well.

For instance, I know of a business with a strict overdraft limit at the bank of £500,000. The MD complained to me about the bank's behaviour when it called him in when the overdraft had risen to £800,000. He didn't seem to realize that he had broken his promise to the bank and had run up a huge debt. The businessmen argued that this was only a temporary state of affairs and that the bank should expect fluctuations in cash flow; the business was still sound. I can sympathize with the bank manager faced with this sort of customer.

Banks are not there to take risks and breaking the overdraft limit rang alarm bells.

Take another example of what I consider unprofessional behaviour. Some businessmen I know have turned up at the bank seeking a business loan without anything resembling a sound business case. Put yourself in the bank manager's shoes for a moment. If somebody you hardly know turns up asking for an overdraft facility of £10,000 without collateral and little more than the germ of a good idea, how would you handle it?

So entrepreneurs need to learn how to manage banks if they are to get what they want. They need to start by accepting that they approach each other from very different backgrounds and points of view.

Entrepreneurs by nature are optimistic, good at selling, future focused and can see the big picture.

Bank managers are selected because they are good on detail, at planning, procedures and thinking analytically.

So here we have two people who are the complete opposite in terms of personality, characteristics and training. No wonder they fail to understand each other. They view the world through completely different spectacles so that whatever an entrepreneur does, the typical bank manager finds it hard to understand or be sympathetic. Take a leaf out of Neil Gibson's book and start to give bank managers what they want: detail, plans and information. Then they may want to play ball with you. Just as with customers, don't fight them but try to understand them and give them what they want. If you treat them like the enemy, guess how they are likely to behave?

Having said that, treat banks like any other supplier and don't be fooled by terms like 'relationship manager'.

I was informed that I had reached the stage in my business when I merited a 'personal business adviser'. At the first meeting he asked if I had a pension, insurance or needed a mortgage. He was a bloody salesman! Make banks fight for your business and ask the rough questions.

I discovered a business friend of mine enjoyed a 2 per cent less borrowing rate than me for the same amount of overdraft. I asked my bank and they said I could have the same. When I complained 'why I have been paying 2 per cent extra for 10 years' they said 'you never asked before'! Yes, I know you might think I am a wimp but we all have to learn these embarrassing lessons. Negotiate, be tough and treat banks like any other supplier.

How banks evaluate risks

How do bank managers evaluate you as a risk? All bank managers use a set procedure and increasingly less of their own judgement to evaluate a business proposal.

Top of the list is an assessment of your character, then comes the question of your past experience and capability, your financial status and the nature of the business.

When it comes to lending money, banks expect you to be able to contribute at least 50 per cent of the resources you will need from your own resources, although there will be exceptions, particularly with capital-hungry business propositions. And of course your ability to repay the loan needs to be assessed.

Having ownership of assets that can be disposed of to repay the loan if the business fails is obviously a factor, but more important is the evidence that your business idea is well thought through and has a good chance of success. In other words, you need that strong business case.

It helps to have a track record – one reason why 'beg, borrow and befriend' makes sense for first-time business owners – especially evidence that you understand cash flow and have handled it in the past. Your credit rating will go up if you can show that your past record has outperformed the average business in the same field.

Once the loan has been agreed and you draw on it to develop the business, you must remember that to a bank no news is bad news. So you need to keep them informed in a proactive way, sending them copies of your accounts and informing them of any changes in your business strategy or in trading conditions and cash flow. Bank managers, like you, hate surprises.

You will find that bank managers like to be invited to visit your premises, and to be told the truth. Use an open and honest approach, and don't patronize them with waffle. Remember they are smart people.

You want to build bank managers into your valued network of contacts and supporters, so take them out to lunch and treat them like any valued network contact. If you do that, when you need them, they may be there to help.

One thought to cheer you when you find the bank being awkward or unsympathetic. They don't always get it right:

> Mr Levi, I am afraid that we will not be investing in your little blue jeans business. We cannot believe that anyone is going to follow a trend set by a bunch of cowboys.

An example of bank evaluation criteria

Character	Assessment of person's character
Ability	Ability and experience
Means	Broad financial situation
Purpose	Is it legal? Business expenditure, not lost profit
Amount	Amount required – 1:1 ratio preferred by banks; however, a higher ratio can be obtained, but would be dependent on commitment from owner, strength of business plan, type of business etc
Repayment	Ability of business to pay back loan
Insurance	Security, assets, other income, etc
Interest rate	Currently 4–7 per cent above base rate, but is negotiable
Commission	Set-up costs, usually £50–£100
Extras	Credit check, additional set-up work

You and the accountant

Another of the prevailing myths about entrepreneurs is that they don't keep proper accounts and do all their calculations on the back of an envelope. Quite apart from being illegal, it makes for very poor business practice. Working with hundreds of successful entrepreneurs, I have yet to find one who hadn't come to appreciate the value of having a good and trustworthy accountant to keep an eye on the bookkeeping and a finger on the trends within the company.

Accountants are vital to the control function. A good accountant will help you sleep easy in your bed by:

- providing you with information you can trust;
- creating credibility with the bank, invaluable when the going gets tough;
- helping with commercial decisions and investigations, including costing, pricing, profit planning, and acquisitions;
- bringing a different perspective to debates and discussions.

So in hiring an accountant entrepreneurs cannot afford to go for the cheap option.

Speaking from personal experience, I can recall a time in my own business when we thought we had a good accountant. Unfortunately the forecasts and information he provided to me and the bank turned out to hopelessly out of line with the true state of the company. I can assure you that this was a highly embarrassing and stressful experience.

So here is a tip. *Get the best company accountant you can.* Use your network, ask around, speak to other entrepreneurs; you should try to find one through personal recommendation.

Knowing your numbers – monitoring the four critical financial indicators

Having an accountant doesn't mean that entrepreneurs can shuffle off responsibility for keeping a finger on the pulse of the business. The financial health of your business is far too important to leave in the hands of the bean counters alone. But seriously, in practice financial success comes from getting the business right, which is your job. If you leave it to accountants to supply such financial information as they consider relevant to the company, you may soon be flooded with profit and loss accounts, balance sheets, and other arcane artefacts that make sense to them but not to you. In fact the basic control information you will need can be produced in a simple form that is meaningful to you and to your staff. I am much indebted to the work of Brian Warnes in this regard.

Brian researched companies that failed and those that survived a crisis for his book *The Genghis Khan Guide to Business*. He found that failure was often due to a breakdown in monitoring and controlling four key factors in any business. So his biggest service has been to identify the four simple but critical financial measures which entrepreneurs need to track regularly if they want to keep control of their business, measures which tell you at a glance how the business is faring.

You control your business by knowing your numbers.

1. Gross margin

The first of these measures is gross margin, the percentage by which your sales are exceeding the running costs of your business, leaving aside the fixed costs, such as rent and rates and staff wages. These costs are called 'variable costs'. With a modern computer accountancy package it is easy to track costs from day to day and to calculate the percentage by which the sales exceed these variable costs. Printed as a graph these figures display the trends and flag up early warning of trouble ahead.

If the trend on gross margin is downwards you are faced with three alternatives:

- putting up prices;
- cutting variable costs; or
- cutting fixed costs.

In these days of low inflation and cut-throat competition the first option is seldom available.

2. Cash flow

The second key measure is that of cash flow – the flow of cash into and out of the business. You soon learn as a businessperson that cash flow can be a major headache. *In fact most business failures are a result of poor cash flow rather than a lack of profit.*

The ultimate measure of cash flow is cash in the bank. Ironically the faster your business grows the greater the danger of a cash-flow crisis – you may simply run out of cash. So you need to check your cash flow daily, particularly when you are up against any limits imposed by the bank.

But if you can see a cash-flow crisis looming, how can entrepreneurs prevent it happening?

One essential measure is to define clearly your terms of trade and make sure your customers are aware of them. Twenty-eight days to pay an invoice seems reasonable and anyone who fails to do so needs to be chased up and harried, especially since some customers will be using you to ease their own cash-flow problems! (In 1996, you may remember, the then UK trade and industry minister, Michael Heseltine, confessed to doing just that in the early days of his business.) A well-managed credit control system is therefore a must. Supplement this with an imposed limit on spending and daily cash-flow projections during difficult times. Any half-decent bookkeeper should be able to supply these figures.

3. Debtors

A customer who fails to pay is a menace so the third vital piece of information you will need is on the status of debtors. Since prevention is better than cure, your best protection against bad debts and poor payers is to make proper credit checks on all new customers requiring credit terms. There are commercial agencies that can supply this information cheaply. Start by asking your accountant.

You also need that rigorous credit control system to manage slow payers. Getting people to pay on time or even earlier can make a tremendous difference to cash flow in most companies – even rescue a failing company.

Remember Tom Hunter: he persuaded his large retail partner to pay his invoices in less than 90 days and it saved his business.

There's another class of prospective customer you need to take notice of – the one who constantly presses for discounts on your quoted prices. Many people in the buying departments of other companies are trained to ask for them as a matter of course and a polite refusal normally causes no offence. Take a stand and stick by your pricing policy. If you *are* pushed into a corner and feel forced to negotiate, you should always try to get something back in return:

> OK you can have a 2½ per cent discount but I want a written confirmed order for the next six months and you agree to a price rise of 3 per cent next June.

4. Creditors

The amount owed to creditors is the last of the four vital measures. You should recognize that suppliers face similar problems to you and need paying on time too. Being slow to pay only creates bad relations between you, and may destroy a very useful chance to build a long-term relationship. But you need to hold costs down, so don't be afraid to negotiate deals, just as your customers try to do with you.

One way to motivate those in your company who do the buying is to set a strict cash limit on spending that can be made without authorization. Above that limit either yourself or a trusted colleague should have to sign the cheque.

You'll find control of spending works best when it is under the control of one person who has access to the latest cash-flow position. If you instigate a simple purchase order system, signed off by this person, you can minimize creditor risks.

Monitoring your recipe

We saw in Chapter 4 that successful entrepreneurs have swapped the formal business plan approach for something much more meaningful and more motivating, the business recipe.

So you need to have a system of control that will monitor your recipe and make sure it is working. If it is not working as you anticipated, it needs to be changed.

You can devise a method of doing this to suit your business. You need to make a list of the ingredients and decide how to measure whether you are achieving your goals or not. No two businesses are the same and you will have to devise your own recipe and the method of checking progress.

But to help you, the most important ingredients of the recipes used by our entrepreneurs are listed in the box, together with key questions you will need an answer to.

Testing the recipe

The ingredients in the recipe that entrepreneurs most often monitor include the following; add any ingredients relevant to your business:

Recipe ingredients	*Measures of success/failure*
Market share	Is it growing or declining?
Customer retention	How many do we keep or lose?
Customer satisfaction level	How many delighted customers do we get?
Where customers come from	Source of prospective customers (leads)
Competitor activity	What are they up to now?
Sales forecasts	Actual sales against forecasts
Share of customer spend	Is it increasing or decreasing?
Conversion rates	Business generation conversion rates
Cross-selling	Amount of cross selling with existing customers. (Existing customers reorders and new orders)
Price competition	Is it getting tougher or easing off?
Return on capital	Return on your investment
Gross margins	Are we improving or declining?
Profit by product and customers	Where do we make our money?
Delivery performance	Is it getting better or worse?
Quality levels	Are we improving them?
Internal efficiency	Are we getting better or worse?
Productivity	Are we getting better or worse?
People's motivation and performance	How well are we managing our people?
Team working	How good is it?
Opportunity creation	How many new opportunities do we create?
Networking	Is it productive and helpful?

Add any others that apply specifically to your business.

If you want to learn how the big boys control their businesses, many use specialist software such as Hyperion. Sixty of the top 100 US businesses use it, as do 40 of the FTSE 100.

Mark Dixon of Regus used Hyperion to help him create his £1 billion company in just 10 short years. Group Financial Director Peter Jenkins:

> We are running it as a tool to help us control our business.
>
> Part of the reason Regus grew so successfully and has been able to realize its vision is that it has underpinned rapid growth with careful business management. This was made possible by Hyperion.

Tom Hunter who created Sports Division also invested heavily in control systems, which has helped him create his £300 million business.

Drawing up a system which keeps you in touch with the key ingredients in your recipe is a vital business tool. It has to be efficient and cost-effective. Since other entrepreneurs have already been down this road, this is another area where your growing network of business contacts will prove invaluable. Talk to your fellow entrepreneurs and find out how they do it.

building **your business**

- Gardening, not hunting
- Building a business generating system
- Networking
- PR on the cheap
- Ploughing money back into the business
- Forming a team
- Creating consistency
- Learning to manage

Congratulations if you have come thus far. Hopefully by now you have the bit between your teeth with your vision clearly etched on your brain, and have taken the first steps to set up your own business.

If you have been entrepreneurial you will have spotted an opportunity, marshalled your resources and built the capability to start your business successfully.

The next stage is to master the skills of building your business.

The entrepreneurs whose collective wisdom and experience is the basis for this book have all built successful enterprises. They are not people content to run a one-, two-, or three-person business – they have their sights on higher goals, driven by their own personal vision.

They are also not fans of the business book – with its emphasis on systems and controls and, inevitably, bureaucracy. Instead their behaviour can only properly be described by creating a fresh vocabulary. This applies as much to building the business as to starting it up.

So in this chapter we'll meet phrases like 'gardening, not hunting' and 'preventing fires' as important business concepts. You'll also find that 'business generators' and practices such as 'ploughing back' can be used to help transform businesses, merely ticking over, into throbbing engines of growth.

However, this chapter is not about growing a business which is already big, a process dealt with in Chapter 9. This chapter is about helping the fledgling business to put down some sound foundations in order to secure its future without putting the whole enterprise at risk.

Gardening, not hunting

Entrepreneurs are often seen as thrusting, restless people, impatient to build their empire, forever straining at the leash to expand into new areas. They are depicted as hunters tracking down and capturing new markets and customers. Richard Branson is again a popular role model – his Virgin empire has grown from music to embrace airlines, railways and financial services.

In fact most successful entrepreneurs don't grow their businesses in this way. They are not hunters but, in their own words, gardeners. What do they mean by that? Once they have established a customer base – determined by the opportunity they have spotted – they cultivate it, nurture it, and it grows naturally through repeat business and word-of-mouth recommendation. It is a much more reliable means of growing a business than rushing around looking for new markets to exploit, and much less exhausting. Successful entrepreneurs don't give hunting for new customers a high priority.

To put it in business terms: *the easiest way to build your business is to seek to sell more to existing customers rather than try to create new ones.*

The business rationale for *gardening, not hunting,* is well established. Your existing customers have already bought from you and if you've delighted them, they will be open to buy more from you. It is far cheaper to retain existing customers than it is to find new ones. To be precise, sales people have long established that it costs around five times as much to create a new customer as it does to keep an existing one.

This is what Neil Gibson told me:

> The company has grown because of the new service we provide to our existing customers rather than working for twice as many customers as we used to.

Of course, not all businesses are the same. Some will have many customers, some only a few, and by their very nature some will have many who are unlikely to repeat their business anyway. Tourism is a good example. People will come to a city like London to see the sights and will move on to Paris or Rome the next time round. But that doesn't mean the principle of gardening doesn't apply. Deep Sea World, for instance, caters for many passing tourists who may never come back to Scotland or to the Forth. But Phil

Crane has seen his attention to customer satisfaction pay off handsomely.

> We are in the entertainment business so we set out to try to make it fun for all our customers. Our staff work very hard to exceed our customers' expectations and this pays off in repeat business and recommendations.

Delighting customers, therefore, makes just as much sense for Deep Sea World as it does for Neil Gibson or Ann Adlington. Even where Phil's customers never come back, their word-of-mouth recommendations bring in a steady flow of new customers without a huge spend on marketing and advertising.

The gardening approach is not based simply on offering outstanding service to the customer. Our entrepreneurs take a proactive stance on customer delight. They have found that engaging customers in dialogue allows them to discover needs that the customers themselves have never dreamt of. It is the same old problem-solving approach. You uncover the problems they face and provide solutions for them.

Anne-Marie Jackson of Handcast Design demonstrates this principle in practice:

> We have a long-standing relationship with a German customer who manufactures beer steins. He wanted to sell specifically into the collectables market in the USA and to achieve competitive advantage he needed to make the lid of his beer stein very intricate and three-dimensional. We did sketch designs and sculptured prototypes, particularly to his brief, and then manufactured it for him. This is a totally different product to the rest of our line. It would be a stein that would represent a German castle or tourist area of the world. It is not a standard trinket box or photo frame that we would supply to the rest of the world.

So if you want to develop your base as a company then cultivate existing customers. You will find that a quiet bit of gardening will create lots of new opportunities for your business. It is also very cost-effective compared to hunting in the drive for new customers.

Later, in Chapter 9, we'll look in more detail at successful gardening techniques, including cross-selling, building partnerships and joint ventures.

So for smaller businesses, share of customer spend as opposed to market share is a tough but a useful indicator of the true effectiveness of your business; how well you are delighting customers.

One of the processes successful entrepreneurs use to evaluate their potential for increasing their share of the customer spend is to conduct a customer perception survey. This provides objective honest feedback which entrepreneurs can then act upon.

Really successful entrepreneurs conduct and act upon customer perception surveys on a regular basis. In fact it has become one of my test questions when I am trying to establish the real levels of commitment to customer service with a client:

Q. How regularly do you conduct and act upon customer feedback?

Measuring customer satisfaction: a quick guide

Here are some practical tips on how to conduct a customer perception survey:

1. Surveys are best done by telephone or face to face. You get much better information. Avoid tick box 'happy sheets' that hotels and restaurants seem to favour. Aim to speak to 50–100 customers randomly selected from your customer database.
2. If you are doing a telephone survey (quick and relatively cheap compared to face to face), inform your customers by letter of your intentions.

Ask them the following questions:

To assess their buying criteria:
Q. What do you really look for in a supplier?
Q. What disappoints you about suppliers?

To assess your weaknesses:
Q. On a rating scale of 1 to 10 how well do we perform on your key criteria?

To benchmark your competitors' position (compared to yours):
Q. On a scale of 1–10 how well do our competitors rate?

To determine your improvement priorities:
Q. What are the three things we need to improve to really satisfy your requirements?

To build your business:
Q. What would we need to do to do more business with you?
Q. What three words would you use to sum up how you see our business?

You can add any specific questions relevant to your business, eg:

Q. What level of technical support do you look for?

You should make sure that your interviewer records precisely what people actually say and does not reinterpret. They might also ask for examples or probe gently where appropriate for more information.

3. The next stage is to summarize the information and identify your strengths and weaknesses. It might look something like this.

Criteria	Rating
	Bad 1 2 3 4 5 6 7 8 9 10 Excellent
Delivery on time	
Quality of product	
Technical support	
Price	
Customer service	

Your ratings ——

Your major competitor · · ·

Based on this feedback your action plan would probably be:

- Improve delivery performance quickly.
- Re-emphasize your product, quality, and competitive edge.
- Develop your customer service asap.

4. The final stage is to redo the customer survey regularly to check that your improvement actions have been recognized and that you have the basis for doing more gardening with your existing customers.

Building a business generating system

The feast or famine syndrome

Most people who run their own businesses discover soon enough the 'feast or famine' syndrome. One entrepreneur described this effect to me:

> One month I am making so much money I am thinking of retiring to Jersey, yet the next I am thinking of signing on the dole because we have no business.

But what causes it and how can we can escape from the cycle?

Feast or famine arises when a small business lands an order that takes up so much of the capacity available that efforts to secure future business have to be put to one side until the pressure eases. As a result sales dry up and there is simply not the work available to keep the business running smoothly when the order has been completed. The result is a roller-coaster sales curve that can test the nerve of the most determined entrepreneur. Take, for example the experience of Laurence Young with his hotels:

> We have to cope with the variations in sales due to the seasonality of our business. We have a very flexible rate policy, looking far ahead at potential future demand on a day-by-day basis in order every night to fill up. But fill up at the best possible rate. So in the winter we will offer crazy rates and we will almost buy people in and then in the summer it's the opposite. We know that that road out there is going to be very, very busy.

In my experience the feast and famine syndrome is the single biggest obstacle to building a successful new business. Entrepreneurs often lie awake at night worrying about whether the latest slump in orders means the end of the business. Fortunately our entrepreneurs have found a solution which aims to create the consistency of business that lets budding business people sleep easy in their beds. They build *'business generating systems'*.

How it works

Most entrepreneurs balk at the idea of 'systems' – the dreaded 'S' word. And of course systems are often bureaucratic and counter-productive. But the 'systems' created by the most successful small business owners are thankfully very simple and straightforward and provide essential control.

So let's get started.

I rarely meet entrepreneurs who tell me that their big problem is having too many highly profitable customers, and having to turn them away! So the task of a business generating system is to create enough of *the right kind of paying customers in the selected market and at a consistent rate.*

This nirvana is not as difficult to attain as you might imagine. In the business to business world it requires just three steps: 1) creating sales inquiries; 2) submitting proposals; and 3) winning sales orders. It involves planning and organizing the right amount of sales activity needed to hit the monthly sales targets, taking the highs and lows out of sales performance and eliminating feast or famine forever.

In the retail or service sector it means creating enough potential customers and making sure you sell to them when they visit your business. For example, Adele McGee of Inspire, who specializes in motivational training based in Blyth, Nottinghamshire, found that in the ladies fashion business, where personal service was offered, 75 per cent of ladies who try clothes on actually purchase:

> The priority therefore is to make it easy to try clothes on by having enough attractive changing rooms and well-trained staff to encourage customers to try clothes on.

Brian Fairey of Countrywide Leisure, a caravan business with six retail outlets in the North and Midlands, found that 70 per cent of customers who said they needed to think about purchasing a caravan and left his site never returned. The priority is therefore to try to clinch the sale while the customer is on site.

Think of the process as being built around three platforms – a market platform, a working platform and a buying platform.

The *market platform* holds the tools you need to create new customers. The market platform should contain a method for generating 'leads' or, in plain English, potential customers. It could be based on advertising, direct mailing, marketing by telephone, networking and problem-solving, or might major on exhibitions and seminars, referrals from other customers, or simply personal contacts.

The point is to choose the method most suited to your business. You can experiment to find the most effective sales method because the database should supply you with the necessary feedback.

Here, for example, is how Richard Holt, a business consultant from Chester, evolved his sales methods using a simple analysis of the data being recorded.

Holt Associates provide innovative ways of supporting entrepreneurs using my EntreNet model. They found that sending mail-shots alone directly to potential cold customers resulted in only 1 in 200 moving from market platform prospect to working platform – a quotation for business.

> I realized that I needed to do something differently, so I paid an agency to follow up the mail-shots with a telephone call, which resulted in an improvement to 1 in 100 opportunities to quote.

He still was not happy. He had noticed, however, that when the potential customers attended a taster event, ie a short personal presentation to a group of potential customers, at which he explained the benefits of the EntreNet, then his conversion rate improved to 5 out of 10. Of these five, three joined his programmes – buying platform.

> I decided to refocus my marketing and invite potential customers to taster events and it worked like a dream.

He was able to develop his business because he had collected platform data, which enabled him to take corrective action.

Feedback of this type should be recorded in the system and used to construct your own effective business generating system.

Once built up, the customer database becomes a vital tool in creating new business. The beauty of using a computer-based system is that you can programme it to remind you to call customers, send them a newsletter or offer, or invite them to lunch – whatever sales method works for you. Contacting them once every three months is about right. Too many contacts conveys the message 'I am desperate', too few demonstrates that you don't really care about them as a customer.

But you must never forget that computers are only an aid to sales. Your strongest business generation asset will remain always yourself and your personal relationships with customers.

While the *market platform* holds the information on potential new customers and tracks your contact with them, the next stage – *the working platform* – is concerned with turning inquiries into firm orders. At this stage potential customers become prospective customers, and you pitch for the work by submitting detailed proposals and quotations. Not all quotations will result in firm orders, but you can calculate from past experience your probable rate of success. You can also work out how long it takes the average proposal to become a firm order; information that is vital if you are to keep the flow of work consistent.

The last stage of the BGS, *the buying platform*, is when firm orders are finally placed. The aim is to create a database of existing and potential new companies and to use this base – linked to an electronic diary – as a means to keep in contact with them regularly. The information on this platform controls the resources that have to go into the two previous stages. For instance, the order book may be too small to match the capacity of the company, meaning lost opportunities for profit and lost jobs – in that case the system advises on the extra resources needed in the selling process. This can be in the way of an extra sales effort or a changed sales strategy, or both. It might also provide the extra pressure on the company at the *working platform* level to apply gentle pressure on firms to reduce the time between quotation and placing the final order. Too little work on the working platform can also act as an incentive to increase the flow of work coming from existing customers – concentrating on the gardening.

Where the load of work on the buying platform is greater than the company can reasonably handle, the system feeds this information back, flagging up the need for new capacity or for adjustments in the sales effort at stages one and two.

Gathering the information must be done religiously, using the step-by-step approach you'll find below. It also has to be on an ongoing basis. There is no point in going through this exercise once a year or in a desultory and irregular way: it has to become part of a regular routine, once a month at least.

You start by calculating your last year's turnover and how many orders it took to achieve this. This helps set a target for next year's business. You also need to know the average number of sales approaches needed to deliver a serious sales inquiry and the proportion of inquiries to a firm order. These 'conversion rates' help determine how much sales effort you have to put in to run your business at its present and planned future capacity. Follow the steps outlined below and you have the makings of a BGS. You can buy in a ready-made model. Many of the successful entrepreneurs I know use the ACT system, which is marketed worldwide.

A business generating system

Stage	Activity	Key indicators
1 Market platform	• Introducing products/services to customers, making sales presentations.	• Value (£s) of potential business. • Conversion rates (%) people spoken to, to serious inquiries.
2 Working platform	• Making firm proposals to customers. • Customers deciding to purchase.	• Value (£) of quotations submitted. • Conversion rate (%) of orders received to quotations submitted.
3 Buying platform	• Orders received.	• Value (£) of work in hand.

Milestones

You need to know the lead time between stages if you are to make the necessary links between the quantity of orders needed to keep the business running at full capacity, the number of jobs you need to quote for, and the number of potential buyers you need to reach.

The stages can be seen as milestones.

	Milestone 1		Milestone 2		Milestone 3		Milestone 4
Market platform	Quotations made	Working platform	Order received	Buying platform	Sales invoiced	Terms of payment	Cash in bank
Defined prospects		*Quotes in the pipeline*		*Existing customers*			
Time ———▶							

Ten steps to building a business generating system

Step 1   Calculate target annual sales.

Step 2   Calculate average order size from historical records. To do this you divide the value of all sales by the number of orders:

$$\frac{\text{Total Sales Value}}{\text{Number of Orders}} = average\ order\ value$$

Step 3   Calculate number of orders required for year:

$$\frac{\text{Target Annual Sales (step 1)}}{\text{Average Order Value (step 2)}} = number\ of\ orders\ required$$

Step 4   Decide how many orders will come from existing customers. (This can be determined roughly by analyzing the information gathered on the buying platform. You can also set targets for winning new business from these customers.)

Step 5   Determine how many new orders will be required to hit sales targets. Calculation: *Number of orders required* to meet annual sales target (Step 3) *less forecast sales to existing customers* (Step 4).

Step 6   Calculate conversion rate of quotations for work to orders from *working platform* information, eg three quotations sent, one order received = 3:1.

Step 7   Calculate *number of new quotations for work required per year and per month*.

Calculation: multiply number of new orders required per year by the conversion ratio (Step 5 × Step 6) At this point divide the answer by 12. This gives *new quotations required per month*. Build in any seasonality, eg no orders at Christmas!

Step 8   Determine conversion ratio of *new prospects* (potential new customers) to *quotations*, eg four new prospects to one quotation = 4:1.

Step 9   *Calculate number of prospects required per month.* Calculation: Multiply number of new quotations required by this conversion ratio to ascertain number of prospective customers who must be contacted (Step 7 × Step 8.) Now divide by 12 to obtain monthly figure.

Step 10   Determine how new prospects are best created in your business, ie mail-shots, telephone calls, adverts, exhibitions, etc.

Plan to undertake enough of this activity monthly to create the level of prospects required at Step 9.

To help you do this you need to follow a *sales activity plan*.

Sales activity plan

A   Determine last year's turnover _____

B   Determine total number of orders last year _____

C   Calculate average order size (A ÷ B) _____

D   Establish next year's turnover _____

E   Calculate total number of orders required next year (D ÷ C) _____

F   Determine number of repeat business expected _____

G   Calculate number of extra orders needed from new customers (E – F) _____

H   Determine how many quotes needed to win an order (eg 1 in 3) _____

I   Determine how many customers visited and how many quotes issued (eg 1 in 2) _____

J   Determine how many potential customers mail-shotted and how many appointments gained (eg 1 in 10) _____

K   Number of quotes to be issued (G × H) _____

L   Number of customers to be visited (K × I) _____

M   Number of mail-shots to be sent (L × J) _____

Notes: This is a dynamic model and the figures need to be constantly analyzed in order to ensure that the established target turnover is achieved. The vital ratios are:

■ number of quotes issued to orders won;
■ number of customers visited to orders won;
■ number of customers mail-shotted to appointments gained.

These will indicate, on a relatively short-term basis, the effectiveness of the promotional approach being used, and where there are any 'weak' links. If these ratios change then the sales activity rates need to be either boosted or curtailed.

This sales platform method also ensures that the company is aware of the resources necessary in order to achieve the stated objectives in terms of:

■ people resource requirements, ie the time 'on the road';
■ availability of sources of data/potential sales leads;
■ office resources and equipment, eg computer/word processor.

The sales platform should be updated on a monthly basis to monitor performance and to adjust promotional activity accordingly.

Software requirements

Once the figures are calculated your sales platform can be managed either manually using a diary system or by computer. There are several software packages available that link together:

■ sales platform;
■ your database of customer contacts;
■ a diary planning system.

One system that is used regularly by entrepreneurs is ACT.

Networking – building relationships with key people

We've already seen the value entrepreneurs place on 'networking' in the early stages of a company's life. Getting out and meeting people who can help your business, befriending them and calling on them for help when you need it, that's what networking is all about.

My first book, *The Hallmarks for Successful Business,* identified networking as a key business building skill, a conclusion that was subsequently borne out by research done in Australia with entrepreneurial companies using the *Hallmarks* model. The researchers found a very strong relationship between networking and profit growth. In fact *it proved the strongest predictor of long-term success.*

But what do we mean by networking? It is perhaps easier to describe what networking is not before describing how entrepreneurs do it effectively.

Some of you will have already got the wrong idea in your minds. Boozy lunches and convivial golf games can be very pleasant but if you are serious about building your business then avoid them. Listen to how Simon Haslam discovered why they don't make business sense.

Simon runs a marketing consultancy business in Glasgow.

> When I first started I used to attend every breakfast, lunch and dinner meeting I possibly could to try to build up useful contacts. I did not create one jot of business but I did put on 2 stone! I learnt the hard way that you need to pick and choose, so I now only network very selectively.

Simon must be doing something right because his business is highly successful.

You have my permission to indulge in such frolics once you are successful – if you choose to!

Again, you might think that going to a local Chamber of Commerce meeting to hear someone give a lecture might qualify as networking, but there are misconceptions here too. Meetings where local business people come together are only of use if these people can provide useful contacts or solutions to your problems.

Entrepreneur's dictionary:	
Networking	Building strong personal and working relationships with people who can help build the business.

So who should be in your personal supporters' club and how do you go about building it?

Ideally you need to build in all those people who have information likely to be useful for your business. The information is as likely to be informal as formal. For example, bank managers can give you formal information about how much they'll charge for an overdraft, or how to organize your accounts to maximize the interest on your bank assets. However, they will also know a lot of local business people and be aware of things you are not. If your business is offering a service or a product they might know a company that is looking for just that. The term I use to describe these people is 'sign-posters'. They stand at a crossroads and information may pass through their sites from a number of directions. Another example may be the MD of a big local firm who has his fingers on the pulse of local business. He may know who can be relied on as suppliers, or which companies are looking for what particular service or product. When you ask the 'sign-poster' for help you are making connections with his or her own network, which might be extensive. For instance, someone once said to me: 'We are never more than three phone calls away from anybody or any business.' 'Sign-posters' – at the cross-roads of information flows – are the most valuable members of any network.

Here's an example from one of our entrepreneurs.

Jimmy Lawana of the Eastern Province Agricultural Union in Dimbaza, South Africa, is an excellent sign-poster. Les Holbrook of the Border-Kei Chamber of Business in East London finds Jimmy an invaluable source of contacts.

> If ever I want to find out who can help me with a particular problem I call Jimmy. He knows everybody and with one telephone call can normally sort out any problem or point me in the right direction, because he is truly wired into everything that happens here in the Eastern province.

As well as sign-posters your network could include suppliers, advisers, key customers, and fellow entrepreneurs.

That's who we need. But how do you go about assembling your personal network, your own supporters club?

Think of it as a *five-step* process.

Step 1 – Existing key contacts list

Start by making a list of your existing key contacts in your business. As we have discussed, these might include:

- key customers;
- suppliers;
- the bank manager;
- business contacts;
- and advisers (both official and unofficial).

Once you have done this, consider whether your list is as comprehensive as it should be. For example, does your spouse, your family and your personal friends appear on the list? We know that successful entrepreneurs learn best through social contacts and that family and friends often play a vital role as a sounding board for ideas and a source of moral support. So add them to your list.

Step 2 – Extending the network

The trick is now to extend your network to include people who can help you resolve business problems or act as sign-posters for your new customers. How do you go about it?

Talking to our entrepreneurs about how they made these contacts often throws up a range of possibilities.

One obvious source of intelligence is a local forum where other entrepreneurs meet. We've seen how Tom Hunter found the support he needed in just such a place – Entrepreneurial Exchange networking with successful entrepreneurs in Scotland. Others found much same range of contacts at their local small business club.

Clive Lunn, Managing Director of hallamtechnic Limited, uses Sheffield Business Club and is now a committed member.

> We have formed a relationship with other members from which we have both benefited with orders worth thousands of pounds to each of us. Attendance by us at Sheffield Business Club is compulsory enjoyment that is always profitable.

Making the most of such contacts is not simply a matter of going along to meetings and asking for advice. You need to learn the trick employed by almost all successful entrepreneurs – make it a two-way exchange. You need to throw in the offer of sharing with them and even collaborating in order to deal with the particular business challenges you face.

Roger Clegg of R & M Services of Welshpool exports lighting equipment around the world. He cannot afford a full-time export salesperson:

> We use the Export Association shared export salesman scheme, it basically means that I don't need to put a full-time sales person on the road. A number of local companies get together and share the service of a person going into the area you are trying to sell. That means that expenses are much reduced, and so you get much more for your money. Plus the fact that they can speak the language, it certainly puts a much more professional view of your company to the potential customer.

But how does it work?

> Basically the sales person or marketing person would come in to our factory and find out a little bit about our product and how we make it and as much as he can, and he would go out as your representative. It costs £250 each for which we would expect to get at least 10 very good new sales opportunities.

Exchanges like this can be the foundation stone of an invaluable support network. We know from research that it is the buzz created by the exchange of ideas that in part accounts for the phenomenal success of Silicon Valley in California. Clusters of similarly minded people with complementary skills operate in Britain in places like Cambridge and Sheffield, home to the Sheffield Business Club. Membership is growing by 25 per cent per annum and the local economy is a bright spot for successful new enterprises. Once you have been to the meeting point of local business and made contact with helpful fellow business people, add these to your list.

Now look around your local business landscape to identify possible sign-posters, people that run larger companies, or have their finger on the pulse locally. It could be a bank manager, or someone employed at the local business support agency. Not anyone will do. The person must have a reputation of being valued by other entrepreneurs. (Again your contacts at the local business club might point you in the right direction, albeit wittingly or unwittingly.) Tom Farmer (the entrepreneur who founded Kwik Fit, the successful UK motor maintenance business just sold to Ford) has provided many entrepreneurs with both good advice and moral support.

Here's another example.

Bethan Jones is a sign-poster for many export companies. The local entrepreneurs value Bethan for being able to resolve their problems quickly. As Anne-Marie Jackson of Handcast Design can testify:

> Our first port of call would be the Export Association. We have found them very useful, Bethan makes things happen and always seems to be able to connect you with the right people. This is invaluable support.

Roger Clegg also testifies to Bethan's sign-posting skills:

> Bethan is very helpful, you need somebody who speaks the same language as yourself and provides hands-on support in a fast effective manner.

In every industry or geographic region there are people who know what is happening. They sit at the interface where many networks meet and overlap – they might belong to industry bodies, employers' associations, local business support organizations. They are wired into the intelligence in the industry.

Once you have found these key people they too need to be added to your network. They can help you overcome difficulties and open up new business opportunities, simply because of the store of formal and informal knowledge they hold. They can point you in the direction of other successful entrepreneurs who will also be able to help if you approach them in the spirit of reciprocity (better expressed as 'I'll scratch your back if you scratch mine'). They are an invaluable source of quick, cheap, up-to-date information. The advice of one successful entrepreneur can be worth that of 100 consultants or so-called experts.

You must also add customers to your list. Treating them as part of the network means you don't simply ask them about the service you've been offering them. You find out where they gathered the information about suppliers like you, you find out who or what influences their thinking, and who they turn to for advice.

Some customers will be far more useful than others because they too will belong to networks, and you will find out who are the people who shape their thinking, and who they can turn to for advice. Seek to add these key players to your network.

Lastly you will have some access to 'paid business advisers' – people like your bank manager, your lawyer and your accountant – whose livelihood ultimately depends on business people like yourself. Make them work for their money by asking them who you should be talking to and put these in turn on your network.

Step 3 – Refine your list

By this time you probably have a long list of sign-posters, supporters, role models, helpers and sources of intelligence on your network – more than you have time to handle and cultivate. So you need now to edit the list down to manageable proportions. Do this by 'talking' to each of them either by telephone, e-mail or face to face. Decide which ones will be helpful to you and put the others on the back burner for the time being.

Step 4 – Making your list work for you

Put your edited list of contacts into your telephone directory or better still onto your computer database and aim to keep in touch with them at least once a quarter. Find out what interests them and when you find relevant information, call them or send it in the post with a short handwritten note. Remember that networking is a two-way street, you need to nurture your contacts. You can't call in favours from contacts in a crisis if you have not spoken with them for 18 months!

Step 5 – Keeping the network in working order

Now that you have established a relationship you can ask for help when you need it, but be sure to make your thanks well known to them if they do help you. Thanking people need cost very little but it will repay itself many times over.

Public relations (PR) on the cheap

> We concentrate enormously on our public relations and on our marketing. We get food journalists up here as much as we can and get our name into the marketplace, into the gourmet columns of the food magazines. We have been on the Keith Floyd television show. Television programmes in fact visit quite frequently. At least two or three a year come here because we lay on something special such as grading oysters or serving oysters, or smoking salmon.
>
> Photography costs a fortune, about £700 or £800 a day. So when a photographer comes to illustrate an article for a magazine we ask for a negative. We have got superb views of our oyster beds, which actually didn't cost us very much to do.

We have already seen how valuable magazine stories about his business benefited John Noble and his firm. He is a master of effective publicity on the cheap. Some of the journalists were even kind enough to put his address and telephone number at the end of articles, making it easy for chefs and restaurateurs to find him. It is a shining example of the benefits of beg, borrow and befriend.

So how can your business tap into this valuable source of free advertising?

You first need to do some simple research. Get a copy of your local or regional newspaper or industry magazine and look for the name of the journalist responsible for producing stories about the kinds of things you do.

Call them up and invite them out for lunch: journalists seldom refuse this sort of invitation if it comes from somebody who sounds interesting. You don't need to spend the money on lunch if you don't want to: you can suggest you call into the office at a convenient time.

But how do you sound interesting? First of all you have to sound confident. It may help to remember that you may be doing them a favour. Most journalists have a target number of stories to produce each week. If you appear to have an interesting story to tell, this will help enormously.

It repays the effort of doing your homework here. You should read their newspaper or magazine to pick up the style, length and type of stories they produce. You can assume that the journalist will be looking for stories with genuine human interest at the heart and most entrepreneurs have interesting stories to tell.

I once sent a press release to our local newspaper, along the lines of 'Ex-building site worker creates successful 120-person consulting business from nothing'. The *Daily Mail* got hold of the story and published it with a picture. We got lots of telephone calls mainly from existing customers who complained I must have been overcharging them. What I did not know was that the *Daily Mail* added 'Millionaire Hall' to the picture!

So be warned: ask to see the copy before it is printed.

There must be something about yourself or your business that is interesting in this sort of way. Could it be that you are a local businessman who has made good? Or do you have an employee who is an interesting character? It maybe that you have done nothing more than been to a lecture given by Bill Gates or Richard Branson. (Local man meets Bill Gates.)

You will gather it is better to have an unusual angle or to exercise some creativity in the way you pitch the story.

To really make an impact you need to do more than just think about such things before you meet the journalist. You should take along a crisp A4 press release with your story written up in the style of the paper or magazine. If you are no good at writing then ask a friend who is to help out. That's what friends are for, but remember to do them a favour in return as soon as you can.

Your well-written press release helps the journalists do their job and enables them to stay in the pub a bit longer. (Only joking, my journalist friends.)

Once you have had that first meeting and made contact at a human level you can go on to develop regular contact. Send in stories when you can, and give them exclusive rights to them if it is really interesting.

My business flourished on a diet of cheap publicity for years. Nothing more than a string of press releases achieved it. Business journals are a particularly fruitful field, because they are often short of stories and they are read by many of your potential customers. We used to send a press release every week, built round a soft-sell story, and most got published unedited. Many people commented that we never seemed to be out of the press and media.

Another example of how effective this can be comes from Paul Darwent of Mini Gears in Stockport. Paul's business manufactures world-class components for the crème of the motor trade, including Rolls Royce, Cosworth engines and many others. Paul first appeared in my TV series *Winning*.

> Appearing on television did wonders for my confidence. It encouraged me to write press releases and become my own PR manager.
>
> I made contact with the editors and journalists in the motor trade media and sent them articles and press releases about Mini Gears. We get free coverage now every month and customers really know about us.

But how has it helped Paul's business?

> Since appearing on *Winning* when I started my PR crusade our business has grown fourfold.

There have also been additional unforeseen benefits:

> Recruiting highly qualified engineers is a nightmare in the North West. But because of our PR campaigns, people seem to know about us and we get lots of quality applicants for key jobs.

A word of warning. If you decide to take the lazy route and hire a PR company to write and place press releases, make sure you pay them on a results-only basis. Avoid retainers unless you need to reduce your profits for tax purposes! Even then I could still think of more useful ways of wasting money.

Ploughing money back into the business

The popular image of entrepreneurs as 'get-rich-quick merchants' couldn't be further from the truth when you look at successful start-up businesses. It hasn't surprised me that one of the four predictors of the long-term survival of a business is conservative financing. That was the key finding of Arie de Gaus when he studied companies that had lasted more than 400 years. In his book *The Living Company*, he found they had been frugal and unwilling to risk their capital foolishly. They understood the usefulness of having cash in the kitty, allowing them to pursue options that their 'in debt' competitors simply didn't have. While most good entrepreneurs don't aim to be around for 400 years or so, they do share the ambition of founding a business that will last and grow. And their reluctance to borrow money to finance expansion or to pay for lavish premises, far less than to finance lavish lifestyles, has certainly stood them in good stead.

Here, for example, is how Norman White found that survival depended on keeping capital in the business.

What became apparent very quickly after starting the company was that raising capital was not going to be easy. We knew before we started that the £0.5 million wouldn't take us very far, we thought maybe six months and then by that time we would have secured proper, what we call first-time funding. The second half of the first year was one of survival in a real sense. All employees had to take salary cuts and some of us stopped taking salaries altogether. We learnt some hard lessons in those early days about conserving cash and only spending it on the real necessities.

So having a 'cash mountain', no matter how small, has spelt survival for many a new business. And if entrepreneurs do indeed have surplus money in the bank they usually know how to spend it wisely. They apply distinctly practical criteria on what is worth spending money on.

Dick Watson of Keepmoat plc has reinvested back into his business at critical points in its development:

We reinvested all the profits over many years back into the business and have only taken dividends in the last few years. We used our vision and values to guide our investments. For example, we invested heavily in developing our customer service 10 years ago because our mission is to delight customers and partners.

But what about reinvesting in their people?

In 1994 we invested £250k in training all our people in visioning and maintaining a positive mental attitude.

We also invest on an ongoing basis in developing all our people in the key skills required by our business, particularly problem solving and decision making. Our people have responded by helping us grow our business from £5 million to £150 million.

The lesson is that successful entrepreneurs reinvest profits back into their business to help them grow. Again it is the gardening analogy. They plough them back to create an even better harvest in the future. This means foregoing many desirable short-term attractions, like going on extended holidays or splashing out on that conservatory. Entrepreneurs do this because if their aim is to create a valued business over the long run, it makes sense to nurture the plant. It also means that in the long term the profits go to you, not to the bank!

In my business, before I sold it, we had a rule for the use of annual profits: 25 per cent for the tax man, 25 per cent for the shareholders and employees in bonuses and 50 per cent reinvested in the business.

Forming a team

> Whenever I see anything accomplished anywhere there is normally a turned on team behind it.
>
> (Tom Peters)

Accepting the need for team working is often one of the most difficult lessons to be learnt by entrepreneurs. Entrepreneurs by nature are egotistical and independent, so forming a team is not a natural process.

But if you want to grow your business to a turnover of more than 1 million pounds a year it is something you will have to learn to do. It is rare for some entrepreneurs to build a business beyond that limit without any help. The reasons are obvious. Businesses need the four capabilities – driving, doing, selling and controlling, and it is all but impossible for a single entrepreneur to possess all four.

If you can't make the transition from one-man band to team-run company the business will hit its natural ceiling and stick there. This is a lesson learned by Tom Hunter, now one of Scotland's wealthiest entrepreneurs:

> Teamwork has been the most crucial thing. Many people can be successful small businessmen, but there is not that many make the transition to a successful large business. When I started I was literally a one-man band but I found I needed to bring people in. I had to find the right people and then get them to buy into the vision and the enthusiasm. If you can't create that, you can't create a big business.
>
> That vision and enthusiasm is the key to our success. People need a vision to buy into, to feel part of the business, and as you grow bigger this can very easily be lost. As a result the efficiency of the business will suffer. My job is to keep making sure people feel part of the business, that they still feel they have a role to play, that their voice is heard and they are not just directed from the top. One of my goals is to make sure this company still stays 'small' as we grow to a very large company.

Building a team when the company is still quite small should be relatively easy. People who join you should feel included and part of the organization. So there should be no need at this early stage to introduce formal structures; informality and flexibility should be the watchwords.

Here is how Tom Hunter did it when he first got started:

> We used to meet as a team on a Monday afternoon and discuss all kinds of things. People felt part of the process, particularly as I encouraged them to ask questions, debate issues and take action. This pioneering phase was very rewarding and good fun.

Teamwork is about creating something together, the 'together' being the key element. At its best, team working produces that strange arithmetic when $1+1+1 = 5$. But how can we achieve this magic outcome? For a start it cannot be achieved where there is gross incompatibility between the personalities involved, or where the staff divides itself into cliques. This implies careful selection and an open management style.

Many entrepreneurs have learnt the hard way that a commitment to open and inclusive management does not, however, mean rule by committee, or even by democracy.

Phil Crane sums it up like this:

> I believe in teams, but not talking shops. You need to involve and consult people and make them feel a real part of the business. But at the end of the day the entrepreneur is normally the one with their house on the line, so they need to take the tough decisions.

So here are a few tips from our successful entrepreneurs on the pitfalls you need to avoid if you are to get your team building right.

Bleary vision

If there is no clear vision at the top as to where the business is going, the team cannot operate efficiently. Everybody concentrates on their own individual enthusiasms or obsessions. They are all busy but the business is going nowhere. In the entrepreneur's dictionary it is called 'busy fool' syndrome.

Unclear roles

If the entrepreneur hasn't made it clear what the role of each team member is, there is friction and confusion over who does what and when and with whom.

Entrepreneurs really do need to know the answers to two critical questions: 1) do we have a shared strategy? and 2) do the members of the team each have three clear objectives that will ensure that the strategy is successfully delivered?

Here is a very simple way of getting the answer to these questions in two minutes flat.

At a team meeting ask your team to write down individually what they believe to be the three priorities for the business and their three key personal objectives. Then discuss the results.

A word of warning: whenever I do this with organizations large and small the entrepreneur is often amazed at the results.

'We do not seem to be working for the same business' is a fairly typical response. That's the reason for doing it – remember to clarify roles.

Lack of trust

Trust is the glue that holds teams together; it can be hard to establish and easy to destroy. It requires consistent behaviour on the part of the entrepreneur and honesty in dealing with issues as they arise. Before you make a promise to your team you need to be sure you can deliver it, and show them you really mean what you say in the way you behave subsequently.

Spending time with people in the business and access to top management can be a great help, as Adele McGee found.

Adele was helping a large UK hotel group improve its customer service. A customer survey revealed that customers valued the friendly nature of the staff on reception but felt that the bar and waiting staff were indifferent and had no time for them.

Adele got the whole team together to explore the problem. One brave young waiter raised his hand and said nervously: 'The reason is the management tell us to stop talking to people and clear the tables or fill the optics.' Encouraged by this bold young man, a waitress joined in: 'More than half the staff here are part-time and we don't get training like the full-time staff. They treat us like second-class citizens; we want to do a good job with customers but we are not taken seriously. It's crazy, when you realize we are usually here at the busiest times.'

The management were inadvertently creating poor service by their obvious lack of trust of their team.

A silence fell on the meeting, which was eventually broken by a very embarrassed general manager who 'promised to look into it...'.

Contrast this with Paul Cox of Lovekyn Garages of Kingston Upon Thames:

> We encourage all our team to run our business as if it were their own. We give them all our accounts and any information they want. We encourage them to develop themselves. We find if we treat them like adults and partners in our business, that's how they behave.

Lack of care for each other

It may sound a little un-businesslike, but unsuccessful teamwork often stems from the absence of caring between team members. Emotions matter in business, and generating the wrong emotion is very counter-productive.

Members of a poor team often expend much time and energy on scoring points against each other or playing games, rather than getting on with the business in hand. Most of us will have experienced that sort of behaviour – a disease big companies are particularly prone to – and can appreciate how toxic the atmosphere can become.

So how can we avoid the disease infecting your growing business? The formula that works for most entrepreneurs is a simple one. Everyone in the company must treat each other with respect, and with dignity. Make that a rule and come down heavily on anyone who breaks it – in a dignified and respectful way, of course.

Martin Vincent installed that rule in CompuAdd and he asks his staff to hold him to it personally. 'We work well together now as a team,' says Martin. 'We have got rid of much of the "shadow side" in our business.' The results are impressive too. CompuAdd's profits have increased every year for the past three years, Martin believes as a direct result of their new healthy culture.

No attention to team process – only to the task in hand

Even people who make natural team workers won't automatically form themselves into a good and productive team. Just dealing with the immediate task in hand can take up all the time available unless space for team building is levered in.

You need to nurture team behaviour. That means making sure the team members meet together regularly (at least once a month) to assess progress and to discuss the latest challenges facing the concern. Team meetings should be short and focused – everyone's time is valuable and they have their own job to do – and should concentrate on the team processes, communication, decision making, and how the team works. Look upon them as opportunities to reaffirm the longer-term objectives in the face of any short-term difficulties that may have arisen.

You will also find that an agreed code of behaviour can do a power of good, as long as the code is visibly seen also to apply to you.

Simon Keats' team at North Staffs Caravans was once very task oriented. He now tries to manage the team process:

> We have a time out and ask people how the meetings are going and how we can improve them. We take minutes and circulate them within one hour of the end of the meeting. We banish competition and encourage collaboration, particularly between department heads, and that has worked wonders. We now prevent problems rather than fire fight. People seem to look forward to the meetings.

Unhealthy competition between individuals

Businesses in a free market are kept on their toes by competition. So it is perhaps natural to think that competition within companies must also be a good thing. Some companies even have pay and reward systems that encourage just that sort of behaviour. For example, in some shops the salesperson's earnings depend heavily on commission and there is a marked reluctance on their part to call on other sales people (who might have more expertise), to the detriment of the customer.

In fact this is wrong-headed thinking. Competition between individuals within the same company destroys team spirit. In the worst cases it creates a situation where management resources have to be devoted to policing staff behaviour to curb dirty tricks and other destructive game playing.

Poor leadership

Those of you who take an interest in sport will appreciate that even the most talented teams need to be properly led. Someone has to provide leadership. But too many new businesses confuse leadership with dictatorship. The best leaders in my experience bring out the best in their teams through example, encouragement, and a display of personal enthusiasm for the task in hand, not through crudely laying down the law. Everybody in the team needs to feel valued and any team exerts its own disciplines upon its members through a sense of sharing and joint responsibility. But no one would argue that it is easy to strike the right balance as a leader. But here are a few hints from entrepreneurs who have proven that they have found that magic touch:

> Make sure you treat everyone the same, you cannot afford to have favourites, this just creates internal mayhem.
>
> (Simon Keats, North Staff Caravans)

> Try to catch people doing things right, rather than always finding fault. Positive reinforcing goes a long way and most teams do not get enough of it.
>
> (Dick Watson, Keepmoat plc)

> I know I have done my bit when my team believe that their success was entirely down to their own efforts.
>
> (Dave Osmond, CompuAdd Computer Group)

Team leadership: how to build teams that really work

Let's try to sum up the lessons of team building. If you use this as a checklist to help you build teams that really work, you will be well on the way:

1. Establish and get buy-in to a team vision. What do we want in three years' time?
2. Pick the right people to work together.
3. Manage the process and establish ground rules for communication and decision making. Draw up a code of behaviour.
4. Encourage collaboration and banish competition.
5. Banish conformity and encourage diversity in thinking.
6. Care for people and encourage them to care for each other.
7. Build trust by keeping your promises.
8. Provide team leadership.

Building the team assessment

If you want to access the quality of team working in your business, ask you team to individually complete the following questionnaire (Photocopy it – you have my permission.) Share the results as a team, identify and resolve as a team to deal with any blockages to your performance.

Totally   Totally
disagree   agree
1   2   3   4   5

1. Our team consistently produces results beyond expectations.	1 2 3 4 5
2. Our business objectives are clearly understood and owned by all our people.	1 2 3 4 5
3. We have established high levels of trust in our team.	1 2 3 4 5
4. Teamwork is a major asset in our business.	1 2 3 4 5
5. Our people have commitment to our business overall not individual departments or cliques.	1 2 3 4 5
6. Our team leadership is excellent and inspires the team to give their best.	1 2 3 4 5
7. We consistently exceed our customers' expectations.	1 2 3 4 5

---

8. We get more ideas than we really need from our team.   1 2 3 4 5

9. Our team collaborates rather than competes internally.   1 2 3 4 5

10. Internal communication is a strength in our business.   1 2 3 4 5

Total score _____

× 2 = _____ %

As a general guideline, scores of:

80% +	=	Excellent teamwork
60–80%	=	High average score
40–60%	=	Teamwork needs some work
Under 40%	=	No. 1 priority for your business

Creating consistency in your business

Many entrepreneurs have left behind big companies because they hated the systems, the bureaucracy and the time spent in unproductive meetings. The last thing they want is to re-create such conditions in their own businesses. They enjoy the new-found freedoms of making decisions in nano-seconds rather than months and are exhilarated by occasionally flying by the seat of their pants. For entrepreneurs, freedom, speed and spontaneity are to be celebrated and encouraged.

But you know what's coming next, I suspect....

Eventually the new business gets to a size where the absence of formal structures begins to show. Cracks start to appear, customers are let down, deadlines missed. The quality of the product or service can no longer be taken for granted; squabbles occur internally. You are facing your first major real crisis.

If you are not careful, from now on you will spend much of your time *'putting out fires'*, dashing from one crisis to the next sorting out the problems, getting things back on track. That way lies disaster.

So how do successful entrepreneurs reconcile the need to keep themselves free to go on developing the business and the need to keep the company nimble so that it can fully exploit market opportunities, with the absolutely vital need to maintain standards and deliver consistently in product and/or service?

The answer is develop a *'fire prevention'* system. A way to build consistency without losing the entrepreneurial flair, energy and spirit.

The way to build consistency is to establish a few simple one-page guidelines for people.

Setting standards – an example

Standards for making customers/visitors welcome

- Send a map to all new customers and confirm appointment time and car park space availability.
- Ensure car park space available on day.
- Ensure customer name is on welcome board in reception.

Standards for sending information to customers

- Check customer name, how it is spelt and their job title before sending out correspondence.
- When sending faxes, call customers and check they have received their fax and it is legible.
- Reply to all customer queries the same day.
- Ensure all customer telephone enquiries get an answer the same day. Minimum standards: 'Mr Jones is away all day but he will call you tomorrow at 9.00 am.'
- Record all customer complaints in the logbook, taking name and details. Do not answer complaint, promise somebody will call back within 1 hour (if person currently unavailable).

Alf Barratt, the Plant Manager of Birtley Building Products, Galvanizing Plant near Newcastle, provides a good example of creating consistency.

Alf established one-page bullet point standards for the six key customer interactions with his business. In three years, sales and profits have increased fourfold, which might be related to the fact that his customer service key indicator scores are constantly in the high nineties.

Learning to manage a bigger business

First of all, let's start with you and your role. Do you need to change what you are doing? How much management and supervision do you provide on a day-to-day basis? Too much or too little? If you spend all your time managing, the business is going to suffer because it depends on your skills as an entrepreneur.

Tip 1: Hold short action-oriented management meetings that last for an hour maximum once a week. Make sure you don't cancel every other one.

Tip 2: Establish simple objectives or agreements with people. Help them keep to them. *'Delegate more to control more'* is the message.

Tip 3: Decide on what aspect of the business you need to continue to run in a hands-on way, and which parts can be left to others. Tom Hunter made these decisions and got them right. He recognized that as his business grew he still needed to oversee one key aspect of his business personally, the buying:

> Even today I still control all the buying, because that is a crucial part of the business and I feel I have a special talent in spotting trends and bringing the right product to the marketplace. I also decided I had a key role in making sure that we keep the company thinking small as we grow big.

Tom keeps an idea on how the business is doing generally by meeting weekly with key managers. He makes it plain that it is up to them to reach agreed objectives through leading and motivating their teams:

> I get together with my senior managers once a week. I also make a point of getting together with the senior buyers and the warehouse managers every Monday night to discuss last week's business, what's happening this week and thrash out any issues. They in turn have meetings with their people.

Tip 4: Make a point of being consistent in your own behaviour. Remember you are a powerful role model and whatever you do will influence the way the company functions.

The rules are:

- Be consistent in how you treat individuals. That means no favouritism.
- Keep your promises. Always try to do what you say you will.
- Encourage people to be open and honest with you. Be authentic in all your dealings.

Tip 5: Build consistency within the company by establishing a few simple ground rules, guidelines for the staff to follow. Terry Bramall did this when he laid down *'The Keepmoat Way'* (see page 59).

Tip 6: Prevent fires rather than fight them. Identify the area where the cracks have been appearing in your business and then, working with your team, establish some simple controls. Your aim is to prevent problems rather than fix them. Later we shall see how entrepreneurs in large organizations control their business using key indicators but you probably do not need them yet.

Tip 7: Take time to discuss issues openly with your team. The purpose of these meetings is to solve problems and that will operate most smoothly if you remember people do not normally come to work to screw things up. These should not be 'gotcha' meetings or opportunities to point the finger or lay blame. Assume instead that people are trying to do their best and look for fault not in the individual but in the procedures or the lack of them. Very often it is the lack of system that causes problems; the best procedures may never have been defined. If you identify causes and fix things as a team you will have everyone pulling in the same direction, and 'fire prevention measures' can be put in place. The very fact that you discuss issues openly in this way will help you project yourself as both consistent and fair, invaluable attributes for the person at the top.

take **stock of your progress**

If you have come this far and have successfully started a new business or have taken a stagnating business and put it back on the road to growth, you should be really pleased with yourself. Perhaps you have not yet begun the task but have started to see possibilities you didn't see before.

This chapter is designed to allow you to take stock and to test your progress. By now you should appreciate the importance of having a vision, a dream of where you want to take the business. You also know that at the heart of successful entrepreneurship lies the ability to *spot opportunities*, and that superior opportunities can deliver growth and ultimate fortune.

Turning vision into reality requires resources and it is the job of the entrepreneur to find them, at the lowest cost. Although many start-up businesses are under-capitalized, using the principle of *beg, borrow and befriend* you should be able to put those resources together. You will also appreciate that no business can flourish without the four capabilities of *driving, doing, selling* and *controlling*. What steps have you taken to make sure your business has or will have these capabilities?

The value of turning to other entrepreneurs for help and advice, and the supreme importance of *building your network of contacts and supporters*, should not be lost on you. Hopefully you have already taken steps to put such things on a sound footing.

On the customer front you should have uncovered the truth that the best way to win and keep customers is to provide a *solution for problems* they face as human beings, and to *deliver customer delight* – to exceed their expectations of you.

To put the business on a long-term trajectory of growth you will now know the importance of building a team, both in selecting the people you need and in weaving them, with all their disparate talents and character traits, into a winning combination.

While doing all this you should not forget the importance of control over the business nor ignore the usefulness of a simple business generating system.

Hopefully from now on you will also have a better and more productive relationship with your bank manager!

The easiest way for you to take stock of your progress is for you and maybe your partner or a trusted friend to complete an assessment. The assessment below is based upon the personal qualities and the key tasks that our entrepreneurs identified led to their success.

Try to answer the questions as honestly as you can. There is no point fooling yourself and others. Don't worry if you get some low scores, you can address them later. The key point is to be open and honest with yourself. I found it helpful to talk this through with my partner Ellen; she does not hold back on giving me honest feedback!

When rating your performance try to be as objective as possible, for example:

Q2. We spotted a superior opportunity.

A 5 score on this would mean your opportunity met all the criteria set out in Chapter 3 on spotting superior opportunities.

A score of 3 would mean it probably meets three-quarters of the criteria.

A score of 1 would indicate it does not meet any criteria. Try to be as factual as possible.

A self-assessment exercise

Totally untrue			Totally true	
1	2	3	4	5

1. We have set out to build something of value from nothing.	1 2 3 4 5
2. We have spotted a superior opportunity.	1 2 3 4 5
3. We have a dream of where we want to take our business.	1 2 3 4 5
4. We have marshalled the resources we need to build our business.	1 2 3 4 5
5. We have been very successful at building the capabilities we need in our business.	1 2 3 4 5
6. We are excellent at problem solving.	1 2 3 4 5
7. We have built good relationships with other entrepreneurs, who help us regularly.	1 2 3 4 5

---

8. We served an excellent apprenticeship, which helped us start our business.	1 2 3 4 5
9. We are obsessively committed to the success of our business.	1 2 3 4 5
10. We have learnt how to cope with ambiguity and risk.	1 2 3 4 5
11. We have built an excellent network of invaluable contacts.	1 2 3 4 5
12. We enjoy the benefits of delighting customers.	1 2 3 4 5
13. We are good at getting resources on the cheap.	1 2 3 4 5
14. We manage our creditors and our cash flow exceptionally well.	1 2 3 4 5
15. We have been successful at picking the right people for our business.	1 2 3 4 5
16. Our business generating system ensures we have enough new customers to meet our needs.	1 2 3 4 5
17. Teamwork is a real asset in our business.	1 2 3 4 5
18. We monitor our recipe very effectively.	1 2 3 4 5
19. We control the key financial ratios very effectively.	1 2 3 4 5
20. We have excellent relationships with our bank and advisors.	1 2 3 4 5

Total score _____

_____%

Notes: The overall score is less important than your highs and lows. Any score of 1 or 2 probably needs some attention, so go back into the book and see if you can get any clues about moving forward. Scores of 4 or 5 are strengths. Well done.

Action points

Discuss your scores with a relative or a trusted confidante:

- What do they tell you about your business?
- What can you do today that you could not do 12 months ago? What lessons have you learnt?

■ What do you see as the challenge for the future? Is your vision still relevant, do you need to upgrade it?

■ What areas should you focus upon? This questionnaire is quick and dirty. You may want to check out your personal progress with others or by getting some more facts.

I hope the questionnaire and the process of reflection has helped you take stock and plan for the next phase of being an entrepreneur – developing your business.

creating **new growth opportunities**

- Growing sales and profits
- Penetration
- Advanced selling skills
- Market development
- Exporting
- Creating new products from your existing offerings
- Adding complementary products

For most entrepreneurs, growth is something that happens rather than something planned. As we've seen, they usually develop businesses by taking specific opportunities presented by markets, products or processes without the benefit of a grand plan or blueprint corporate strategy. Growth develops naturally out of the day-to-day successes in solving problems. So not only does problem solving = learning in the entrepreneurial world, it also produces growth.

Being more specific, *entrepreneurial businesses grow by developing profitable products or markets (becoming more effective) or by improving the way they do things (becoming more efficient).*

We saw earlier that the entrepreneurial process can be summarized as shown in Figure 9.1.

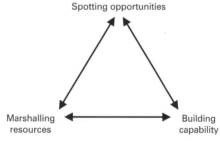

Figure 9.1 *The entrepreneurial process*

This chapter focuses on helping you create new opportunities, the next focuses on building your business capabilities to take up new opportunities.

But while entrepreneurial development leads naturally into business growth and development, it is no simple process and most businesses fail to make the journey from a small business to a successful large one. Eighty per cent of companies in the UK have ceased to grow or are in decline and the figure is surprisingly high even in the USA.

In this chapter, to help explain how growth can be achieved, we will look at a number of examples of successful business growth and try to tease out the common threads.

Let's start by looking again at the factors that predispose companies to growth.

To grow, companies need to have spotted the superior opportunity, to have secured the resources necessary to exploit it, and put in place a team with the necessary capabilities. They need, too, to have the necessary control systems in place, and to have anticipated future restraints on growth and sought to remove them.

One way to assess how well prepared your company is for growth is to complete the following assessment exercise. The rest of this chapter will help you to grow your business successfully.

Assessing your readiness for growth

This questionnaire is designed to help you access your readiness for growth. It will help you identify your business strengths and those areas that might need developing.

Answer the questionnaire as honestly as you can; you might also consider asking members of your team to complete it.

Totally disagree			Totally agree	
1	2	3	4	5

1. We have identified superior opportunities to grow our business.   1 2 3 4 5
2. We have the funds available to meet our growth needs.   1 2 3 4 5
3. Our core business is healthy and profitable and this new opportunity will not detract from that too much.   1 2 3 4 5
4. We have the technology and resources to take up this opportunity.   1 2 3 4 5

---

5. We have sufficient management time and people resources to take up this opportunity.   1 2 3 4 5

6. We have the necessary capabilities in our business to take up this opportunity.   1 2 3 4 5

7. Our business is well controlled, we have good information systems.   1 2 3 4 5

8. The new opportunity fits well with the focus and direction of our business.   1 2 3 4 5

9. We will be able to build a strong team to take up the opportunity.   1 2 3 4 5

10. We have identified and have plans to remove the obstacles to our success.   1 2 3 4 5

Total score _____

× 2 = _____ %

If your score is 80 per cent + then you are already probably well on your way to success.

This is a tough questionnaire designed deliberately to get you to ask the questions successful growth entrepreneurs ask themselves.

Low scores of 1 and 2 might be areas to consider taking action whilst scores of 4 and 5 are almost certainly strengths.

Growing sales and profits

As we have already seen, *spotting opportunities* is the skill entrepreneurs most need to acquire. Most successful businesses get started to exploit a gap in the market where a need is not being adequately fulfilled. As the business matures, however, the business can only grow by uncovering new opportunities. Often this can be done through using simple marketing techniques. For the growing business, marketing becomes the key driving force.

One of the big differences I have noticed between British and US entrepreneurs is in their attitude towards marketing. In the USA marketing is seen as vital if a business is to have a long-term future: in the UK it is often reduced to no more than designing brochures or a new logo. Much of this difference in approach is culturally derived. In Britain entrepreneurs are influenced by the role model of the traditional corporation, cautious about investing for the future, unable to appreciate the difference between profit and building long-term value. Traditional British business attitudes are in turn driven by the UK financial markets whose only real interest, it seems to me, is in making a fast buck.

You can make a fast buck by cutting overheads, squeezing suppliers, reducing the spend on training and on research and development, and cutting back on marketing effort. But while this produces short-term financial rewards it does nothing to sustain the long-term future of the British economy. British investment houses don't invest enough in growth markets such as telecoms, the Internet, computer software, or even pharmaceuticals (US investors significantly now own more than 50 per cent of Glaxo-Wellcome, Britain's most successful pharmaceutical giant), sectors where companies are valued at 30 to 50 times earnings. Instead they prefer to put their trust in traditional British businesses involved in old markets and selling on average at only 10 times earnings.

It is no wonder then that many British entrepreneurs fail to create valued businesses with real long-term profit potential. Too many end up competing on price, and in declining markets: they reap the consequences – declining profits. As a result they are failing in their entrepreneurial mission, to create the long-term valued businesses the economy needs.

One way of growing a business, which for some reason gets missed by many businesses, is simply to improve your product or service. As Tom Peters said: 'If you give people something worth paying for they will pay you for it.' If you don't then your product is a commodity and you will be competing on price just like everybody else.

Another conclusion from working with successful entrepreneurs is that the most successful ones *achieve their aim of creating a valued business by developing valued products and services.*

This is a direct relationship, as we have seen in the case of Phil Crane, Tom Hunter, and the rest in this book.

So if you want to grow your business the start point is to improve your product or service so you have a competitive edge. This means applying the first and most fundamental marketing principle: listen to customers and give them what they want. This appears to be very hard for some companies to do in practice.

Yet, it doesn't have to be like this. If entrepreneurs give priority to marketing they can create companies operating in the growth markets of the future and build excellent long-term profit streams.

By marketing I don't mean the sort of activity you will see in the marketing department of the large corporation, where marketing budgets run into millions and a single three-month campaign might cost more than the entire turnover of the average British company. What young growing businesses need is not massive spending on advertising and promotion – which they can't afford – but the application of sound marketing principles.

There are four ways to do this, which are simply described by Igor Ansoff's box (Figure 9.2).

Products/services

Existing   New

	Existing	New
Old	**1** Penetration	**3** Product development
New	**2** Market development	**4** Diversification

Markets

Figure 9.2 *Ansoff's growth box*

Ansoff found that businesses grow in four distinctive ways.

Firstly they can sell more to existing customers, which he called *penetration*: old markets/existing products. Secondly, they can try to sell their existing products into new markets, either geographically, ie export, or new industries. This is termed *market development*: existing products – new markets.

He also found that they develop new products for their existing customers and this he called *product development*: new products into existing markets.

Finally he discovered businesses that grew by developing new products for new markets, which he called *diversification*.

A key lesson from our entrepreneurs is that although you can in theory pursue any of these four approaches in any order, successful entrepreneurs normally follow this order:

1. *Penetration* – selling more of *existing* products and services to *existing* customers. This is the easiest because you already have a relationship and track record. It is always easier and cheaper to make sure you have optimized sales to existing customers before moving on to the next way.
2. *Market development* – sell *existing* proven products and services to *new* customers. Existing customers will help you build your business if you delight them. But customer delight also leads to recommendations to potential new customers. The word will get around and you need to exploit the opportunities.
3. *Product/service development* – developing *new* products for *existing* customers. Working in collaboration or partnership to build new products or services.
4. *Diversification* – selling *new* products and services to *new* markets. New

products/services to new markets is always the hardest and the riskiest to do because both products and markets are new and unknown. Yet if entrepreneurs can adopt marketing principles they can build valued businesses.

Let's see how our entrepreneurs tackle these approaches to growing a business.

Penetration – selling more to existing customers

Selling more to existing customers makes sense, as we saw in Chapter 7. You already have a relationship with them, and your product and services must be to their liking or they would not come back for more.

Just what the potential is will depend on your existing share of their spending on the kind of products and services you offer. If they spend £10,000 a year on your kind of business and you are selling them £9,000 you are already doing quite well. But if you currently only sell them, say, £1,000 there is a real opportunity here for you to sell more.

You obviously need to begin by finding out just what percentage of their present needs is being supplied by your company. So how do you go about it? Your sales representative is normally a good source of intelligence and you should begin there. If you draw a blank you will have to make use of your network to find out what you can. As a last resort you can look at company accounts to get some idea of their spending on your type of product.

Having secured the figure you should next consider the fact that few companies would risk putting all their eggs in one basket by having just one supplier. Unless you can offer a truly unique product or service, or have some special relationship with the customer, you are unlikely to secure 100 per cent of their spending. Again, buyers will generally tell you what the policy is on suppliers if you ask for it. Some companies will not purchase more than 30 per cent of products or services from any one supplier but others may well purchase much more.

Armed with this information you can assess the opportunities available for your business and prioritize your marketing activity accordingly. The information might also help you decide whether to stick with penetration as a strategy, the lowest cost option, or move on to the more expensive strategies of market or product development. (See subsections 3 and 4 below.)

You will see from all this that share of customers' spend is a key entrepreneurial indicator.

There are well-proven ways of opening up opportunities for increased selling to existing customers. They don't cost much and so have a natural appeal for the true entrepreneur.

1. Conduct a customer perception survey

Ask your customers to provide you with feedback to enable you to improve your services to them.
Ask:

- What do you look for in a supplier?
- What disappoints you about suppliers?
- How do you rate my company as a supplier?
- Who are your best suppliers and what makes them special?

and finally the key question:

- What do I need to do to do more business with you?

Put into practice what you learn and you will increase your sales.

2. Cross-selling

Cross-selling is the process of selling additional products and services to existing customers, making sure that your full range is offered to your customers. Many high street retailers now make a substantial part of their profit from cross-selling accessories, insurance policies and maintenance agreements. The same principle can be applied in almost any line of business.

The opportunities are probably greater than you imagine. In surveys my firm carried out for client firms we found that again and again a firm's customers were often completely unaware that a supplier might be able to meet their needs in other areas. Simply making them aware of what you have to sell is enough to create profitable new sales opportunities.

You need to check with your customers personally to find out if they know enough about your full range or services or products to enable you to sell them on. Levering out these extra sales can hugely increase your profitability, helping to create the resources you will need to develop and grow the business.

Just how much you might benefit can be illustrated by the experience of two firms I have had dealings with.

The first is Simon Keats of North Staffs Caravans, the caravan retailer we met in Chapter 7. The average selling price of a caravan is about £11,000, but if his sales team could sell accessories and services the price could be quite easily raised to around £13,000.

Here are the details:

New caravan sale	£11,000
Finance deal	£600
Insurance	£130
Tow bar	£150
Spare tyre	£60
Annual servicing	£120
Accessories – averaging	£200
Awning	£800

After an initial hiccup with the sales form he had designed, and some staff training, he quickly raised his turnover by £750,000 a year and his profits by about £80,000 – meaning that he more than doubled his profits.

Another entrepreneur who was quick to grasp the potential of cross-selling was Kevin Smith of ACT Controls. His firm, which makes vision inspection and systems to control management processes, also recognized the benefits of cross-selling:

> We appointed a sales manager to sell what we call 'Site Services' as a package to anyone who wants it. We sell instruments and it occurred to us that in the future they would need servicing, recalibration and quite possibly repair. So we offer them a long-term maintenance plan – I believe this is a tremendous opportunity for us. We make money and we gain experience in other aspects of the business, so that in the end we have an option to grow our services side.

ACT Controls has seen the business grow dramatically and cross-selling has played a significant part without the need for expensive marketing. Look at it this way. If you don't maximize your potential for cross-selling it is like inadvertently leaving profit on the table.

3. Problem seeking – problem solving

One great advantage of working with existing companies is that you are in a position to influence their buying policy in so many ways. Cross-selling is one example. Problem solving offers another way in. In fact, engaging in dialogue with your customers can lead you to establish a need they did not realize they had, for which you can then offer help.

The problem-seeking questions covered in Chapter 3 can really help drive this process. Have a look at them again and if necessary devise your own questions.

Here, for example, are the questions I use when I want to sell top management training to companies:

▓ How do you build the capability in your top team to deliver your strategy?

▓ How do you ensure your training links directly to your business needs?

▓ How do you evaluate the benefits of your investment in training?

I ask these questions because I know from experience of dealing with large companies that this is often where they have problems, which then become my opportunities.

So think about your experiences with your customers. Where do they have real problems and pain? What keeps them awake at night? Also ask yourself what has worked elsewhere for you.

Design and ask your own problem-seeking questions, then stand back and get your order pad ready!

4. Build strong links at all levels with key customers

There is a fourth technique that will allow you to increase your sales with existing customers, one that is used by big companies to keep their competitors at bay – cosying up to the key decision makers within the companies who are already your customers. Some of these key decision makers will be at the top, but they are found all the way through a business.

In most companies, between three and six people are involved in any buying decision. Marketing experts call this the 'decision-making unit' but I prefer the acronym used by some of the entrepreneurs I have met. They refer, chauvinistically you might think, to the MAN. The MAN refers to the people who are concerned in any buying decision: people who control the **M**oney, people who have the **A**uthority to make the decision, and people with the **N**eed for services and products. In some small companies the MAN may in fact be only one person but normally 'he' is spread across several people and departments.

The entrepreneurial trick is to build relationships with as much of the MAN as possible. This means marshalling your resources to make contact with as many of them as possible. If you have technical people then they need to be encouraged to make contact with the technical people at the customer end as regularly as possible. Sales people should similarly be building relationships with the buyer and your sales administration people with your customer's administration staff.

Cosying up to the MAN can be an extraordinarily effective way of building sales. One of the 'winners' in the BBC TV series *Winning* was Raj Samuel, the Managing Director of Elm Refrigeration in Glasgow. Elm was a small company then, but it had won a large contract to supply refrigeration equipment to Marks & Spencer. Raj made it a policy to take the key movers among his customers out for dinner, along with his own senior staff, and to follow this up by maintaining social contact at all levels within those customer companies.

This enabled his team to build strong links with the MAN.

Spreading your contacts within the customer company means the network of contacts will still remain even if your most important contact goes off to work for someone else, something which happens all too frequently.

Some of the smart larger companies go further. They exchange staff between themselves and their customers, hold joint training events and collaborate in many others ways. Out of these activities they hope to create new opportunities for business, increasing their sales. More often than not this is exactly what happens.

A primer on advanced selling skills

Quotations and proposals

Basic selling skills were covered in Chapter 5, when we looked at business start-up. These skills come into their own when submitting quotations or proposals – a high success rate at a good price will allow you to grow and develop your business.

To build your capability to sell more effectively, take some lessons from our entrepreneurs.

Dave Osmond, the Operations Director of CompuAdd Computers, learnt how to sell effectively the hard way – he has done the job for many years and was often taken advantage of before he got smart.

The first important lesson he learnt was about timing. Sending in the quotation or proposal at the wrong time can cost you dear.

> If your customer tells you they will make a buying decision on, say, Friday at 12 noon then make sure your telephone offer goes in at 12 noon and not before. You will find that if you send it in three days before it gives your customer time to go elsewhere and negotiate a better deal, from their point of view of course. Never show all your cards until you have to.
>
> If you submit it bang on the deadline it gives you a chance to negotiate from a stronger position. For instance, if the customer is hesitating, you can always ask what you would need to do to win the business. It puts you in the driving seat.

But how, you may ask, do you delay sending the quotation in early if the customer is pressing you for your proposals? Here is Dave's advice:

> Tell the customer you are still working on some information to allow you to finalize the details of your bid. But check at the same time whether Friday at noon is still the decision point.

Another reason for not sending in quotations early is that a more astute competitor may well pip you at the post.

Let the customer experience it

Another sales tactic is to encourage the customer to try the product or service on offer. Certainly Adele McGee found that it paid big dividends in retailing. Fifty per cent of customers who experience the products end up buying them – one reason why smart car sales people get you behind the wheel as soon as possible.

Even if you cannot get people personally to try the product you can try setting up a demonstration of the product in use. For instance, Simon Keats of North Staffs Caravans increased his sales of barbecues, from an average of three a weekend to over 100, simply by lighting a barbecue and handing out sausages and burgers to customers' children.

One reason why demonstrations pay off so well is that – as the old saying goes – a picture is worth a thousand words. In fact a product demonstration is worth a thousand pictures, but personally experiencing the product is much better than either!

Handling the price objection

Another advanced selling skill is knowing how to deal with customers who tell you your goods or service is too expensive – the price objection. Adrian Norton has his own technique when he meets such a customer:

> Don't get flustered but ask – expensive compared to what?
> This helps the customer make an objective comparison between your offer and your competitor's. Very often they are comparing chalk with cheese. You need to encourage them to compare like with like.
> One way of doing this is to ask your customer to list the features of your products and then compare them with what they get from competitors. It brings it home to them that your offer contains many more benefits to the customer. They have worked it out for themselves.

Adrian has a further shrewd bit of advice – if such a comparison does not work out to your benefit you need to ask yourself: Do I deserve to get the business?

The secret in handling the price objection is to help your customer understand the difference between cost and value. This helps especially when it comes to discussing possible discounts.

Adrian Norton again:

> Remember, many people ask for a discount just to test you out. So don't fall for it. Ask them how will that help your business? In 50 per cent of cases they will say almost embarrassingly 'I always ask and you would be surprised how often I get offered one. But fair enough, I'll take it.'

Another Norton piece of selling wisdom:

> Try saying: It is not our policy to give discounts because... and then re-peat all the features and benefits of your service. The other 50 per cent will cave in at this stage. This means I don't ever need to offer discounts.

If some customers still insist on a discount then you need to understand the economics of giving discounts.

What most business people don't realize is that you have to increase the volume of your sales enormously if you are to offset the sum you have lost by giving the discount in the first place. The narrower the profit margins (gross margin) on each sale, the greater the sales volume increase you will need.

Look at Table 9.1 and work it out for yourself.

Someone with a gross margin of just 5 per cent would need to increase the volume of sales by 67 per cent to offset a paltry 2 per cent discount. Even some-body with a more comfortable margin, say 30 per cent, needs to increase the volume of sales by 20 per cent to counteract a 5 per cent discount. Let me assure you that a 5 per cent discount is most unlikely to achieve that sort of result.

Such simple facts about discounting are often totally ignored by sales people.

Table 9.1 *Cost implication of price cuts on business profitability*

% Price reduction	Existing % gross margin								
	5	10	15	20	25	30	35	40	50
	% Volume increase required for same gross margin								
2	67	25	15	11	9	7	6	5	4
3	150	43	25	18	14	11	9	8	6
4	400	67	36	25	19	15	13	11	9
5		100	50	33	25	20	17	14	11
7.5		300	100	60	43	33	27	23	18
10			200	100	67	50	40	33	25
15				300	150	100	75	60	43

Interestingly enough, the same economic facts demonstrate the benefits of even a modest price increase if you can pass it on to the customer. As Table 9.2 shows, volume of sales would have to fall by more than 29 per cent before the extra income from a 2 per cent increase would result in less income for your business. This is not to say that should be your policy if you are in a highly competitive field where price is the only way to compete. But it reinforces my point that businesses need to compete on quality and value, and/or on some unique feature rather than on price.

The old adage *'Sales for vanity – Profit for sanity'* is appropriate here.

Table 9.2   *Cost implication of price rises on business profitability*

% Price increase	Existing % gross margin								
	5	10	15	20	25	30	35	40	50
	% Volume decrease to generate same gross margin								
2	29	17	12	9	7	6	5	5	4
3	37	23	17	13	11	9	8	7	6
4	44	29	21	17	14	12	10	9	7
5	50	33	25	20	17	14	12	11	9
7.5	60	43	33	27	23	20	18	16	13
10	67	50	40	33	29	25	22	20	17
15	75	60	50	43	37	33	30	27	23

When you are driven to make a discount, you should always try to get something back in return. You can say to your customer: 'I will give you a one-off discount of 5 per cent to win your custom, but in return, I need you to give me a one-year contract, or to agree to hold stock for me, or to put me on your lists of preferred suppliers.'

The rule is clear: always get something back. If the customer changes his or her offer, you change yours.

Partnerships with the customer

Finally an advanced sales skill that should be in the locker of every entrepreneur – the skill to grow the business through building *long-term customer partnerships and alliances*. Seek to sell partnerships with customers in order to undertake joint product development, joint training and joint marketing and promotion.

Raj Samuel was good at this. His aim was to understand his customers in the area of his specialism better than they do. So when a customer says: 'I was thinking about…' Raj replies with 'Yes, we have been developing one of those for two years.'

This approach led Marks & Spencer to help fund Elm's development programme for a clever electronic monitor (now known in the trade as 'The Plastic Chicken') to be placed in the M & S stores. It sits in the cooling cabinets and refrigerators automatically transmitting data on the temperatures of the various products to a central control.

Forming this kind of long-term partnership where the customer invests in the joint development of new products is an impossible act for competitors to follow. Raj and his team had achieved the ultimate in selling – creating a sustainable non-price-sensitive partnership. Eureka!

Market development – existing products/services to new markets

Conventional business wisdom would say you need carry out in-depth market research before committing any resources to market development. The smart entrepreneurs would agree: they just do it differently.

The traditional marketing approach is to research the proposed market in detail and to then produce statistical reports. These are often based on secondary (published) data. Such surveys cost a lot but, in my experience, market research of this sort is often undertaken to provide a case for the product and service *after* someone in the organization has made the decision to go ahead and requires to justify the decision to themselves or head office.

By contrast, entrepreneurs want the research to be much cheaper and to be more meaningful. Their method is to do their market research by going out and talking to people face to face, making use of their networks to find out as much as possible about the target market. In particular, they try to identify whom the movers and shakers in that market might be.

It means going back to the basics we covered in Chapter 3, a question of spotting opportunities.

Market development for entrepreneurs means going back to the same processes used in starting and building up a new business. The difference now is that the entrepreneur has learnt lots of lessons and has a proven product or service to take to new markets.

Since exporting is a major form of market development we will look at it in detail, because there are lessons here for everyone.

Exporting

In the mid-1990s the Development Board for Rural Wales noticed something rather extraordinary was going on in Mid Wales. There had been a steady growth in exports, particularly to Europe. In 1996 they asked me to investigate the phenomenon to explain it and see what lessons there might be.

As a result I found myself travelling to Newtown and looking up some of the most successful small firms. That led me on to discover a quite remarkable organization called the Mid-Wales Export Association.

Bethan Jones and her team of people run the company. In my eyes they became the 'Welsh Wizards'. By their efforts they had convinced many local businesses that trading in Europe offered great opportunities and that the perceived barriers facing small companies wanting to trade there were largely mythical.

Take for the example the *language barrier*.

Many companies felt inhibited by their lack of competence in speaking and understanding a foreign language. There were people with language skills employed by these small companies. They found they did not need them. Over much of Europe English has become the common language for business.

R and M Services of Welshpool markets specialist lighting for pool and snooker tables. They are a small firm employing just eight people but 40 per cent of their products are exported, mainly to northern Europe. Roger Clegg is the MD:

> In Holland everybody speaks English better than we do, our Swedish agent speaks extremely good English and in Germany most of our customers speak English too. It helps that I have a smattering of German and I can open the door and order a beer for them.

For R and M Services the French-speaking countries have not been so easy to crack but another local business, Makefast, has found a way to disarm French suspicion of 'les Anglo-Saxons' – albeit coming from Wales. Makefast manufactures non-corrosive buckles and equipment for the yacht market and employs 28 people.

Brenda Brown is the Managing Director:

> We believed we could not sell in France because the French only like buying from the French. We had problems with going the distributor route because they 'cherry pick' products and do not take all the range. So we made an arrangement with a Frenchman, and set up our own company where he owns 52 per cent so that it is important to him that it succeeds, and four British companies own 12 per cent each.

Another perceived barrier is that European companies are poor payers – they simply do not pay up in time. This is another myth exploded in Mid

Wales. In fact they pay up providing you have a system to monitor payments.

Makefast has shown just what to do. Brenda Brown again:

> We don't have too much of a problem in getting paid because we are manufacturers selling to other manufacturers, and if they don't pay they don't get any more goods which stops their manufacture. Most people pay within 60 days although sometimes from Europe it takes longer. When we first started we used the Export Guarantee system and had an arrangement with the bank. But our exports were so small that the charges were too expensive and the administration too time-consuming, so we now just sell on open credit. We tell them 30 days and get paid in 60!

A third myth about exporting that has been dispelled is the idea that nobody should venture into the export business without first reading a DTI market research report on the country and type of business concerned.

The Welsh entrepreneurs often got started by visiting an exhibition in the country of their choice and made sure they responded quickly and efficiently to the enquiries that arose. In addition to following this simple principle there were four other prerequisites for success:

1. You must have developed and established a good and well-established product or service before making your foray into foreign markets – such markets are no place for experimentation, which is better done closer to home.

   Roger Clegg had done this:

   > We had developed our product in the UK. We started to look at export markets three years later because we knew a lot of our type of product was going abroad.

2. There has to be a willingness to adapt the product or service to bring it into line with local tastes and preferences.

   One person who displayed this last quality to perfection was Anne-Marie Jackson, the Marketing Director of Handcast Designs. Handcast make gifts from moulded resin – trinket boxes, photographic frames and various table-top accessories bought mainly by women. They now export 25 per cent of their production. As Anne-Marie told me:

   > Over the years America and Japan have been markets where our product is highly in demand; it is the 'Englishness' that has made it popular

157

to market. That is one of the reasons why we don't supply to Germany as such, because our product is definitely not to German tastes and for us to supply that market we would have to create a whole specific collection which is really is not viable.

3. You need to understand basic export procedures and generally the 'rules of the export game'.

Bethan Jones of the Export Association has found:

You do not need a degree in exporting to understand the rules of the export game. But there are well-established basic export procedures which new exporters need to follow. That is where we can help new exporters, with these important basics.

4. Most of all they need an open mind and a willingness to listen and learn.

Anne-Marie Jackson again:

We were not very experienced in exporting but we were very proactive in the UK market. We went to trade fairs, and exhibited at international trade fairs and from that we picked up exporters. It was actually from exhibiting ourselves at the trade fairs.

But Handcast did not get going in exports for some time:

Four years after we started, we were still exporting passively from the point of view of almost accepting the first customer that came along from one country and taking them on board. Of course that isn't necessarily over the long term the best way of going about developing customers. I think it was three years later when we finally developed the resources to be a little bit more selective or target the market a little bit better.

So how did Anne-Marie target her market?

America is a huge market, therefore there must be potential, but having said that it is a very sophisticated market and very competitive and not necessarily the easiest or the best market to attack at the start. Germany on the other hand we went to because the Trade Fair is the biggest in the world. We then were able to pick up a couple of customers from around the world, not just Germany. In fact, the German market in itself is not an ideal market for us.

But do they operate differently in difficult countries?

> In Japan we used distributors. It is obviously a difficult market to deal with directly, so we have a distributor. In America we have done both, we have tried distributors and the complexity of that market means that using distributors you are several times removed from the end purchasing. You have very little control on how the product is presented. In France, we specifically selected agents, so we can market to France directly.

But what makes a good agent for Handcast?

> It is what makes a good agent for anybody, it is somebody who is willing to understand the product that you have and that has a very good customer base themselves. Somebody who has a relatively small number of principals so you can make sure that they actually take your product as seriously as the others can. Usually we find agents by approaching people in the trade to find out who has a good reputation.

Once they have fulfilled some initial enquiries and decided to expand by exporting, the real challenge is to find and manage good distributors or agents. This is the biggest blockage to successful export growth

What about the problems of managing distributors? How do Handcast do that?

> With a distributor I think the most important thing is making sure that the product is right for them and for their market. A distributor could have a very large number of products in their portfolio, yours is going to be one of many. You have got to put yourself in the forefront of his mind if he is going to then support you. With a distributor it is much more of a partnership relationship. Unless they are going to make money they are going to lose interest very quickly. So again the usual things are important, servicing them, making sure that you deliver on time, make sure that what they are getting is correct. The biggest thing is that you are always aware of what they actually need in terms of product and if necessary make the product, even though it is not necessarily the normal portfolio but will help them succeed in their market.

So the real problems in exporting are finding and managing your distribution channels. In 1999 we need to add exchange rates to these two primary processes.

Finding and managing good distributors or agents is the biggest blockage to successful export growth. The Mid Wales companies have successfully broken through, with the help of the local Mid-Wales Development Board, which has provided support with translations and contracts, and help with the paperwork

Even with a strong pound and a strong dollar, exports can still be a profitable way to expand your business.

Creating new products and services out of your existing offerings

An innovative way to grow your business is to create new products or services out of your existing offerings.

There are at least five ways our entrepreneurs use to create marketing space and develop new profitable products.

1. Do the opposite of the traditional industry norms

This means either raising or eliminating features above or below the industry standards.

For example, Keepmoat changed the way they deal with local authorities, building partnerships rather than getting into confrontation by claiming extras on contracts. This led to many more opportunities to negotiate rather than tender for work. It also made the competition look like dinosaurs.

First Direct, the 24-hour telephone bank, transformed banking. They were helpful and friendly, which was a shock to most people used to getting 'verbal muggings' from their unfriendly bank manager. First Direct are more than a bank, they are more of a social service – much better than Relate. I call them up when I fall out with my partner for somebody nice to talk to! Only joking!

But seriously, First Direct has transformed banking, with the rest, who now look like dinosaurs, struggling to catch up. This is about increasing service levels beyond expectations.

The opposite also works. We will shortly see how Walmart stacks 'em high and sells 'em cheap. 'No frills' retailing. Again they changed the rules in the USA and stole a lead over the competitors. How can you apply these principles to your business?

2. Copy substitutes

Ask yourself the question: What are people buying instead of our products?

This does not necessarily mean your competitors' products; it could be that they are buying substitutes – something instead of your product.

Center Parcs provides a good example. Instead of taking holidays in the UK British holidaymakers are now enjoying the sun in Spain or Florida. This is hard to compete against if you are a boarding house in Blackpool and it rains 8 days out of 10. Center Parcs decided to copy this substitute and bring the sun to Britain, creating large enclosed areas with Mediterranean temperatures. People might not choose to spend their two-week summer holiday there but they do seem to be prepared to spend long weekends or weeks at the facility. Learning from and copying substitutes is a creative way to grow your business.

3. Change the appeal

Most products or services are purchased on price and functionality; largely their appeal is rational. Others compete on feelings and their appeal is emotional. For example, in the USA coffee was a commodity purchased on price. Commuters drank it as part of their daily routine. The results were low margins by selling coffee as a commodity in packets. Starbucks changed the rules; they sold a retailing concept – coffee purchased in a very nice environment: the coffee bar. They turned ordinary people into coffee connoisseurs for whom a $3 dollar cup seemed value for money. Starbucks became a national brand with no advertising and margins around five times the industry norm.

Conversely Anita Roddick shifted Body Shop in the opposite direction. Few businesses are more emotional than cosmetics; on average, packaging costs 85 per cent of cosmetic companies' overall costs, as the old marketing slogan says: 'In the factories we make cosmetics, in the perfumeries we sell hope.' By stripping away the expensive packaging Body Shop made significant cost savings in an industry that had a very fixed, established way of doing business.

4. Reinventing the product and targeting niche markets

This calls for the true entrepreneurial flair and imagination. Mareena Purslow from Mareena Purslow Funeral Services in Perth, Australia shows how.

The Purslow funeral business goes back four generations. Mareena decided in 1989 to set up a separate division for women. Women as carers were the target niche. She decided to reinvent the service, moving away from traditional black cars, pin stripe suits, dour music and the solemnity of the funeral industry.

Mareena introduced maroon cars and outfits, employed women only, and introduced loudspeakers for graveside gatherings, to play more modern music.

She now employs 24 people with a turnover of £3.5 million and has enjoyed rapid growth while the rest of the industry is in decline and is restructuring.

> I deliberately recruited women with no funeral experience or preconceived ideas about the industry to help me reinvent the business and target the female-only up-market niche.

It worked well, because she sold out handsomely to US-based Service Corporation International.

5. Working back from the price point

In markets where price and volumes are under real pressure, one way of growing the business is to identify the customer's price point and develop your offer accordingly. It calls for true entrepreneurship in action. Here is how it works.

The price point at which customers can sell to their customers or are prepared to pay becomes your opportunity (in our entrepreneur's process model).

You then seek to get the resources to provide the product at the price point and build the business's capability to deliver it profitability.

Paul Darwent of Mini Gears explains how he uses this approach in his business:

> A customer in Devon wanted to purchase a gear from us at £10.50 each. It was a big order overall, £250,000 per annum. We could only make them for £11.00 with our current methods and processes. So I set out to meet the customer price point.
> I worked really hard and travelled around Europe and eventually sourced some new blanks in Italy for £2.00 and purchased some new drill cutting equipment second hand which enabled us to make the mini gears now for £6.50. I am still trying to find ways to get the price down to £5.00 so we make a good margin.

William Mow of Bugle Boy Industries of Los Angeles, USA also used the price point approach to create a billion-dollar jeans business.

> My customers fixed the price at $24.00, so I needed to make them for $12.00 to make my margin. I sourced the cloth in Asia and got them made up to the customer specification in several factories spread around Asia. This allowed my customer to make their margin and me to make mine, a good deal for both parties.

This growth strategy calls for real entrepreneurial skill and flair.

Adding complementary products and services

Another way for entrepreneurs to develop their business is by adding complementary products or services to their existing range of offerings.

The first thing is to recognize that new products cannot be designed behind locked doors from first principles without any testing with potential customers. So another arm of a marketing strategy must be to conduct low-cost experiments by engaging customers in concept design, prototype development, and product or service trials.

We have already seen the advantages that flow from such a process when it comes to maximizing the sales of existing products or services. By working with your customers you begin to understand the nature of the problems they face, and the buying criteria they operate by.

As well as demonstrating you are really interested in their business, it builds relationships and provides a source of free market research and testing. The whole process means that the customer feels a sense of ownership, a gateway to a lasting commercial relationship, which is not price specific.

The best possible outcome is to engage with customers from the very inception of the business idea, through its development – involving the customer in needs analysis, product concept, assessment of the business prospects, and even through to product design and launch.

Collaborating with customers is the way David Latham of Labtech, makers of microwave technology circuits, did it and grew his business dramatically:

> Our main competitive advantage is the technology of the circuits and we have been working with some of our major customers on projects that won't actually appear for three or four years yet. We collaborate on needs analysis and the product concept and even share the product design and development.

As we have already seen, his relationship with Ericsson, one of the world's largest manufacturers of mobile hand-phones, gave his business a tremendous boost:

> Once Ericsson realized how good the product was, they put us on their internal system. A company like Ericsson is worldwide, so we then started getting unsolicited business coming in from other divisions of Ericsson. What is true of Ericsson is true of many other big companies. If you're in motorcar component manufacture it could be Ford or Datsun. It is the principle that entrepreneurs need to recognize.

Neil Gibson of JHB Group is another who has grown his business through adding complementary services:

> We now have only half the number of customers we once had, but they provide better business, and our offer of a cleaning service and the fitting of thermal insulation has meant we now have loads of other business coming in from related areas.

One deal on thermal installation alone meant business grew by 20 per cent:

> We took on a thermal insulation contract last year that added on half a million a year. That's a big progression for us in itself. We can't go out and think that each new customer is going to give you half a million pounds a year – we would find it difficult to cope. But there is lots more growth in the pipeline.

Forgive me if I do not dwell on Ansoff's fourth growth process: diversification – which is selling *new* products and services to *new* markets.

Diversification is a much more expensive option and much more risky for the smaller but growing business. Many studies show that only 1 in 10 diversifications are successful because you do not know the product or the market and this learning curve proves too steep for most businesses. They do not fare much better in the world of the big corporates. A recent study revealed that 90 per cent of mergers and acquisitions fail to deliver the promised improved stakeholder benefits. Customers also fail to notice any improvements. The major beneficiaries appear to be the top management and their city advisers. So remember the principle – *gardening, not hunting* – and you cannot go far wrong.

building **your**
business's growth
capabilities

- The journey to growth
- Investing in innovation
- Growth projects
- Improving internal efficiency
- Removing obstacles
- The business development processes
- Management for growth
- Leadership in growth

Spotting new opportunities is the spark that ignites the growth process in entrepreneurial businesses, as we saw in the last chapter.

The next step on the journey to growth is for the entrepreneur to build their business's capability in order to take up the new opportunities and to grow profitably.

Working with growth entrepreneurs has helped identify the business development processes they use to grow their enterprises, including 'letting go', 'backfilling', 'getting into bed together', and leadership.

Once again these are not the processes taught by traditional business schools.

The journey to growth: investing in innovation

The traditional wisdom about growth suggests that all you need to succeed is to set objectives for innovation, allocate the appropriate budget to research and development, appoint a project manager and make sure you set tight deadlines. Big corporations try to do it this way. But at a cost. The bureaucracy and systems involved often squeeze out both creativity and entrepreneurial behaviour. The result is that most truly creative and entrepreneurial people within the organization want to get out. As we have seen, 50 per cent of all new entrepreneurial opportunities are spotted while working in someone else's business and most successful entrepreneurs have had a previous life fretting within the confines of the big company.

It follows then that to grow businesses organically, entrepreneurs need to nurture the wisdom within their companies, not suffer the same talent drain that afflicts their bigger rivals. They can encourage innovation by being tolerant of their people experimenting, trying things out and taking a few risks, particularly at the edges of the organization. Tom Peters calls such free spirits 'skunkworkers'. There may be no such nirvana as an entrepreneurial culture; there are normally, however, enterprising individuals who should be encouraged.

This means leaving space for people to be creative and in particular being tolerant of low-cost experiments.

Even big organizations like the 3M corporation in the USA had to learn to create space to allow people to innovate and be creative. The guy who developed the yellow Post-it Notes was thought to be a bit of a crackpot to start with, until his experiments turned into a multi-million dollar business.

It means forgetting the idea of setting SMART objectives and producing detailed innovation strategies: such an approach doesn't work at the business start-up stage and it won't work now.

Successful entrepreneurs don't normally create miracles overnight, and don't expect profits to flow quickly in the short term. They invest in innovation rather than push for immediate profit, which is not always easy; keeping true to their commitment to create in the longer term a business of value.

The journey to growth: growth projects – a different way of growing

It may be an uncomfortable truth for those who believe in the efficacy of 'business planning' but the best entrepreneurs in my experience rarely prepare detailed growth plans and, if they do, only when they need funds from an external source, like a bank or an investment agency. Once the funds are in place the detailed plans are normally filed away and never looked at again.

Phil Crane again:

> I grow by projects. My next project is to try to bring the only pirate treasure in the world to Britain.

But how did Phil find this opportunity?

> A friend of mine who did Jorvik in York and the White Cliffs of Dover attraction. He used to come up to Scotland but up here he found people did not do projects, they just did feasibility studies.

Is this the difference between an entrepreneur and a traditional business?

> I don't know, but if the public sector, for example, put as much money into businesses as it does into feasibility studies, then the tragedy in Scotland could be avoided.

So if 'feasibility studies' are not the key to successful growth, what methods do the successful entrepreneurs use? The answer is 'growth projects'– they tackle each growth opportunity as it comes along, each as a single project.

The entrepreneurs who were the object of my research were very project oriented, maybe because projects have a start and a finish, and, as we know, entrepreneurs get bored quickly. They are often dreaming up their next three projects, while starting out on today's scheme.

The project process often followed by entrepreneurs can be broken down into distinct steps, and anyone with half a nose for business can copy the practice successfully.

In short, it begins with an idea that the entrepreneur finds interesting, and first puts to a rough-and-ready test by discussing it with trusted colleagues and friends. Only after deciding there is indeed a market opportunity will the business invest time and resources in experimentation and refinement of the idea. The whole process needs support and encouragement from the top if it is to work at all.

Entrepreneurs rarely produce detailed project plans but in my experience often loosely follow a process like the one detailed below. If you want to use any of the ideas in this chapter to grow your business you may find it useful to use the entrepreneurs' project process as a template to help you think through your idea.

The project approach

1. Find an idea that interests you.
2. Discuss the idea with people to test it out.
3. Assign someone (or a team) to investigate whether it is an opportunity.
4. Allow space for experimentation and learning.

5. Provide resource and support.
6. Demonstrate commitment and enthusiasm for the project.
7. Invest in the project if it looks promising.
8. Celebrate success or learn the lessons for next time.

Where projects involve developing new markets or products ('external projects') there are a number of additional steps at step 7, which are added to the internal process:

7a. Assess market potential and whether the project has the basis for competitive advantage.
7b. Produce financial projections:

   - cash flow;
   - funding requirements;
   - balance sheet and P & L projections;
   - feasibility studies.

7c. Determine resources requirements:

   - additional resources required;
   - scale of operation;
   - people skills needed.

The journey to growth: growth through improving internal efficiency

In Chapter 11 we cover some areas under the banner 'revitalizing your business'. These may be worth visiting at this point because these are also a means to grow a business by improving efficiency. You can turn them into a 'project' (or a series of projects) and devise your own schemes to tackle the obstacles to efficiency.

So project one may be to remove blind spots, project two could consider cost reduction opportunities, project three examine 'system slippage', the fourth project might be to introduce methods of continuous improvement, while the last could set itself the task of 'redoing strategy'.

Such 'revitalizing' processes may not be seen initially as entrepreneurial but they are because they create space and resources for investment in innovation, which is a key element in our entrepreneurial model.

The journey to growth: removing internal process blockages and disconnects

There are, however, more radical ways of achieving the same effects, making the company internally more entrepreneurial. This is done by introducing supplier/customer relationships within the company, creating opportunities for would-be entrepreneurs to exercise their talents.

As they grow, most businesses change their structure, creating departments managed by department heads, with the aim of improving 'command and control' within the business. However, this throws up fundamental problems, as will be immediately apparent by looking at Figure 10.1.

The process flow, from creating customers through to delivering the service and customer support and follow-up, is horizontal. But this process flow often fails at the boundaries where it has to cross the vertical departmental (or sub-departmental) boundaries. Even when staff are positive and committed to the broader objectives of the business, things can go badly wrong. A quick glance at Figure 10.2 will show how departmental structures can disrupt the flow of the business process.

The case of 'Geordie Engineering Systems'

To give you an example, an engineering company in the North East of England was facing increasing competition for its products used in the engineering industry and sought to respond by improving its customer service.

This seemed sensible because customer service staff were reporting many customer complaints, chiefly about late deliveries. What the company could not easily explain was the fact that its *internal* information system showed that 90 per cent of deliveries were on time. How could this be? Investigation of this apparent contradiction uncovered a very common problem – the departmentalization of the company was leading to gross customer dissatisfaction.

First of all we found a major discrepancy between sales force policy and the production system – while sales people promised 7-day delivery, production allowed for 10 days to meet new orders. The problem was compounded by confusion between departments on what constituted 'a delivery' – sales thought it meant delivery of the entire order (a fair enough assumption you might think), while production managers recorded a part delivery as a full delivery. No wonder they considered that 90 per cent of deliveries were on time!

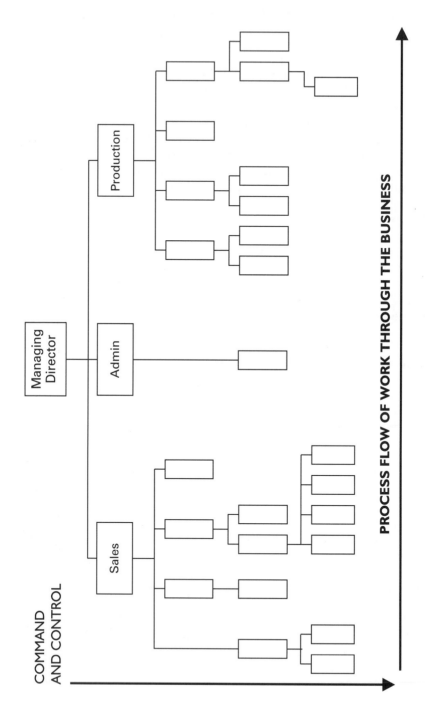

COMMAND AND CONTROL

Managing Director

Sales   Admin   Production

PROCESS FLOW OF WORK THROUGH THE BUSINESS

Figure 10.1 *The fundamental problem of formal organizations*

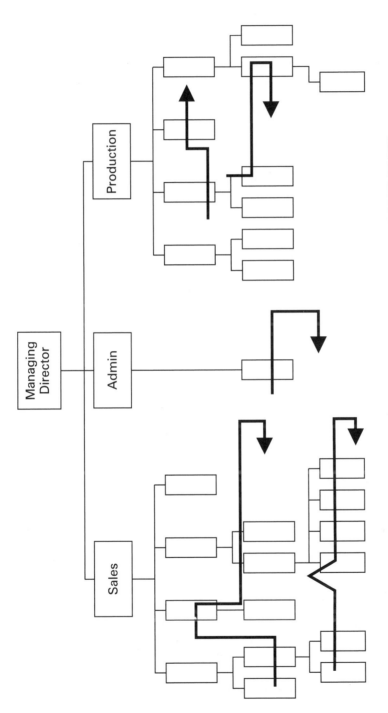

PROCESSES FAIL AT THE BOUNDARIES BETWEEN DEPARTMENTS

Figure 10.2 *Processes fail at functional boundaries*

The bonus system within the production department also worked to the detriment of the customer. In a misguided attempt to boost productivity, pay had been directly related to output. What no one had foreseen was that this meant production giving priority to orders that paid them the biggest bonus, while other customers with promised deadlines were forced to put up with frustrating delays.

If this were not bad enough, internal company politics were a nightmare. Power lay with the production manager, a personal friend of the managing director; doubly unfortunate since he was arrogant and blind to the faults in his own department. He was also a male chauvinist who refused to listen to the advice of the production planner because she was 'a woman'.

This explained the puzzle of why the sales director had resigned in frustration over the issue of customer service when the entire management team had agreed it must be given priority.

It was a classic example of how a business functionally organized into departments can inadvertently create 'disconnects and blockages', which in turn can have a serious impact on the external customer. A 'disconnect' occurs where two departments fail to communicate with each other or have different ideas about the overall objectives. A 'blockage' is where members of one department compete rather than collaborate with members of another department, as happened between the production manager and the production planner.

These problems are sometimes known as the 'silo syndrome' because people operate as if their departments 'were' the business. Unfortunately, internal inefficiencies and conflicts normally spill over into the marketplace, as happened with the engineering company, where it resulted in a 15 per cent reduction in market share and a 20 per cent decrease in annual profits.

There are two ways to tackle the problem. Firstly, the company can create transparency between departments and agree, publish and monitor standards across the company. A better flow of information automatically acts as a restraint on silo building.

But there is another possible approach: a company can create its own internal supply chains, turning departments into customers and suppliers all down the line (Figure 10.3). This provides a stimulus to improved efficiency and will almost certainly improve external performance, and ultimately grow the business.

So how should you go about setting up this internal supply chain?

Start by getting your department heads together to explore where the disconnects and blockages are causing problems for your customers externally, or for internal teams. Make sure the necessary facts have been gathered before the meeting to quantify the problems wherever possible. This helps reduce the negative politics which can spring up between departments, but it also helps to provide a common goal, persuading people to

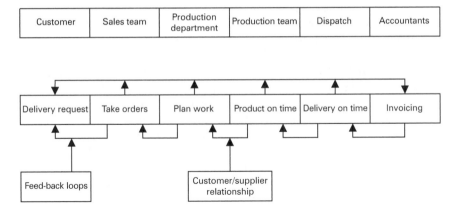

Figure 10.3 *Creating visibility*

build alliances with other internal teams to the benefit of the business over-all. Had the team in our engineering company known that blockages and disconnects were costing the company 15 per cent of its market share and a 20 per cent decrease in profits, they might have behaved quite differently, especially as their personal incomes were involved.

The potential to make major business improvements has existed in every business I have worked with. So have a go at working smarter rather than harder: reconnect the internal supply chains in your business; remove those blockages and enjoy the benefits.

A second example of disconnects and blockages: the case of Waste Disposal Inc.

A waste disposal company in the USA had grown into a national business, competing through good customer service, or so it thought. They consid-ered losing 18 customers out of 100 every year quite acceptable since sales and marketing added far more than this each year. In other words, they were into 'customer churn'.

It was only when we helped their accountant calculate that an 18 per cent customer loss rate meant a loss of $6 million per annum in net profit, equal to their current annual net profit, that the MD saw it differently. He could double profits by stemming the flow. A bit of research then showed the in-dustry average 'churn rate' was just 6 per cent, meaning that there was something seriously wrong with customer service.

The solution was simple – the customers were lost because when they cancelled contracts in writing, the hard-pressed customer service staff did not respond quickly enough. A staggering 70 per cent of the churn could be cut out by the simple expedient of phoning the same day contract cancellation notices were received to investigate why the contracts had been,cancelled and then doing a bit of customer relationship rebuilding.

Interestingly, this business had all this information themselves, yet no one had calculated the consequences in financial terms. The profit and loss account did not include *customer loss rate $6 million*, so no one took any notice. So here we see disconnects between the customer service staff, the marketing department and the finance function. It was only when somebody reconnected these departments that the opportunity to grow the business by improving internally efficiency become apparent. Incidentally, many of the really significant profit improvement opportunities rarely appear on a traditional profit and loss account. That's why they don't get identified easily.

The journey to growth: the business development processes

Hopefully this chapter will have already made some business people sit up and think about how their business is being run and what steps to take to achieve a better growth performance. But one of the most revealing and exciting parts of my research into how successful entrepreneurs really operate has been to do with the business development processes they have used to take their business onto a growth trajectory.

These processes are not generally taught by business schools, and certainly not in the down-to-earth language entrepreneurs use to describe what they do. When I got groups of them together I found they were again using an *'entrepreneur's vocabulary'* all of their own, not to be different but because they claimed traditional business language did not adequately explain how they actually did things.

Process 1 – Letting go

For the business to grow successfully into a larger enterprise, entrepreneurs must literally at some point 'let go' of many aspects of the role they have created for themselves within the business. The good news is that entrepreneurs provide much of the energy and commitment to start and build a business. The bad news is that eventually their continued involvement in all aspects of the business becomes a real blockage to progress. This is a hard lesson to learn for entrepreneurs like us, with independent streaks and large egos, and to deal with comfortably.

The reason we need to 'let go' is that, as the business grows, we cannot possibly continue to be all things to all people. There are simply not enough hours in the day. Letting go and delegating to people is not an easy transition for most entrepreneurs to make, as Mary Conneely, who runs the West Melton Lodge, a 42-bed nursing home at Brampton in Yorkshire, confessed.

How long does this take?

> I find it very difficult to trust a business of this type to just anybody. Every element has to be taken care of, right down to the smell of this place. Which I find very hard to come to terms with. As a result of that I am doing spot checks all the time, which takes up most of my time.

But Mary is learning to let go:

> If something goes wrong it goes very wrong, and it's people's lives all the time that I am dealing with, that worries me. But if you have a good workforce I think you can pass on the responsibility, but that is one of my difficulties.

Mary has put her finger on one of the really big problems facing any entrepreneur who accepts it is time to let go – can others be trusted to do the job as well as they have been doing it? This gnawing doubt that others may not be up to the job is one of the major blockages to successful business growth. In some cases the worry is that they might actually do the job better than us!

The trick is let go of the lead gradually. Work with your team and share your vision and your concerns with them. Select those you feel you can trust most and delegate tasks and projects to them over time. As they develop, your confidence in them will grow and you will find it easier to delegate and sleep easy in your bed.

The alternative is the deep-end approach.

Some four years ago I was off work quite ill and my doctor ordered me to work only one day a week. I had been totally unprepared to let other people do parts of my job but in the circumstances I was forced to let go. It was stressful and difficult, but I am pleased to say I came through it and so did my team. However, given a choice, I would have much preferred the gradual approach that so many of the successful entrepreneurs have followed.

Dave Osmond of CompuAdd Computers had to learn to let go, which he found difficult. So he followed this approach which he found personally very helpful.

> I learnt it does not have to be all or nothing – there is an in between gradual approach which worked for me in practice.

Letting go – a gradual approach

Step 1   Select the right person to whom to delegate some of your work.

Step 2   Identify a project or piece of your work which you can delegate.

Step 3   Agree objectives in outline with your selected person, eg: 'reduce buying costs in admin. by 10%', or 'keep customer service level at 92% satisfaction'.

Step 4   Ask the individual to produce a one-page bullet point action plan on 'how' they will achieve the objective.

This has the benefit of:

- giving them personal ownership;
- allowing them to think for themselves;
- conducting a mental rehearsal before committing to any action;
- giving you an opportunity to check their thinking and provide any coaching input.

Step 5   Once you are happy with the simple action plan, give them the authority to implement it.

Letting go means delegating and sharing power, picking people you can trust, and giving them clear directions and the space to learn and grow. Business books make 'delegation' sound simple but it isn't. It is a special problem for entrepreneurs because they have invested so much emotional capital in their business. 'Letting go' is something parents have to learn to do when their children reach maturity. That is why, for entrepreneurs, it is a better word than delegation – it recognizes the emotional dimension. There is an emotional barrier that we have to recognize and conquer. It has to be tackled if our growth aspirations are to be realized.

Process 2   Backfilling

We have already seen how entrepreneurs grow through projects, not plans; their 'next project' excites them. While it can drive the growth process, it has an undoubted downside. The entrepreneur may become so excited about the new project that the existing business suffers, as we will see in Chapter 13, which can sometimes cause businesses to fail.

So an essential business process is what entrepreneurs refer to as 'backfilling'. It is based on the metaphor of someone digging a trench and then turning round to find that they need to fill it in behind them afterwards. Backfilling is an important growth process because it consolidates the core business.

Much of the backfilling work is not of the sort most entrepreneurs will enjoy. It involves establishing systems, finding staff to do the essential routine jobs that only bore the entrepreneur, people who are good on detail and who find satisfaction in tying up the loose ends and completing the job. (Many entrepreneurs are very bad at such tasks, because they are driven and exited by new ideas.) However, many people find such work very much to their liking.

So methods of backfilling will include:

- appointing people to backfill positions;
- establishing new systems and procedures;
- training people to manage the core business.

Laurence Young, who runs the Lodge on the Loch Hotel near Onich, Fort William, has backfilled several hotels to allow him to continue to grow:

> As we took over more and more hotels we recognized the business could only continue to grow if we could apply the successful formula we had developed to each of the new units. So the first year of running any new hotel was spent putting in computers and putting in systems and procedures, to better enable the running of the business and to establish control.

Backfilling may also include a decision to 'outsource' parts of the existing business.

Backfilling – building a team to manage growth
Phil Crane, Deep Sea World:

> We had a brilliant team, absolutely brilliant team. We had a team that thought they could do miracles, and they did. That is the secret of it, I think, getting a team that nothing can stop them. 'We can accomplish anything we like.' The difference between success and failure is a man's will, and we had a team that just didn't know how to give up. But it was also very well organized. I had a superb operation team.

The second biggest blockage to business growth is quite strongly linked to letting go, building a team that really works.

We have already looked at the principles of basic team building in Chapter 7. To take a business on to the path to sustainable growth requires a more sophisticated approach, as Phil Crane found when he was developing the video business that provided a launch pad for Deep Sea World. We need teams that not only share a vision and have the energy to take it forward, but have the range of skills required within the growing business.

The benefits strong teams can bring to a business are well rehearsed in countless business books:

- Teams allow everyone to focus their energy on their strengths rather than their weaknesses.
- Teams can increase productivity and efficiency. Team members are often closer to the customer and can see opportunities every day to improve the business.
- Teams can improve communication. Team members need to communicate effectively to create success and the business of a team is to share information and the delegation of work.
- Teams make better use of resources. Teams are a key to focusing people and their brain power directly onto problems.
- Teams are more creative because they combine multiple perspectives and share knowledge.

In this chapter I want to look at the question of team building from a different perspective.

One of the principles of marketing is that if you seek to understand customer needs and then meet those needs you will be successful. So can we apply this approach to teamwork? Start from the point of view of team members: what do they want from their team leaders and other team members?

I have conducted surveys of the expectations of team members and there is a huge area of common agreement about what they wanted from their team leader (in this case the entrepreneur).

Team members want to be treated in an honest fashion, they want to have clear goals to work towards, and they want to feel everybody in the team is treated as an equal. Most of all they want to be trusted and treated with respect.

What team members want from their leaders

Preferred approach	*Frequent expressions*
1. Be honest with us	'Tell us as it is.'
	'Be straight with us at all times.'
	'We can take bad news.'
2. Give us clear consistent goals	'Tell us what is expected of us.'
	'Don't change the goal posts every five minutes.'
3. Treat us all equally	'No favouritism or stars.'
	'Treat us as a team, not a set of disparate individuals.'
4. Trust and respect	They also felt that it is critical for team members to trust and respect each other. They felt trust and respect for each other are at the centre of effective team working. The leader must set the example if it is to work.

Speaking to entrepreneurs I was struck by how many of the most successful ones recognized the importance of the trust and respect principle. Mary Conneely put it this way:

> I treat my staff how I would like to be treated myself. Unless you have respect for the staff it is very difficult for them to have respect for you. I maintain a very friendly relationship. While I don't believe you should be too closely involved with staff, you should understand their personal needs and their emotional needs. In my opinion, if you think about your staff everything will tick over nicely. They become very loyal, it is two-way, you give and take on a two-way basis.

Mary Conneely intuitively seems to have known how best to bring out performance from team members. She recognized what they emotionally needed from the team relationship and then offered it to them.

So here are the ground rules for good team building:

■ Be willing to listen, open and as fair as possible at all times. The logic is simple. If we want to create trust in people, treat them in the way you want them to behave with you. So, for example, the more you listen the more they will.

■ Support all team members equally as Mary Conneely does:

> We train everybody and encourage them to go to university, even if that means they may go off and take work elsewhere. This applies to everyone. We had one young woman who suffered from dyslexia; she received a special computer for dyslexia sufferers and it changed her life. She is now at London University doing Law and Criminology. But in the summer she comes back to work for us.

■ Do not talk behind individuals' backs – this kills trust stone dead.

■ Be authentic at all times. The most powerful thing you can do to build trust is to put into words what you are experiencing at all times. 'Fred, you don't seem to be happy with this idea – what is the problem?'

■ Respect the opinion of everyone in the team. Gossip kills respect, so don't indulge in it. Remember: as a Yorkshireman would see it, trust without respect is like fish without chips.

■ The way to build trust is to show sensitivity and loyalty to all team members.

These skills are now recognized at business schools as the 'soft skills' – skills which treat those in the workplace as emotional and rounded human beings, not cogs in a wheel. Adopting these soft skills does not come easy if you have an egotistical view of the world, as entrepreneurs invariably have. As Phil Crane put it:

> The soft skills turned out to be the hard skills for me, because they are hard to do in practice. But when I did force myself to exercise them I did them well and we created a team that was unstoppable.

There is plenty of evidence to support my view that building team spirit in this way really pays off. At the Academy for Chief Executives run by Sue Cheshire, based in Hertfordshire, a recent survey of entrepreneurs who had followed a course there for three years found that they rated the acquisition of soft skills the most beneficial part of the experience, helping them to build strong teams.

Process 3   Getting into bed together – building partnerships and alliances

'Letting go' and 'Backfilling' free up the entrepreneur to concentrate on the future development of the business. The most successful ones carry forward the benefits of networking, taking it to a new level. They call it 'Getting into bed together'.

Building partnerships and alliances was highlighted as a key entrepreneurial growth process in my first book *The Hallmarks for Successful Business* – a study of 30 growth businesses. I found that successful entrepreneurs spent a minimum of 50 per cent of their time outside their business talking with customers, partners, and other key players, and often striking up informal partnerships with them. Further research, based on that book, has been carried out by Dr Tim Mazzarol of Curtin Business School in Perth, Western Australia. He used my Hallmarks 'templates' to track the progress of fast-growth Australian businesses over a four-year period and found that the *building partnerships and alliances* factor was the highest predictor of profit growth. Similar results have been found in studies at Babson College in the USA and Durham Business School in the UK.

Getting into bed together, the process of building partnerships and alliances, is a logical follow-on from networking and finding help covered in Chapter 7. The rationale for the process is simple.

Most businesses have a fairly narrow set of business competences – the things they are really good at. For example, Keepmoat plc is good at refurbishing council houses but this did not mean they were not good at all types of construction. So if businesses are to build their capability in order to take up opportunities that come along, they need to work with other organizations that already have the skills they need. The aim, as I said before, is for 1+1 to equal 5.

The general narrowness of the competencies of even a large business is daily evidenced by the wish of many big corporations to concentrate on the 'core business', selling off the peripheral businesses. The trend is for large organizations to build partnerships in order to take up opportunities they feel unable to tackle on their own. The giant Microsoft has recently got into bed with BT, and Virgin with Stagecoach, the UK-based but international transport company. Other examples appear in the pages of the financial press daily, as traditional market segmentation boundaries are ignored by companies anxious to exploit new opportunities. The starting point for building partnerships, as always as in any entrepreneurial activity, is spotting that opportunity.

Where partnerships fail it is often because no one has spotted a real opportunity to create something of value. A good example is the partnership between government agencies like Business Links and Chambers of Commerce in the UK. They have become adept at accessing financial resources from Europe or the DTI so they form 'partnerships' and spend the funds. Unfortunately, often partnership becomes the purpose of the exercise, not the opportunity to create something of value. Without that opportunity standing at the centre, it is impossible to know who can add value to the partnership and the 'great and the good' pile in to ensure they get their share of the spoils. As I discovered when I had my business, the purpose becomes the maintenance of the 'partnership' rather than creating value for customers.

So we must start with the opportunity and then seek the appropriate alliance. In exploiting the opportunity there will be skills and competences you do not possess as a firm. Look for somebody who does. You need to be convinced that this company really does possess the skills and that you can work together. This can be tested through a pilot project before signing up to a formal partnership. It may seem a great deal of trouble but it pays off, as Keepmoat found out.

A guide to building partnerships and alliances

The process used by entrepreneurs to build partnerships and alliances is as follows:

1. Spot a superior opportunity – see Chapter 3.
2. Clearly identify your own business core skills. What are we really good at? This is a much more problematic task than might be first appreciated. It is hard to be objective about these issues so here are some questions you might ask to help you:

   – What allows us to do business?
   – What can we do that others cannot?

- What do our customers or contacts say is different about us?
- Where do we make and lose money?
- What is our business recipe?

3. Find out what skills are required to take up the opportunity, which you do not possess. This might include:

- access to market;
- technology;
- network contacts;
- funds;
- special skills;
- valued experiences;

or any others.

4. Investigate who possesses the skills or resources you require. This is a job for the resource investigator in your team. These are the people who always seem to know people or can find resources to get the job done. Invite people who can really contribute to the partnership rather than being there for purely 'political' reasons, as is the case in many public–private fiascos.

5. Explore the possibility of collaborating. Could you trust them? Have they really got the skills you need? What is in it for both parties? Is it important enough for both parties to make it work? Is it possible to work together on a pilot basis to find out whether you can collaborate? Talk about building trust together and what needs to be done to build it effectively.

6. Draw up a partnership agreement. If both parties decide to collaborate, set out rights and responsibilities, intellectual property rights and all the details. Do not skimp on this; get good lawyers involved and try to cover all angles. Make sure you share the risks and rewards in any deal.

Dick Watson of Keepmoat plc helped to pioneer partnerships and partnering with local authorities for the regeneration of local communities. Whilst Keepmoat could provide management and construction skills and finance, the local authorities had ambitious plans to regenerate run-down communities and they also owned the land. They also had skills in working with local communities in a bid to revive local pride and employment. With the resources available from central government and local taxes, everything was in place for a public–private partnership that provided not only homes and facilities but employment and opportunities for training the unemployed or the never employed.

Partnership agreements clearly defined the rights and responsibilities of all parties and in some cases provided for development profits to be shared and reinvested in the particular project. The operation has proved to be a significant success for Keepmoat as a business and the company has now set up a Partnership division to form new alliances.

Once partnerships are up and running, founded on sound principles, focused and clear management is needed. Partnerships are akin to marathons, not sprints.

Partnership principles

Commitment	The reason the partners are working together must be important enough to get people involved. It cannot be half-hearted.
Win–win	The aim must be mutual benefit for both sides in the partnership. One must not be seen to be constantly gaining at the expense of others.
Long-term view	Partnerships are long-term, between stable organizations; short-term relationships are not partnerships.
Openness	Both partners should keep each other informed. Surprises can be deadly.
Development of trust	Trust does not happen quickly. It takes time to develop.
Effective representation	Both sides need a champion to marshal resources and make things happen.
Integration	Both sides need to be integrated and supplied with information and systems.

The journey to growth: management for growth

To be a successful growth company you need to learn to manage. That might sound a little strange. Haven't entrepreneurs been managing up to now?

Up to this point there has been management but it has probably been of a *de facto* variety. Small companies can manage well without too much in the way of formal management, as we have seen. But now with the company growing fast the task is to learn to manage in the more conventional sense of managing people and processes but most importantly *without losing the entrepreneurial spirit.*

This is a real challenge. You can become deluded into believing that holding meetings, writing reports, filling in forms and generally spending lots of time in your office is contributing to the development of your business. Many entrepreneurs fall into the trap of becoming bureaucratic managers. You should know better than that.

Management is about planning, controlling and coordinating any business in order to achieve its objectives. Managers are paid to take action and make things happen. In order to achieve this they need to manage processes and people. Whilst this book is not about formal management methods – there are sufficient tomes written on this subject – it might be worthwhile to review the current thinking on managing a business.

I am indebted to my friend Professor Gerard Egan of Chicago, who summarizes many of the problems in management in his excellent book *Adding Value*. So here goes.

Numerous studies show that managers do not manage well. This is not necessarily their fault; it is often due to the lack of a system for managing. Consider this:

- Managers are often selected as managers because they are good at something else (professional or technical).
- Once in the role they receive little training as managers.
- Their managerial role is often ill defined.
- They often have few effective management role models to copy.

So therefore:

- Managers pick up whatever skills they can as they go along.
- They normally value their technical role over their managerial one.
- They have no system or model for managing.
- Management skills are nearly always undervalued.

So why does this happen?

- New managers say nothing: 'Don't rock the boat.'
- Managers in other organizations are no better; as one said: 'We are no worse than anyone else.'
- Pressure of work prevents people from thinking about it.

But unfortunately the emperor often has no clothes.

This is not the fault of managers. They were often thrown in at the deep end and they either sink or swim. In 1998, 40 per cent of CEOs in the Kompass business directory were 'changed' or 'left'. A recent Cranfield Business School study found the average tenure of a UK CEO is only four years.

To manage effectively, managers need to manage the systems, culture and people in their business.

So the role of the CEO or managing director is to set the strategy for the business overall and ensure they select the people capable of implementing it. The managerial tasks in growth therefore include:

- Get a shared strategy.
- Pick the right people with the potential to manage.
- Provide good data for decision making.
- Incentivize good performance.
- Provide an effective role model for managing the business, particularly of the business's core values: 'How we do things here.'
- Encourage teamwork and collaboration.
- Encourage experimentation, innovation and risk taking.
- Provide feedback on performance.
- Manage the business processes effectively.

Perhaps most of all you will have to learn to recruit the right kind of staff and manage them effectively as individuals.

Recruiting individuals has already been touched on in Chapter 5. You need to follow the same process as you did then, but now you will be looking for people with the leadership qualities necessary to lead a team. You have to be sure that all members of staff are given clear and focused objectives and that you can provide the support and training they will need.

But here I want to concentrate on just three aspects of the managerial job: providing motivation, giving feedback, and developing a system of rewards which reinforces behaviour that contributes most to the company goals.

Providing motivation

Most people who come to work want to do a good job. If you have picked the right people they will be naturally motivated to do a good job. Should this not appear to be the case maybe you are to blame. My problem as a manager was that I sometimes used to blow hot and cold on people, depending on their performance on that particular day, without making allowances for the things that affected them as people.

People can be expected to get 80 per cent of their motivation from doing the job (if they are not getting that then possibly they are in the wrong job) but your job is to coax that extra 20 per cent. The influence of good leadership and people-handling skills can be very marked. A colleague of mine, Adele McGee, used to coach and manage retail sales staff for a ladies' fashion group. Their head office always knew which store Adele was working in in any particular week simply by monitoring sales. The store with the best record was invariably the one she had taken under her wing, because she had motivated and fired-up the retail shop assistants.

Providing feedback

Many people in business seem to dislike giving people honest assertive feedback on their performance and indeed many avoid it like the plague. This is a weakness that any company bent on growth will have to tackle, since a lack of feedback, or less than honest feedback, does not help the company achieve its aims nor does it allow individuals to adjust their performance. In the saddest cases, people are asked to leave because of serious problems with their work when they have had no reason to believe their cards had been marked. This is clearly not fair.

It is not that the people responsible for giving feedback do not know how to do it; it just seems they feel uncomfortable with the process in practice. If the feedback process in a growing business is not what it should be then it is time to act. Feedback comes with the job; so get on with it and stop being a wimp.

Rewarding success

Rewarding success is clearly a key priority if you are to get the motivation right. It needn't cost a bomb either. The most under-used words in the manager's vocabulary are 'Thank you' and 'Well done'.

When I was speaking with one entrepreneurial team recently I asked how they knew they were doing a good job. The reply was 'When we don't get our backsides kicked'. A very motivating environment! If people achieve success it is important to acknowledge this publicly. Saying thank you and meaning it also sends a powerful message to everyone else in the team. (Yes, I know it's stating the obvious, but why then do managers not do it?)

A study of the top 200 CEOs of European companies in the early 1990s found that they considered that a key part of their success was their skills in 'persuading people to do things'. This included their people, customers, the City, suppliers, partners and many more.

These 'soft' interpersonal skills, which are often ignored by conventional business wisdom, appear to be the key managerial task entrepreneurs need to learn if they are to grow their business successfully and produce the results needed to fuel further expansion.

Sue Cheshire again:

> Our CEOs normally join us to achieve hard bottom-line results. How-
> ever, after a few meetings the discussions are generally around getting
> the most from people – the so-called soft skills. In my way the soft skills
> are the hard skills in that they are hard to deliver in practice yet when
> people do them well they turn into hard results.

A checklist to help coach and manage individuals effectively

The process for doing this well involves:

1. *Picking the right people*: 'Round pegs in round holes.'
2. *Giving them clear objectives and focus*: 'Tell me what's expected of me.'
3. *Ensuring they have what they need to get the job done*, including training, resources and your time: 'Give me the tools to do my job.'
4. *Providing motivation* and energy for people, fire them up, get them going: 'Inspire me to really give my best.'
5. *Providing feedback* and coaching on their performance: 'Tell me how I am doing.'
6. *Rewarding success* and helping them learn any lessons: 'Reward me for my efforts.'

The journey to growth: leadership

My work with entrepreneurs suggests that we need to make a distinction between managers and leaders. Managers make businesses work by planning, coordinating and controlling activities in order to hit budgets, targets and objectives, producing results to expectations. Leaders who make the business better, however, drive business growth: producing results beyond expectations. Dick Watson, Managing Director at Keepmoat, is a leader. He consistently exceeds everybody's expectations by producing outstanding results, and as we saw earlier, they became one of Britain's top private companies.

So what are the elements of leadership at this level which we need to promote and cultivate?

1. Establishing a clear vision

Over the past 10 years it has become the fashion for most companies to have 'mission statements' which are displayed prominently in the boardroom and workplace. In my experience these are largely a waste of paper. The staff are cynical about such initiatives, seeing them as the product of some new management fad – all fur coat and no knickers.

We need a practical vision that we can use to measure progress and provide motivation across the board. The best way to drive the point home is to look at a company vision that seems to be achieving its goal – that of the high-tech glass-manufacturer, Solaglas.

Solaglas – the three-year vision

■ *To have established 'partnership' trading arrangements with selected customer groups and suppliers.*
This part of the vision is translated into a specific strategy document naming the customer groups and suppliers and setting a time-scale for achievement. It has become a reference point for the board, the shareholders and the company's strategy department.

■ *Achieving a minimum of 15 per cent net margin.*
A self-explanatory target that is easily measurable and publicly available. The general message is that this is a company that intends to grow and fight off predators.

■ *Achieving targeted customer satisfaction levels.*
Again, the target customer satisfaction figures are defined within the company and regular information on performance is fed back to the staff at all levels.

■ *We are the company everybody wants to work for.*
The measurements designed to show this is true are the natural wastage rate (very low and getting lower) and the ratio of job applications to vacancies.

■ *Solaglas name established in UK at same or better level as Pilkington.*
Again it is possible to measure progress towards this objective and to take corrective action if the graphs do not appear to be heading in the right direction.

■ *Nationally co-ordinated specific sales and marketing activity.*
This part of the vision is directed to improving the performance of sales and marketing and again has specific targets.

■ *Best Information Technology and Management Information systems operating internally and with customers and suppliers.*
This part of the vision combines elements of an aim and a boast. It sets targets but also makes people feel proud to be working for such a progressive company.

■ *Human Resource System in operation to provide appropriate training, to guarantee terms and conditions, and to ensure rewards are fair and motivating.*
The aim is cement the good relations between company and staff. Targets are set for the training programme and there are regular reports on the number of people being trained.

▪ *Cost-centred production units.*
The commitment here is to delegate the responsibility of meeting financial targets to the production units themselves. People feel more in control and the company aim of keeping a tight rein on expenditure is achieved through workforce involvement.

▪ *Barrier-free, open communications culture.*
The last element of the vision commits the company to a free flow of information wherever company law allows it. The commitment emphasizes how much the company trusts its own workforce to be responsible.

This is the sort of vision growing companies need to create, a vision which is realistic, challenging and inspiring all at the same time.

2. Encourage everybody to contribute ideas

Companies that want to grow need to establish a competitive advantage by mobilizing all the best ideas within the company. Leaders need to inspire people to contribute ideas from all levels. Ipswich Town Football Club put this policy into operation and was surprised to find that most of the good ideas came from junior front-line staff.

3. Translate the best ideas into projects

Companies need to adopt the 'working on the business' approach we look at in detail in Chapter 11. Turning the best ideas into projects acts as an antidote to the common assumption that ideas put into suggestion boxes are not generally acted upon. Ipswich Town FC has managed to convert 60 per cent of the ideas suggested by their teams into projects to improve their business.

4. Create a climate of learning

We saw in Chapter 5 that innovation comes through free thinking and low-cost experimentation. A corollary is that the company must tolerate mistakes when they are made. Making mistakes can be a great learning experience. A climate of learning will only emerge if we observe the rules of respect and even-handedness.

To take one example of how not to do it, a CEO complained to me that his people would not take risks, resulting in my visiting him and sitting in on some of his meetings. In one meeting he delegated a project to an individual in a style straight out of the manager's guidebook on how to delegate. Just when I was puzzling over why he had a problem the individual got up. As he was walking towards the door the CEO bellowed at him 'and don't screw it up'.

5. Encourage people to be persistent

We saw in Chapter 5 that one of the marks of all good entrepreneurs is persistence in the face of setbacks and disappointments. To keep the entrepreneurial spirit alive, leaders must encourage staff to be persistent, especially during difficult times. All projects have setbacks, and good leaders help people to maintain the enthusiasm and commitment that will often see them through to a successful conclusion.

One entrepreneur who impressed his staff and me was Martin Vincent of CompuAdd. When the going got tough or when people made mistakes he sought no scapegoats and never attempted to fix the blame on individuals or groups. He supported people right at the time they needed it most. His team rewarded him by the most enthusiastic support.

6. Celebrate success and learn the lessons

Leaders need to demonstrate at regular intervals – not just once a year – that they appreciate the efforts of the workforce and positively celebrate the achievement.

You don't necessarily have to go to the lengths of Raj Samuel, the Managing Director of Elm Refrigeration in Glasgow, who makes a point of taking the team out for a beer and a celebration whenever the firm wins a big order. But you take the point.

When mistakes are made it is important to hold a post-mortem and try to draw out the lessons in a positive, non-blaming way: it is only when there is no learning from the error that they become more costly than the company can bear.

None of this of course is rocket science; we are back once again to the 'soft skills' that people seem to find so hard to remember to do in practice. You should know how to do this, so make time to do it and watch your business take off.

The journey to growth: being the business

Leaders, by definition almost, set an example for others to follow. Many traditional business leaders don't seem to appreciate the power of the positive role model. Far too often they behave in the way they feel their position in society entitles them to behave and when they get caught out it can have disastrous consequences for company morale. Yorkshire Water (now renamed) has taken years to live down the consequences of its ill-guided share option perks for directors, in the face of a drought that made customers very angry and put their own employees at the risk of at least verbal abuse.

Conversely, most entrepreneurs I have ever met seek the ethical. They start with the advantage of being people who have built up a business, often at some considerable sacrifice to themselves. So it is maybe easier for them to behave as business leaders should. Entrepreneurs should also try to behave in line with the business priorities. If the business needs to delight its customers, the entrepreneur needs to be seen to delight customers. If part of the business recipe is to treat each other with respect, it's patently obvious that if the entrepreneur is a bully then the recipe is more likely to be 'dull obedience upwards – sheer brutality down'.

It is my view that behaving in line with the company priorities as an example to everybody is one of the most powerful ways to develop a business.

Successful entrepreneurs learn the lesson of 'being the business' in their behaviour and they usually find that their people follow their lead.

Business leaders will often look externally for a benchmark against which to judge their own style, sometimes friends, teachers, former bosses or even historical figures. There is a fashion, for instance, for business leaders in the West to look to Machiavelli and even ancient Chinese military textbooks. The source of inspiration will vary from country to country. In France, the civil servant is seen as a good role model, whilst in Greece, Alexander the Great is admired by many business people. In the USA Bill Gates and Warren Buffett are entrepreneurs who are greatly admired, while Nelson Mandela is seen as having commitment and moral authority in South Africa.

Sometimes role models like these are adopted at peril. In Australia they used to admire entrepreneurs like Alan Bond until his spectacular downfall, while in Britain Robert Maxwell has helped give the whole idea of business a bad name.

At present Richard Branson is admired in the UK for his sense of adventure and taking on new business ventures as well as treating staff well and making business fun; we certainly need more like him.

revitalizing **your business**

- The limitations of benchmarking
- Removing blind spots
- Cost reduction
- Revitalizing the business by teamwork
- Redoing your strategy

The skills of the entrepreneur play a crucial role in starting up and growing businesses and so far this book has very much dwelt on that role. No business can survive and flourish without having access to those skills.

The pattern from the past has been pretty clear. Someone spots an opportunity and gets the resources together to exploit it. In the early stage of the business the enthusiasm of the founder carries everyone along and the small scale of the enterprise means it can react quickly to changes in the market. But as the company matures and grows, problems set in. The exhilaration gives way to grind and if you're not careful the sure-footed nimbleness of the gazelle can be replaced by the plodding gait of the dinosaur. Although the firm may continue to move forward under its own momentum for a number of years, growth levels off and the company becomes just another company, often working as much for the bank as for its owners and its workforce.

Maybe 80 per cent of all firms in the UK fit into this category. They have very little to distinguish them from their competitors, no unique proposition to offer customers, and they find themselves competing on price alone, the squeeze on margins making it impossible to fund further expansion. Keeping up with the pace of technological change proves more and more difficult. Not only that, they find that customer tastes and needs are changing faster than ever before and that fresh new companies are muscling in on their traditional markets. The owners may still be making a comfortable living but a new insecurity gnaws at their peace of mind. They are stuck just over the hill in the mature phase of the business life cycle and need to revitalize before it gets too late.

Perhaps you might recognize your own company as one facing some or all of these problems.

So this chapter concerns itself with what actions companies can take to revitalize their entrepreneurial spirit, restore their margins, and give themselves a new competitive advantage.

Working with entrepreneurs who have themselves been faced with all these challenges and found a way through has convinced me that addressing the problems using the approaches outlined can transform businesses, merely ticking over, into supercharged new companies by releasing cash for new investment.

The limitations of benchmarking

Benchmarking has been presented as one of the latest panaceas to revitalize businesses. The idea is that you compare yourself with the 'best' and copy them. The promise is that if you work hard enough, in three years' time you might just be as good as your competitors – big deal! There are major pitfalls. For example, who to benchmark against? Once you have a business to benchmark against, often their recipe has been developed over time and proves impossible to copy. There are often many contextual factors and tacit learning that you simply cannot possibly re-create. Take a tip, forget benchmarking and develop your own recipe for your business.

The five arms of the revitalizing strategy are:

- removing blind spots;
- adopting cost reduction techniques;
- eliminating system slippage;
- revitalizing the company through teamwork;
- redrafting the business strategy.

Removing blind spots

In the early days of the company the entrepreneur spotted an opportunity and found a way to exploit it in order to get the business off the ground. The entrepreneur had his or her finger on the pulse of the company. But as companies mature, entrepreneurs can find themselves drawn into the daily grind of running the company, cutting them off from the real world outside. Firms develop blind spots: they can no longer see the world out there as it really is. Bad enough in itself, but made worse by the fact that they are unaware they have lost touch: the problem with blind spots is that by definition we do not know we have them.

A pig is a pig, isn't it...?

It helps to recognize that our perspectives on any issue depend on where we stand as observers. Take something from everyday life, something as easy as describing a pig.

The common view is that a pig is an animal with a snout, small 'piggy' eyes, a plump body, and a curly tail. To make it more graphic, the description might include the fact that it is pink, bristly, probably smelly, and almost certainly dirty.

But how would a farmer see a pig? He might see it as a particular breed, weighing 100 kilos, pleasingly lean, and worth £90. An animal rights activist might say 'poor pig' and a boar pig might think, if the pig were female, yippee!

Businesses, like pigs, can be seen from many different viewpoints. The owner sees it in one way, those who work for it perhaps in quite another, and customers from yet another.

The gulf between the views of the owner and the customer can be staggeringly huge. I once asked an entrepreneur how good his business was at customer service. His view was that it was very good: there were very few complaints. But when we conducted a customer perception survey, only 40 per cent of customers were found to be even vaguely happy with the service being provided. This was particularly unfortunate since the 60 per cent who were unhappy were all businesses in their own right with customers of their own. Many of them would be going around telling people who were potential customers about the lousy service.

The survey cost very little and effectively removed a very important blind spot. Once the owner could see how poor his customer service really was, he could start to put it right.

Every business has blind spots, some far more than others do. We have to discover what they are and try to deal with them.

As well as customers' perceptions there are the perceptions of the workforce, of the investors and shareholders, and of the suppliers. All can tell owners and directors something significant about their business. Closer to home, so can your family and friends.

Although businesses can find out what these are by asking each 'stakeholder' directly, learning to think the way they do can be very helpful. For example, when I asked one entrepreneur to stop thinking as the managing director and think about his business from the perspective of the investor, he started to ask different and tougher questions of his management team.

Other blind spots are not about perceptions, but about practices within the company.

Simon Keats is a young entrepreneur from Stoke-on-Trent who runs a caravan retail business, North Staffs Caravans, with a turnover of £3.1 million a year in 1998. Because the firm was small, employing only 20 people, he imagined he knew about everything going on within the business. Then he happened to spend a day in the accounts department checking invoices:

> We had a price list for the caravans we sold and I found it strange that none of the invoices seemed to reflect our current pricing policy. When I looked into it I found that my sales people were giving regular discounts of up to 10 per cent on the prices.
>
> Then I looked at the prices we were paying for the caravan accessories. They seemed a bit high to me, so I phoned round some alternative suppliers and without exception they quoted me substantially lower prices. We had been with one set of suppliers for so long that nobody seemed to have thought there might be more competitive new suppliers out there.

In short, Simon was horrified to find how generous his people had been with his money!

So every company needs to tackle its blind spots and set about removing them. It may not be easy. Even acknowledging that the company view on many important issues might be seriously off beam can be very painful.

Sometimes we refuse to confront our demons and see what it is too emotionally difficult to see. It is not very pleasant to find that a long-held view is based on a fantasy; something we have invested some emotional capital in. Even when we are provided with 'objective facts' or 'credible statistics', which seem to prove beyond doubt that our view is way off beam, it's hard to accept it. (Ask any expert on selling: piling statistics on top of statistics to prove a point is more likely to alienate rather than convince a potential customer.) In the case of the entrepreneur the problem of emotional ownership of our own particular view of the world is greater because we are all egotistical and independent. How often, when advisers or managers push harder to get us to see reality, do we push back even harder with 'that's not how I see it'?

The tendency to shoot the messenger if the message isn't to our liking is a major obstacle to the removal of business blind spots. We need to learn to listen to what other people have to say and acknowledge that: 'Well, yes, he/she might have a point.'

Challenging the tendency to blame outside forces

It is understandable that many people running companies will seek to blame anybody but themselves if they are faced with real problems. Instead of tackling the issue within the company they blame outside forces, forces such as competition, legislation, the government, the bank or even the weather.

Energy needs to be focused not on blaming these outside forces but on finding creative entrepreneurial answers to the challenges the company faces.

Blind spot eradication

The first step is to tackle the blind spot problem. Here is how others have done it and turned their businesses from plodders into gazelles.

Inspect, not expect

The Simon Keats story is a good illustration of the gulf between perception and reality:

> I suppose I made the error of expecting everybody to know what their job entailed and leaving them to get on with it. My going 'back to the shop floor' gave me a whole new perspective on the way the business was operating.

For Simon, going down into the business was a salutary experience, and the lesson is clear enough. We need to know how the staff is implementing company policy, assuming that one has been defined. While I am not suggesting that 'inspection' of this sort should be an everyday occurrence (constant supervision is very demotivating) 'inspection for a day' can pay big dividends. As we will see later, 'inspection' in this case led Simon to take action to improve staff training.

Brainstorming blind spots

Simon might have begun with an alternative approach – bringing teams of people together to brainstorm the question of blind spots. Many heads are better than one, especially if they bring a range of distinct perspectives to the task. It is also helpful to involve people who are close to the action, ie the salespeople, the receptionist or the delivery drivers. They experience day to day the realities of your business, so they are a gold mine of information.

Charlie Fairburn runs a company that makes juggling equipment in London, called rather bravely 'More Balls Than Most'. In fact, they do more than make juggling balls – they actually teach people to juggle. Charlie got his whole team together to try to uncover the company's weaknesses:

> I started by asking them to describe how they thought the company was doing, and what unpleasant realities we were sweeping under the carpet. That was a revelation. I also found they had a very shrewd idea

of where our weaknesses were. The whole exercise brought us closer together and led us to implement a rolling programme of common-sensical improvements that had a real impact on the performance of our business.

Some typical questions to be answered by such a brainstorm are:

- What is stopping us from seeing what is really happening in the business?
- What unpleasant realities are we trying to avoid?
- What blind spots do you believe we have?
- What facts do we need to gather to help us judge our performance more effectively?
- Be brutally honest with me, where are we at risk as a business?
- What potential problems do we face that I don't know about?

Stakeholder survey

A third effective way of identifying blind spots is to conduct surveys with the key stakeholders – customers, suppliers and investors. We saw how to conduct a formal customer perception survey on page 110. Surprisingly, asking customers to complete surveys does not frighten customers away: they often like to think their views are being given honest consideration. Suppliers are generally equally cooperative, feeling it could be a valuable networking experience for them. However, meeting face to face over a cup of coffee or a drink can sometimes be even more effective in unlocking those sought-after and valuable perceptions.

The outside view

Provided a firm picks the right people, bringing in some outside advice can also serve to challenge the 'received wisdom' prevailing within the company. We have all come across situations where a closed group of people only reinforce their own prejudices about the outside world. Letting in light and fresh air can dispel the complacent view that our way must be the best.

Cost reduction

So the first step in the revitalization of a business is to uncover the blind spots. Once that task has been tackled, constructive action can be taken. But of what sort?

One is to reapply the old virtues of *'beg, borrow and befriend'* to the business – in other words, reduce the necessary running costs to a minimum. As companies grow, all kinds of unnecessary costs find their way into the system and need to be rooted out.

Simon Keats is a good example of how this can be done. North Staff Caravans is a family business started by Simon's father 52 years ago and there had been plenty of time for these costs to have built up. When Simon and his brother took over the running of the company they found it was profitable and under no immediate threat. But Simon was not happy to find he was working very hard for comparatively little return. The profits, about £40,000 a year, represented just over 1 per cent of turnover.

Simon, like his father before him, had the ambition and vision of an entrepreneur and was keen to develop the business, but the lack of profits made that job much more difficult. But what if a 'cost reduction programme' could unlock the funds he needed? When I first suggested it to him, he jumped at the chance to try it out.

I had met Simon at a workshop for caravan retailers. Most of the owners were middle-aged and conservative, and distinctly sceptical about the benefits any such exercise would bring. Simon wasn't like that. He took away the whole cost reduction programme introduced at the workshop and set about the task with real energy and zest. It was a question of *Just do it*.

The central idea of cost reduction is to question every cost in the business. Simon used brainstorming and achieved a truly remarkable turnaround:

> My 'awayday' in accounts had been enough to convince me there were lots of costs we could cheerfully do without. We identified where we could save costs within the business, how we might reduce the cost of supplies, and where there were hidden costs on the sales side. I made the rule that no cost cutting was to be allowed, if it meant we couldn't offer at least as good a service to our customers. But we found there were lots of savings to be made within the company and also through reducing the costs of buying in stock and other supplies. Our 'zero-based budgeting' exercise was probably the most valuable thing we did. As well as coming up with real savings internally, it highlighted the fact that some of our lines were very slow-selling – ditching these lines led to big savings on the stock side, releasing the cash for other things.

'Zero-based budgeting' is a great way to re-inject early entrepreneurial values into a company. It starts off on the assumption that the budget for any part of the business should be zero and any expenditure should be properly justified. It is possible to tackle some real taken-for-granted cost assumptions. In other words, restarting the business with a clean sheet of paper.

From a cost perspective, you ask 'Do we really need that' and often the answer is no.

It threw the focus on a number of areas:

- internal costs;
- bank charges;
- press and publicity;
- sales strategy;
- suppliers;
- skills;
- the future.

Internal costs

Simon's team came up with ideas for saving on accountancy by improving internal bookkeeping – savings £3,600 a year.

They suggested an urgent review of the sales strategy in the accessory shop, to cut out non-selling lines – savings £20,000 a year.

Press and publicity

The questions addressed here were how effective was the advertising? Was it going to the right places to reach the customer? It was decided that making big cuts in advertising expenditure made little sense, but that it could be far better focused – featuring certain models with higher retail mark-ups.

Sales strategy

In Simon's case the brainstorm came up with huge potential savings. Was it really necessary to give away £100 of free equipment with each caravan? How did prices compare with competitors? Were all models paying their way? As a result of looking into these questions, stock items were cut by 500 and certain lines dropped altogether. The discounts were slashed and some prices actually raised without any adverse effect on the sales figures.

Suppliers

The fact that there were alternative suppliers in the market was exploited to the full. When stocks were required the company should ask for quotes from three separate suppliers (even applying this rule to banking services!), a policy that forced down costs. In future all supplier invoices and prices were to be checked against the agreed price, while the wholesalers were to bear the costs of stock-holding through introducing a 'just-in-time' delivery system. The savings amounted to £20,000 a year.

Skills

It was decided that poor skill levels were costing the company money. A training grant was secured and a staff training scheme introduced based on the real needs of his business. This was based on an industry initiative – 'Profitline'.

The future

A management team was to be set up to review costs regularly and suggest savings. There was to be no slipping back into sloppy ways.

The outcome was that Simon improved his profits in the first three months from an annual £20–£30,000 to around £120,000. As a result he could not only survive but release funds for future expansion. As well as *beg, borrow, befriend,* Simon used such other start-up processes as: *Negotiate hard, Zero-based budgeting,* and *Be like Scrooge.*

It is perhaps worth noting that cost-cutting for Simon did not mean cutting staff. In fact he recruited two extra people over the period.

Another entrepreneur who followed a similar cost reduction/profit improvement programme was Phillip Edwards of Pontypridd Caravans in South Wales. Phillip was just 25 years old, an IT specialist with no business training at all, but displayed the same get-up-and-go attitude as Simon. He used a *Pareto analysis* of his stock by sales value. He was able to cut his stocks by 40 per cent and reduced the amount of capital tied up by £300,000, more than doubling his net profits in one go.

Cost reduction entrepreneurship is not about counting the paperclips or firing people. It is about finding where the business is haemorrhaging costs and stopping it. This is one of the quickest and most effective ways to build a new platform for the future.

System slippage

System slippage is a term used to describe the difference between the systems companies have in theory and the use or lack of use of the systems in practice. In my years of working with business I have been amazed to find the gulf is huge, yet not perceived by management. Yet it is a quick, cheap and easy way to get an immediate improvement in performance and profit.

To take one example, an Oxford-based engineering company I worked with decided to re-examine its selling systems. The issue they focused on was spending on advertising, and the savings amounted to £270,000 a year, a saving of 90 per cent.

The marketing department in the company had devised a system to measure advertising effectiveness. Whenever a sale was made customers were asked to tick a card saying where they had heard about the company and its products. Unfortunately, no one had trained the sales staff as to what the purpose of the exercise was, and they simply ticked a box at random. They thought the important part of the job was to take the customer's money.

The system slippage only came to light when the company discovered that six customers had ticked the box 'TV advert' – when the product concerned had never been advertised on TV. When a subsequent survey found that 85 per cent of new customers came from one source of advertising – the direct mail-shot – they slashed their marketing spend from £300,000 to just £30,000, saving £270,000 – incidentally twice the existing net profit.

You may think that this is a remarkably big saving, and in percentage terms it is. But in 20 years' experience of working with entrepreneurs and helping them to tackle system slippage, the savings have always exceeded expectations, sometimes by a factor of 10. None of these companies had a turnover of more than £5 million.

The potential for savings

System slippage: Example from companies with annual turnovers of less than £5 million

	Value
Not following the process for the selection of suppliers	£400,000
Not following procedures for purchasing stationery	£20,000
Not asking for three quotes from potential suppliers	£50,000
Not completing planning process at commencement of a project (causing project to go off track)	£750,000
Not taking up references for a senior appointment (candidates lied about experience and qualifications)	£20,000
Not following process for 'cross-selling' to customers	£500,000
Not following production planning system (resulting in conflict between sales and production)	£250,000

Eliminating system slippage

Here's a quick guide to the basics:

Step 1   List the systems, checklists, processes and ways of working – formal and informal – in place to control your business.

Step 2   Investigate gently which are being used and which are not. Remember that people may be reluctant to tell you what really happens. It is an exercise guaranteed to raise your blood pressure: finding out what's not happening when a lot of money has been spent on a system is stressful, but is also a fantastic opportunity.

Step 3   Identify why the systems are not being used. Simply threatening with a shotgun will only work in the short term. Here are some common reasons:

- The importance of the system has not been clearly explained.
- The system has been 'imposed' so the users do not feel it belongs to them.
- Staff have not been trained in using it.
- The system is complicated and bureaucratic.
- There are too many systems.
- Nobody supervises it or checks on it.
- There are no incentives to use it.
- There are no consequences for not using it.

Remember people do not normally come to work to screw up, so you need to deal with the reasons why the system is not being adhered to in a proper manner. The real issues are normally to do with apathy or a lack of understanding.

Step 4   Calculate the consequences of not using the system or process to your business on an annualized basis. Doing the economics helps to give you the incentive to sort it out.

Step 5   Ensure the systems are in place and your people are trained or confident in using them. Agree a way of monitoring the system without being too heavy-handed.

If you successfully follow steps 1–4 you will have created enough profit and new opportunity to revitalize your business. In my experience entrepreneurs have released anything from £50,000 to £1,000,000 from within their business by simply completing this exercise. The motto is: *Work smarter, not harder.*

Revitalizing the company through teamwork

Most companies in need of revitalizing already have 'teams' – certainly at management level – that normally meet regularly as a team. There may be other teams brought together for internal meetings, formal or informal, on a regular or intermittent basis.

Unfortunately, teamwork of this sort is not the way to rekindle the entrepreneurial spirit. This is quite simply because, in most cases, these meetings provide a top-down flow of historical information, such as the last month's accounts, or attempt to solve current problems. The problem is that such meetings generally keep the business as it is, providing more of the same. Often the agenda simply recycles that covered at the last meeting, and the issues largely remain the same.

This might be termed working *'in' the business*; carrying out the business of the business. It is not about taking the business and putting it on a new plane. To do that we need people to work *'on' the business*.

This sort of work needs a different approach to teamwork, one based on the Western equivalent of a Japanese method called 'Kaizen', continuous improvement.

Continuous improvement teams are not concerned with what's happened in the past, nor would they find sitting at a table discussing a report very helpful. They are teams of people who set about improving the business by analyzing what they are presently doing and working out ways of doing it more easily, more quickly and more consistently.

The thinking behind the approach is straightforward:

- If we don't work *on* the business it stays the same.
- Standing still is not enough: we need to improve to keep ahead of competitors.
- People in the teams will improve the business only if they feel involved.
- The people at the coalface, doing the work, are most likely to see how to improve it.
- All businesses have lots of unused potential: let's release it.
- People enjoy seeing their ideas being implemented – they find it motivating.

The process is kicked off by bringing your people together, in one big group or several smaller groups. This is for a briefing on what the company is trying to do, why it has to do it, and what the role of the teams is to be. Everybody has to receive this message.

Break the company down into teams coming from various parts of the company – multidisciplinary teams – and arm them with a flipchart and a remit to come up with ideas for improving the way things are done. Ideally it is better if this is not led by a manager or supervisor, but by somebody selected by the group. The managers and supervisors can easily stop the process in its tracks if they throw in negative or know-it-all opinions, which to be honest they are often prone to do.

It helps if the group is asked to focus on one specific issue at a time, such as improving customer service or cross-selling more products, or working more effectively internally; there are plenty of suggestions outlined in the box below. Ideas can be written on the flipchart or posted up using Post-it Notes. If the whole process can be made fun the quality of the ideas will generally be better.

When the teams are brought together to present their ideas to each other there can be some very useful cross-fertilization. Once identified, the best ideas need to be implemented within a timeframe.

Once this approach gets going it can be repeated regularly, and better ways of doing things continuously evolved. That is why it is called 'continuous improvement' – the journey is never over.

Ipswich Town Football Club uses this approach with all their staff, excluding players. At the first meeting David Sheepshanks, the Chairman, led off and got the whole thing going. He had 50 people split up into six or so cross-departmental teams.

After some discussion it was decided by the teams that managers shouldn't be part of them. When the first session produced a staggering 60 improvement actions, some 24 were chosen as the most promising, and within a month 16 of these ideas had been put to the test and found to work – a success rate of 66 per cent.

Since then 20 of the 50 commercial staff meet monthly to identify problems, come up with possible solutions, and then test out whether they work. The results are presented to the management group, who sanctions the changes needed. In this first year, the aim has been to improve customer service generally and to improve takings through 'cross-selling' the services offered by the club. The use of the restaurant bar and function rooms has shot up. At the same time, the drive for sponsorship has been stepped up and many more season tickets sold than before. Ipswich Town Football Club has a set a target of 80 per cent successful implementation and already they are well on the way to doing it with David Sheepshanks at the helm, backed by a highly motivated group of people.

PRACTICAL TEAMWORK – CONTINUOUS IMPROVEMENT

An eight-step strategy

Every business is different but this is an approach that has worked for many businesses in need of revitalization.

Step 1

Get people together in one group. Explain the above principles to the whole team. 'We are going to revitalize our business in order to stay ahead of our competitors/meet our objectives, prepare for exporting' or whatever the reason is in your business.

The whole group is invited to participate in the exercise. It is important that everybody hears the same message together.

Be upbeat, optimistic and tell the team how much you value their input.

You are not calling in experts or consultants. The wisdom is within to improve the business and you are going to do it together.

This initial meeting takes 1½ hours.

Step 2

Suggest the team break into groups of 4–6 of mixed departments and disciplines. Let them decide the groups, provide them with a flipchart or large piece of paper and pens. You join a team as a member but don't lead it.

Tell them it would be a great start if they could identify 20 areas for improving the business. Tell them to identify:

- things that they can personally take responsibility for improving;
- team actions;
- inter-team issues.

Encourage them to avoid external undoable factors like 'exchange rates in Korea' or the old classic 'if only management would…'.

Try to provide some live examples from your own business, eg 'Fred suggested we manned reception over the lunch break to improve customer service.'

Examples of the issues focused upon by entrepreneurs include: cost reduction, system slippage, customer service improvements, internal effectiveness, better ways of working internally, improving the product or service, making it easy for customers to buy from us, improving cross-selling opportunities, and many others. Ask them to write their ideas on the flipchart or paper. Make it fun. Act as cheerleader.

Step 3

Get each team to present their ideas quickly to each other. Congratulate everybody. Often people do not have the precise data or need to so some research or investigations.

Step 4

Ask them how they want to take the ideas forward. Do they want to work in the same groups to implement the idea? Do they want to allocate the idea to natural work teams? The important thing is to let them decide how they want to organize themselves. Encourage them to get the facts so that they make objective assessments.

Step 5

Agree some ground rules for the follow-up. Here are some typical examples:

- Whole group to meet again in one month's time to report on success and progress in implementing the ideas.
- Teams to prioritize the actions, since they cannot all be done at once. Any actions involving change in a process or some expenditure need to be put down on a one-page action plan prior to taking action. You should use this opportunity to see the quality of their thinking and also to give any necessary coaching or input before they commit to action.
- Make sure you agree to undertake at least one action yourself. You are their boss and an important role model. You need to demonstrate your commitment to the process in actions, not just words.

Step 6

Groups implement their action plans. You offer support, help remove any blockages, and show interest as they implement their plans.

Step 7

Groups report back on progress one month later.

Celebrate and reward success and learn lessons. Make it upbeat, positive. Say thank you and well done. Calculate the percentage of actions successfully implemented against the total planned.

Make sure you complete your actions or the whole thing will die before your eyes.

Your challenge is to keep the action-taking above 80 per cent on a consistent basis. (A result commonly achieved by successful entrepreneurs who have used this process for more than four meetings.) Thus, if you identify 20 actions and implement 16 of them, your business just gets better and better. It becomes revitalized and everybody involved gets the feel-good factor.

It might take 3–4 meetings to get to 80 per cent implementations:

the total often mounts steadily along the lines of 30–50–60–80 per cent. In other words, it takes time to build the process into the culture and for people to get the idea that you are serious that working on the business is here to stay. Many will expect it to be dropped after a couple of months: you must prove them wrong.

Step 8

Ask the group how they will maintain this fantastic process of developing your business. Occasionally individuals say 'we are too busy to do this'. You need to be firm and say that this is a new dawn in your business. Everybody, including you, will have to spend some time working on as well as in your business. It's your new way of doing things.

Businesses that do this well normally meet monthly to report on progress and celebrate success. Keep it going; it will revitalize your business if you do it right.

Redo your strategy

A very powerful way to revitalize your business is to redo your strategy. Some entrepreneurs seem to believe, unfortunately, that changing the organizational structure is enough to breathe new life back into their business. In fact, while this gives the illusion of change, it does nothing to revitalize the business, which is what we need to do.

Redoing your strategy means getting back to the basics and thinking as an entrepreneur as opposed to a manager once again.

Picking the right people – to be on the strategy review team

Rethinking strategy should be a team exercise but you need people on the team who are strategic thinkers, and not simply people who may feel they have a right to sit at the table, or people you may feel should be on the team for 'political' reasons. Playing politics probably contributed to your present state.

So you need to think about which of your own staff should be involved internally in the exercise of rethinking strategy. People with a vested interest in a profit centre or department will find it difficult to be objective and see the whole picture of the business: their vested interests almost always colour their judgements. This is particularly true if you might be thinking of exiting the very part of the business they are responsible for managing. This happened to me once and it was an important lesson for everyone concerned.

Frankly, the smaller the team the better. Remember you can always get others involved in gathering information as you need it. Choose people who will not necessarily agree with you but who can be expected to challenge and debate the issues with you: such people, you will find, help you with your own thinking.

However, you have to make sure you explain to those not on the team why they are not involved, something easier said than done. My advice is to be honest with them: trying to 'con' them always makes matters worse when they actually find out what is happening.

Preparation for the strategy review

Information gathering

Gather some strategic information to help you rethink your strategy at your review sessions since there is nothing worse than not having relevant information on the topic.

INFORMATION GATHERING

Here are some examples of the kind of information you will need.

Question to be discussed

A. The current operational performance of the company

1. What has our performance been like in our markets of choice?

Useful information:

- market shares;
- strength of our competitive edge;
- sales and profit trends by customers and products;
- competitors strengths and weaknesses;
- overseas trends in current markets;
- customer attitude survey feedback;
- other relevant factors for your context.

2. How efficient and effective have our operations been?

Useful information:

- Performance measures, to include:

    – quality;
    – efficiency;
    – utilization;
    – wastage.

3. How effective is our process management?

Useful information:

- methods of planning and control;
- provision for flexibility;
- identify where these processes are adding value.

4. Are we making the best of our plant and people?

Useful information:

- qualifications and experience of staff;
- present arrangements for supervision and target setting;
- investment in training;
- technology involved. How old? How reliable?

B. The current financial performance of the company

Useful information:

Profitability	*Gross profit trends*
Break-even Point	
Funding	Gearing
Borrowing	
Cash/Assets	Cash flow
Working assets	

Overall quality of financial control and management

Are the systems being used or have they slipped?

The pre-strategy review meeting

The information gathered needs to be reviewed, understood, and put in summary form prior to the strategy session proper. We should already be using it to help answer some important questions, such as:

- What is it telling us about our business?
- What are our strengths?

- What are our weaknesses?
- What should we focus upon?
- What challenges in the environment should we be responding to?

You will find that attempting to answer these questions should provoke a healthy debate prior to the strategy session, which in turn will set new thought processes in motion.

The strategy review

Strategy making consists of six steps:

1. Design the new strategy.
2. Test it with the key stakeholders. Is this what the investors, managers, customers want?
3. Sell the strategy to everyone. Inside the business and externally to customers and investors.
4. Cascade the strategy internally. Encourage departments to translate the strategy into their own department plans. What does the new strategy mean we should be focusing upon?
5. Implement the strategy. Do it. Much more of this later because this is the hard part.
6. Refine it. Adapt it as the business develops.

Remember that entrepreneurial strategic development is not the same as taught to MBAs at business schools. This should be a jargon-free zone and should be *less about strategic planning, more about acquiring a sense of strategic direction.*

If you are serious about the exercise, and implement the policies decided on by the review, you will find 'redoing strategy' will make an enormous contribution to revitalizing your business.

The strategy review – the details

The entrepreneurial process consists of making a number of decisions.

It can take anything from 2–10 days to answer these questions, probably dependent on these factors:

- the quality and quantity of information you possess, ie the pre-work;
- whether you have a shared process, ie all singing off the same hymn sheet;

■ your experience of thinking and debating strategic as opposed to operational issues.

It can help to have an experienced strategic facilitator to help you work through the process.

The facilitator should stick with the process and avoid getting too involved with the content by asking these questions of the team:

1. What have we learnt from the past about our business that we want to retain in the future?

■ What are we good at?
■ What helps us compete?
■ What is our way of doing things that we should cherish and nurture?

2. What is happening in the world that affects us that we need to respond to?

■ market trends;
■ technology changes;
■ competitors' activity.

3. In answering questions 1 and 2, what business should we be in in the future?

■ scope of business;
■ focus on strengths;
■ exit from loss makers.

4. Where will we be in 3–5 years time?

■ picture of the future;
■ customers, investors, employees.

5. What markets specifically should we be in?

■ growth markets;
■ chance to use our strengths;
■ focus and direction.

6. What products/services should we focus upon?

■ focus on 3–4 at most;
■ exit loss makers.

7. What will we need to get better at in order to deliver our products/services successfully into our chosen markets?

■ core strengths;
■ building partnerships.

8. How will we get those we need to help us deliver this strategy success-fully behind it?

- employees;
- investors;
- partners.

Martin Vincent and his partner Dave Osmond of CompuAdd Computers of Bristol went through this process. Here are their responses to these questions.

Q3. To deliver hassle-free computer solutions direct to UK organizations with volume PC requirements.

Q4. Shareholders:

- Our net profit before tax has increased year on year by at least 25 per cent.
- We are in a position to float or sell at a multiple to earnings of at least 15.
- We have established a business plan for our sustainable profit growth beyond flotation.
- We have chosen and focused on a target market and gained market share.

Customers:

- We have developed a set of customer service and internal standards, which we use to measure our performance.
- We have a set of key indicators to measure our performance.
- We have refocused sales, marketing, technical and supporting functions to match the needs of customers.
- Customers recognize and value the CompuAdd difference.
- At least 80 per cent of our sales are repeat purchases, ie orders from retained customers.
- At least 80 per cent of our new business comes from referrals.

Employees:

- We have devolved the management of the business, creating opportunities for staff development whilst allowing the directors to develop the business strategically.
- We have a working environment, which is conducive to teamwork and encourages initiative.
- We have an improved information system and MIS infrastructure in place providing the tools for staff to work effectively.

- Staff who contribute share in the success of the business.
- We are seen to be one of the best employers in the area.

Q5. Our customers are UK organizations who have volume PC requirements. The principal markets are:

- government;
- departments;
- IT departments of large organizations whose customers are internal departments or related organizations.

Q6.

- Custom configured PCs and servers;
- Peripherals;
- Services required for the installation and use of the above.

Q7. The key issues are:

- Coming from 'box shifting culture' we are not experienced at selling and delivering chargeable services.
- Processes are not simple and procedures don't work consistently.
- We require leading-edge product development normally reserved for large players.
- Life of products not very long.
- Product compatibility, consistency and quality.
- Range of peripherals and accessories vast but wish to offer to keep control of the customer.

Overcome by:

- Work with partners who can show us the way to start with.
- Simplify and automate processes so that quality procedures can be followed.
- Position company as one that uses tried/tested/stable technology.
- Internal skills to monitor market place for opportunities and developments.
- Stock managed efficiently (aim to always have what is required and minimize inventory).
- New products and components tested by skilled technicians prior to being offered for sale.
- Proactive approach to quality control systems – standard configuration for manufacturing PCs (ie consistent slots and drivers).
- Direct delivery service from distributors to customer to reduce stock holding costs, handling, exposure to obsolescence and keep range broad.

Q8.

- Restructure the existing Board.
- Appoint Dave Osmond as Operations Director.
- Set up weekly cross-team meetings.
- Undertake internal management development programmes for supervisors and department heads.

The lessons learnt from working with entrepreneurs who have revitalized their business by developing a new entrepreneurial strategy could fill this book. However, in summary:

- redoing the strategy can really revitalize a business;
- focus on the important issues and keep it simple;
- gather facts wherever possible and note and test assumptions;
- watch out for bias and vested interests creeping into the process.

One final word of warning. It seems that many businesses, quangos and government bodies have been told that getting a strategy is the right thing to do. Many go through the motions, producing elegant missions, visions and values statements which they have trouble implementing. Try to avoid the typical trendy strategy statements, which only devalue the exercise. Phrases such as:

'Work in partnership'	Relationships where $1+1+1=5$ are incredibly difficult to create. Very few really work in practice.
'World Class'	80 per cent of UK companies claimed to be world class, but only 2 per cent matched world-class criteria (DTI Report).
'A Learning Organization'	Organizations do learn sometimes. However, too much emphasis is placed on the sum of individuals learning as evidence of being a 'learning organization', ie 'We put lots of people on courses therefore we must be a learning organization.'

Your people will quickly discover whether your new strategy is for real or is simply a cosmetic exercise. Using words that cannot be delivered does not help your case.

Take a leaf out of the book of successful entrepreneurs like Martin Vincent of CompuAdd. His strategic plan aims to improve customer service by monitoring 'hassle-free delivery' on a daily basis. Similarly, Keepmoat plc reviews how well they are 'delighting customers' once a week.

Use terms that your staff will readily understand. Plain English helps.

A checklist on redoing strategy for entrepreneurs

Here are some of the key lessons from entrepreneurs who have successfully revitalized their business by redoing their strategy:

1. *Use your business memory.* Future strategy builds on your strengths. You need to use the business's memory to think through why you are successful and perhaps what your competitive advantage might really be.

   Test your competitive advantage with customers – is this how they see it?

2. *Know what is happening in the business today.* This should be a review of what is happening in your business world. How well tuned are you to what is happening? Your network should be able to provide lots of data to help you. Check to see whether you have any blind spots or assumptions that are untested.

   Conduct a customer perception survey if you haven't already done so.

3. *Reduce the scope of the business.* This may seem strange, but revitalizing the business normally means reducing its scope. Good strategies provide focus. For example, a building firm might redefine its business in these terms: 'We were in construction but now we are in new homes development.' Can you do the same in redefining the scope of your business? Success rarely comes from expanding the present scope – usually the opposite.

4. *Have something for everyone.* While making the picture as clear as possible, have something in the strategy for all the key people, customers, employees and investors.

   Examples:

   – Launch on the stock market in three years' time.
   – All employees to share in our success.
   – We will build more partnerships with delighted customers.

   Defining the picture in this way enables your people to work at how to prioritize their efforts.

5. *Exit unprofitable markets.* Revitalizing strategy normally means exiting unprofitable markets. Entrepreneurs enjoy adding products and services; they rarely kill them off. Now is the time to consider how to refocus the business. If some of your efforts are producing no return, or incurring a loss, you should axe them. The arguments for staying in an unprofitable market need to be very strong indeed if they are to be endorsed by the review.

6. *Concentrate on profitable products, services and markets.* It is time to go

back to basics. The priorities normally followed by entrepreneurs in order of importance are:

1. Sell more to existing customers.
2. Sell to new customers.
3. Develop new products/services.
4. Diversify – a low priority.

The principle is gardening (sell more to existing customers) rather than hunting (going looking for new opportunities). The principle of business focus is critical. You should aim for two or three market segments, no more.

The pre-strategy work should have helped identify which products/services are profitable and which hold potential and these should be the focus for the future. This is about working smarter, not harder.

7. *Develop 'the skills of the business'*. By this I mean not the skills of individuals within the business but of the business overall. Based on my experience, the skills entrepreneurs most often need if they are to revitalize their businesses are:

   - moving from customer service to delight;
   - developing better control of the core business using key indicators;
   - building strong partnerships and alliances;
   - reducing unproductive costs;
   - working more effectively as a team;
   - making more effective use of IT.

   Clearly the skills your business needs to develop will be dependent on your own particular circumstances.

8. *Share the strategy*. The most difficult parts of strategic entrepreneurship are to make sure everybody understands the plan and getting them to play their part in seeing it is put into practice. Only recently the received wisdom was that, to succeed, a strategy needs to be shared and owned by everyone in the business. But this only happens in an ideal world, one that businesspeople don't inhabit. In fact, most entrepreneurial businesses have to live with real disagreement about the overall strategy. Again, in my experience the strategy stills manages to function effectively because, although people might not agree with some of the decisions, they generally take the view that it is right for the business overall.

reinventing **your** **business**

- Understanding change
- The foundation stones for reinventing your business
- The process of business reinvention
- A guide to blockages

All companies reach a point where they need to reinvent themselves; they get past their 'sell-by date'. This is part of the natural life cycle of business – start-up, growth, maturity and eventually decline. The task facing entrepreneurs is to read the signs early enough to take action. This phase often just precedes the survival stage but if action is not taken, companies can slip into crisis.

In order to reinvent themselves, businesses need to understand the dynamics of change and how to transform themselves.

We have seen that successful entrepreneurs are invariably good learners, and have the knack of staying close to their customers. They are not weighed down by business dogma – most have never been near a business school – and can respond flexibly to opportunities and problems in their business.

Rather than prepare a 'business plan' they develop a recipe for success, which they learn to implement. While this works brilliantly for a while – many of the entrepreneurs I studied have won business awards such as 'New Business of the Year' or 'Fastest Growing Business' in their area – sooner or later most run into difficulties. They settle down to become just ordinary firms – with more and more attention being given to the daily running of the business and less to developing new business or responding to changes in the marketplace. They have lost the entrepreneurial edge.

As Alison Fletcher of ABI Electronics of Barnsley, who won several small business awards in the late eighties, said:

> We were successful and thought we had a God-given right to be so. We then ran into real business problems but we were complacent and only survived by the skin of our teeth. Success almost led us into failure.

By the time the firm starts running into trouble they find it is almost impossible to change: the business has established systems, procedures and a way of doing things. The company culture has set in a mould like concrete – extremely hard to break.

While the business environment changes rapidly they are stuck with a brilliantly conceived business recipe, unfortunately five years out of date.

Part of the problem is that this crunch point is usually preceded by a period of apparent unprecedented business success. Kotter and Heskett in the classic book *Corporate Culture and Performance* found that most of the major business failures in the USA were preceded by a period of success.

The firm developed a recipe that works. It hires managers to cope with the growing bureaucracy. People internally begin to learn they are the best and become more arrogant and stop listening to their customers and stakeholders. They start to believe that their idiosyncratic way is what gives them the edge. A strong arrogant culture develops and the business loses the plot. The only way out of the dilemma seems to be to change the top management almost wholesale or break up the business by selling off its parts.

Recent examples include, in the UK, Sears and Laura Ashley, and there are even questions in June 1999 about the once invincible Marks & Spencer.

Success leads to complacency and few businesses at this stage seem to have fully understood the lead-and-lag between developing a new product or service and maximizing profits from it. The great period of success and profitability reflects work done probably years ago. The crisis when it comes brings the dubious benefit of spurring businesses to change, but by this time it is often too late. But does it need the threat of failure to enable a business to take change seriously? Can it not change before it is too late?

Understanding and managing change

One of the saddest features of the present business landscape is the fact that many more firms are aware of the need to change, but take the wrong sort of action at the wrong time. Those who choose to change when there is no immediate crisis on the horizon are making what I refer to as 'discretionary change' rather than change brought about by a real need or crisis – 'compulsory or non-discretionary change'.

Most discretionary change is inspired by reading business books or is sold by management consultants well versed in the latest 'cool' management fashion or, more properly, 'fad'. This 'fad' is often introduced as the answer to *all* their problems. Whenever I talk to business people, a clear sign that they are engaged in discretionary change is when they claim: 'We are into TQM or Re-engineering or Customer Care.' Unfortunately the fad becomes the end result, the purpose, as opposed to the process of improving the business. Fads by their nature don't last and the constant switching to adopt the 'latest business idea' only serves to create cynicism amongst the management team and staff.

Discretionary change of this sort rarely lives up to the initial hope and promise. According to a study prepared for the UK government's Trade and Industry Department (DTI), 80 per cent of discretionary change programmes are quietly abandoned within two years. This is not because these are necessarily bad ideas, but because they are introduced as fads. In the USA, for example, 60 of the top 500 businesses have started and abandoned at least three management 'fads' over the past five years. Incredibly, despite this record of failure, most of the companies were about to embark on yet another fad: hope, it seems, springs eternal in the management breast!

The record of companies undergoing 'discretionary change' is pretty appalling by any standards. By contrast, those companies who undertake change because they foresee an approaching crisis or a real opportunity have a much better record. 'Non-discretionary change' of this type has to be distinguished from the 'quick fix' approach that might be embarked on in the panic of an actual crisis. It is introduced carefully and with purposefulness and prudence. Companies who want to transform themselves successfully to meet the challenges of the future need to adopt this approach. Below I will take you through the steps that need to be taken and show how this approach to transformation works in practice.

Before I take you through the steps you need to take and give you some examples of how this approach to transformation works in practice, I want to make it clear that there are many pitfalls on the road you will have to avoid.

Most companies who start out on the road of transforming themselves into modern go-ahead companies often fall at the first hurdle. Of every 100 'change programmes' discussed at board level, only 20 ever get beyond the discussion stage. This is the problem of inertia or getting started. Even if they get started, the problem seems to be that boards, having discussed the principle and decide to 'set up a project group to consider it carefully...', then pass responsibility on to managers already overloaded with projects. One such manager said to me recently: '*David, don't give me any more projects – I have 11 already.*' This is a well-known management problem – project overload.

But it gets worse. Even where companies actually begin to implement a programme of change (20 per cent of all companies), only a very few will actually complete the process. Most projects run out of steam and get quietly forgotten or put into cold storage: 'Let's just put it on the back burner for a while.'

These statistics come from my friend Gerard Egan, a Chicago-based management consultant and writer with a special interest in the process of change. He found that just 20 per cent (or a fifth) of the transformational projects progressing beyond the discussion stage were actually completed successfully.

Putting it another way, only one-fifth of the 20 per cent of companies who get started with 'non-discretionary' change actually achieve their objectives – that is just 4 per cent of all companies considering such change.

While entrepreneurs wanting to transform their business need to be realistic before they start on the journey, the odds of achieving successful change are substantially improved if they can learn from the experiences of other businesses who have successfully completed the journey.

Before we look at the lessons of experience, though, a further word of advice. Remember that change is often traumatic and that it increases uncertainty and stress levels among all those affected by it. The role of the leader is to help people through this process and there are good ways and bad ways of going about it. You can bully people into change using an autocratic style of management but it will not produce results in the longer term, especially as it may lead to people using their creative energies outside the business in hobbies or other pursuits. The successful business leader seeks to harness most of that creativity and energy in the cause of the business – taking everybody along with the process.

That said, let's look at the principles of successful business transformation.

The foundation stones for reinventing your business

1. Top management commitment

Commitment does not mean simply giving your time, when you can spare it, to the issue of transformation, or even in writing messages of support to the management and staff promising your full support. In business, actions often speak far louder than words and one apparently unimportant action can torpedo the project from the outset. *Entrepreneurs must champion the change in their actions, not words.*

Let me give you an example. I was once facilitating a 'change management programme' for a large business, a programme critical to the future of the business. The process was to begin with a launch at a two-day workshop in a hotel in England's Cotswold Hills, where the MD was to start the ball rolling. I briefed the managing director on what to say to the top management team and everything seemed set for take-off. Then, the day before the event, his secretary telephoned to say that he had been called away on urgent business but wanted the event to proceed as planned because it was so important. He sent a copy of his address, which was to be read out at the conference.

Next day at the opening session I apologized for his absence, emphasizing that only the most urgent business had prevented his appearance in person. Whereupon one of the senior managers announced to the whole team that the real story was that the managing director had been invited as a guest to a big Manchester United football game and he had not wished to miss it.

I should have packed my bags at that point.

To show management commitment you have to do what you say you will do, give the lead for others to follow, but most of all show by your actions that you really mean it. Follow the example of Dick Watson, Managing Director of Keepmoat plc, who, over a 20-year period of working with me to help develop the business, always said:

Put me down for the first one.

Because he took it seriously, so did his team and the change happened as planned.

2. Engage everyone in the business in the process of change

'Big Bang' change imposed from the top down rarely works. People have got to be involved in the process and allowed to make their contribution in ideas and enthusiasm, but at the same time those at the bottom will only have a sense of direction and purpose if that comes from the top. So successful change needs to be both top down and bottom up at the same time. One of the most effective ways to engage people in the process is to encourage them to 'work on' the business group as a team (see page 203).

Your aim should be to make change an adventure rather than a trauma for people. Giving some assurance on job security, or on the principles of compensation should anyone lose their job as a result of the changes, can help a lot.

Training can help too, if the training programme is directed towards giving people the new skills they will need. But 'sheep-dip' training – where everybody goes through the same training programme – in itself won't be enough. You need to support any general training with tailor-made programmes designed to meet the more specific needs. Attention to individual needs is one way of building the involvement you so desperately need.

3. Do the economics

One real lesson I have learnt from the successful initiatives, which have brought about change, is that the benefits of the change process need to be quantified in financial terms. If the figures point up the poor prospects on the horizon for an unchanged company, you will be surprised how often 'discretionary change' becomes 'non-discretionary'. The impact of such figures can be particularly effective with MDs and boards who have chosen to take a 'Mary Poppins' view of the world and have mentally swept the threats posed in a competitive market under the carpet. Equally, when entrepreneurs see the financial benefits of a process they will tend to take it more seriously.

A word of advice though. Many of the benefits will need a little work to quantify them as they often lie outside traditional accounting practices, even though they impact directly on the bottom line. One good example of this was the waste disposal company we met on page 173, which did not see the significance of 'lost customers'. I have yet to see a profit and loss account that includes such calculations; yet in that case 'lost customers' were costing the company $6 million per annum.

So when your financial people 'do the economics' you need to be sure they enhance their conventional way of looking at figures with some of the 'breakthrough thinking' process outlined in this book.

4. Do the 'political' work

One of the commonest errors made by companies trying to change is to forget that there is a 'political' agenda that needs managing, just as much as there is an economic one.

Change initiatives often create chaos and confusion for people and this has to be addressed.

This means establishing both who will be affected by the change process and who is in a position to affect the process itself. Such a list might include customers and employees, suppliers and investors, managers and supervisors, and industrial or commercial 'partners'. In preparing the list you need to slot them into three categories – allies, adversaries and fence-sitters.

The political task is to identify who fits into which category if you do not already know, ie are you sure the 'allies' are really on your side?

The task then is to work out how to get your allies to champion the change for you, how to get the 'fence-sitters' off the fence and behind the process of change, and how to deal with the adversaries. In the last case it may simply be a case of neutralizing their potential for creating trouble.

The fact is that politics rather than logic kills most change programmes and those who want to spearhead change miss out the political work at their peril.

Look, for instance, at the example of Martin Vincent of CompuAdd whom we met in Chapter 11. When he calculated that improving the delivery performance of his business would have a significant impact on his bottom-line profits and on the long-term survival of the business, he ensured everybody in his business took change seriously.

To see how the listing of people as allies, adversaries or fence-sitters can be used to deliver political benefits within a company, we should look no further than Geordie Engineering Systems – remember them from the Chapter 10? In this business the marketing manager wanted to change the way the company managed customer service. This was how the political map panned out:

	Allies +	Adversaries −	Fence-sitters =
Production team		X	
Sales staff	X		
Accounts & admin.			X
Customers	X		
Managing director			X
Marketing manager	X		

His analysis of the politics within the company proved very useful in devising a 'change strategy'.

He reckoned the production team was against the change largely because being more sensitive to customer needs made life more difficult for them. On the other hand, the sales staff wanted it because they thought improved sales would mean more pay, and were aware that customers really supported the change, as a result of a customer survey.

He reckoned the key lay in winning over the fence-sitters, particularly the managing director, and in convincing production there were benefits in the process for them too.

He enlisted the support of the sales team who took the production staff to meet customers so they too could hear what customers needed first hand.

Meanwhile the marketing manager 'did the economics' of the change, to show that the change could lead to prices holding up (when falling prices had been squeezing profit margins) and to an increase in market share.

When the figures showed the changes would be worth an extra £150,000 on profit during the next financial year, the MD started to warm to the change.

Other elements in the strategy included redesigning the production process – involving the production manager, who was classed as an adversary, to work out a new production plan that meant no one would lose out in the change. The production manager turned out to be a real dinosaur and so he had to leave. These are the really tough decisions that cannot be avoided if you are really serious about change.

Finally he persuaded the company to bring in training for accountants and the general office staff – something they had never had before.

The outcome was a general acceptance of the need to change and a new spirit of enterprise across the whole organization. On the way a few battles had been fought, a few egos massaged, and some harmful myths and assumptions killed off.

5. Build the change into the existing brickwork

Many change programmes fail because they are bolted on as a 'special project'. You know the syndrome: *'The customer care project group meets every other Tuesday at 4.00 pm'* which is also understood to mean *'if anyone is available or can be bothered to turn up'*.

So the more the change can be built into existing processes, the more it is likely to succeed. You can do this by aiming to include the change process in such areas as:

- induction programmes;
- the agenda for existing meetings;
- newsletters;
- interviews used to appraise individual performance;
- the objectives set for individuals within the company;
- team meetings.

In fact, into as many of the existing business processes as possible.

You really do need to be visible and active at this stage talking to your people, constantly reassuring them, but most of all being honest with them.

6. Communicate, communicate, communicate

The last element is as simple as it is important. You need to tell people constantly how things are going.

Even in the smallest company there exists a grapevine of unofficial communication that spreads bad 'news' like wildfire, turning rumour into very often damaging 'fact'. If there is a communication vacuum within your company, the grapevine rumour machine will soon fill it up and the task of reform and change will be all the more difficult.

So don't leave it to the grapevine to screw things up. Send out letters or faxes, or better still e-mails to keep everyone informed. More than that, take every opportunity to sell the change to everybody, particularly face to face. Where successes are chalked up by any individual or department, make sure you celebrate them publicly.

The process of business reinvention

Business reinvention has to be positioned as *a non-discretionary non-negotiable process that transforms the fortunes of the business for the benefit of all*. It involves business leaders taking a series of steps, steps based on the practice of the most successful entrepreneurs, techniques which we have already encountered for the most part in the earlier chapters of this book.

It means taking entrepreneurs, who may have become 'managers' in the bureaucratic sense, and helping them to rediscover their entrepreneurial touch with the object of re-energizing and refocusing businesses which were once entrepreneurial but which have now become in many cases complacent and lethargic – in the most damning sense, ordinary.

The business reinvention process we will look at is linear: you need to do Step 1 before Step 2 and carry on through to the end. It should also be a continuous process if a business is to be really successful. Keepmoat plc, for example, has been doing it for 20 years, using it to grow from sales valued at £35 million in 1979 to over £115 million in 1999, with profits to match.

You will find that this chapter also provides a useful summary of many of the entrepreneurial processes covered in this book.

Business reinvention process – a summary

Step 1 *Redo the existing strategy* on pages 207–216.

Step 2 *Identify and remove any blockages* to the delivery of the strategy.

Step 3 Work 'on' the business as a team. See page 203.

Step 4 *Establish key indicators* to monitor the development of the business.

Step 5 *Develop the customer service process*, creating increased customer delight. See page 78.

Step 6 *Provide development opportunities* for individuals and teams.

Step 7 *Provide the leadership* to make all this happen. See page 238.

Step 1 Redo the existing strategy

The step-by-step process to rework an existing strategy is covered in some detail, beginning on page 207. But then it was used to promote growth in a young company. Here we will be redoing strategy for a different purpose – to transform the mature business.

Getting the strategy straight is always the first job in transforming any business. Drawing up a new strategy in many companies is no more than redrawing the organizational chart, a process that rarely improves the fortune of the business because it does not address the fundamental problems – selling the wrong products in the wrong market. In fact, playing 'musical chairs' in this way can be dangerous because it gives the illusion of progress – we can all relax knowing we have been 'reorganized'.

A new strategy should normally seek to reduce the scope of the existing products and markets, less rather than more, while at the same time focusing on one or two high potential growth opportunities.

The aim of the strategy is straightforward – to secure the existing business and provide a sound platform for the future. At its best a strategy will be simple to understand and will offer obvious benefits, be it increased profit margins, or the opening up of new markets, or more likely the better exploitation of an existing market. The best way to illustrate the principle is to see how it worked in another construction company I worked with based in the south of England, whose name I have changed to protect their commercial interests. The before and after picture shows the results of strategic transformation in living colour.

Southern Construction

	Old	New
Business scope	Building houses in the South of England.	Building homes for single people selling at up to £150,000 on selected inner city sites of no more than 30 dwellings.

Comment: Before the new strategy was drawn up the company was losing money in some areas by its policy of building any sort of house anywhere. An analysis of the housing market showed that there were better profits to be made in specializing and concentrating on building higher value buildings in attractive settings. This led to a much sharper focus.

	Now	Five years hence
3–5-year vision	▦ Turnover £30 million.	▦ Turnover £84 million.
	▦ Profits £1.6 million.	▦ Profits £5 million.
	▦ Good dividends for shareholders.	▦ Delighting customers.

■ A diversified business.

■ Employees share in our success.
■ Continuous improvement techniques to ensure company operates at the cutting edge.
■ Programme to enhance margins on houses built.
■ Building partnerships.

Comment: Under the old strategy everyone was working hard for no great reward. Before I was called in to advise, the company's vision was simply a continuation of the past in which dividends and profits were the driver.

The problem was that none of the staff had 'bought into' the business – what was in it for them? The new strategy took a more modern approach and sought to balance stakeholder benefits between staff, customers and shareholders. The benefits of employee participation in share ownership are now well established – they can lead to dramatic improvement in business performance. A comparison of the index of the share value of companies with employee share ownership schemes with those who have not showed that they outperformed the FT 100 share index by 48 per cent over a 10-year period. This was a lesson learnt by Southern Construction who adopted into their new strategic vision.

Markets	Old	New
	Anything south of St Albans.	Carefully selected sites which match an established set of criteria based on the company track record in the past. For example, where had they been successful and why?

Comment: Southern Construction looked carefully into what factors were present in the past when they made money. Why did they lose money on some sites and make it on others? What were the factors that explained the difference? They identified 10 factors that they used as a simple rating system to evaluate the attractiveness of new developments.

Products	Old	New
	Whole range of houses including starter homes, executive homes, brown field development, housing associations, etc.	Homes up to £150,000 aimed at professional couples or single people living together.

Comment: While the housing market in their area was buoyant, research showed that professional couples and individuals were a fast-growing market. The fact that such people could afford to pay more for housing was an additional reason for targeting this market. There was a further advantage to be gained from being first into this market. As market leaders they would have a competitive advantage against newcomers who ventured to exploit the same market.

Values/Culture	Old	New
	Competitive, traditional building values. The company was divided into specialist departments such as surveying, estimating, and contract management. Unofficial watchwords were: 'Get away with what you can.' 'Build quickly and sort out defects later.' 'Use cheapest subcontractors.'	The company needed to come together in a common effort to delight customers. This meant collaboration, not separation, and the creation of partnerships within the company. Training to be given to all staff, who were to be treated as business people, not just 'builders'. 'Cross-team' working to be introduced based on: ▪ a system of internal customers; ▪ an emphasis on building quality; ▪ better management of the supply chain; and ▪ new partnership status for suppliers and customers.

The new strategy was a brilliant success, leading to the targeted increase in profits and a growth of business of almost threefold – largely due to word-of-mouth praise by delighted customers. With the new training in place, most of the new top management positions have been filled by high quality internal candidates.

Step 2 Identify and remove blockages to the delivery of the strategy

With the new strategy tested and in place, the next step is to get the top team together and ask: What will prevent us achieving our strategy? What blockages could impede our progress?

Blockages are a good metaphor in this context because blockages stop things happening and once removed open the way for the process to flow forward. Martin Vincent of CompuAdd identified a number of blockages preventing the successful delivery of his strategy. He rated them before and after he took action:

Ratings out of 10
1 = Poor
10 = Excellent

	Before	After
Delivery on time	4	8
Selling (pre sales)	5	9
Commercial administration	3	7
Stock control	3	7
Board commitment to strategy	3	9
Management capability at Department Head level	4	8
Technical support (post sales)	5	9

Martin assigned each of these blockages as a 'project' to one of his directors or senior managers with a brief to remove it – taking the precaution of restructuring his board over a period of six months to improve competence and commitment. The scheme was a dramatic success, as the before and after ratings demonstrate, and his business has significantly improved its profits every year for the past three years.

A guide to blockages

In order to try to help entrepreneurs to recognize some of the blockages that impede business growth, I have analyzed 20 client cases from the past 10 years and found these the most common blockages to progress.

1. Top team not all signed up to the new strategy, producing a clash over business agendas and disagreements about future direction

Top team division is hardly surprising since most managers have reached senior positions through having a large ego and strong personal views. It is quite common for top teams to agree on strategy at a meeting only to ignore it or seek to undermine it. While successful entrepreneurs recognize that unanimity is something found only in the grave, they will nevertheless see to it that there is collective responsibility for the implementation of the overall strategy.

If an individual is holding out for the old strategy or refusing to implement the new, the entrepreneur has to question whether this individual is more important than the future of the business. Most board members will acknowledge that at some point the business must come first.

The key to building commitment is to spend enough time in

---

dialogue with individuals and teams debating rather than selling the strategy. Entrepreneurs by nature are often anxious 'to get on with it' but time spent in dialogue and debate with colleagues will pay dividends when it comes time for the strategy to be implemented.

2. No process to engage everybody in understanding and delivering the new strategy

Top teams may decide on the strategy but they rarely are responsible for its detailed implementation. That is a job for their colleagues right across the business. So business leaders need to ensure the staff buys into the new strategy, again engaging in dialogue with them face to face. It is not good enough for a CEO to send all staff a video of himself extolling the virtues of 'his' new strategy, as I have known one big bank CEO to do. The rule is to allow enough time at meetings for genuine questions and debate.

The second arm of a policy aimed at removing this blockage should provide for the staff to be involved in delivering the new strategy through 'working on' the business.

3. Challenging and changing the existing culture – 'the way we do things here'

Any change in strategy in many firms depends crucially on removing the blockage posed by the prevailing culture within the firm. Culture is one of the most difficult things for entrepreneurs to challenge and change in practice, and indeed the topic merits a book on its own! However, we can summarize it like this.

The major culture blockages companies often need to tackle include:

- poor internal team working;
- poor internal customer relationships between departments;
- a lack of respect and dignity in the way individuals treat one another;
- attitudes towards improving customer service;
- refusal to take responsibility for making things happen;
- the attitude that what we do cannot be improved upon;
- a blame culture rather than a 'fixing it' culture;
- a sloppy attitude towards quality – that is somebody else's job;
- a lack of partnerships within the business;
- a dislike of working collaboratively with all stakeholders.

A start can be made in changing the culture by developing a statement that people can buy into – a new way of doing things. See, for instance, 'The Keepmoat Way' outlined on page 59.

It hardly needs to be said that you need to champion the 'new way' while building it into as many existing systems and processes as you can, including induction, training, briefing meetings, appraisals, and reward systems.

I seem to spend more of my time with clients working on this issue than almost any other.

Step 3 'Work on' the business as a team

The process of working on the business is described in detail on page 203.

The key is to engage as many people as possible in identifying ways of improving the business, in line with the strategic priorities. One company in the computer software field (for competitive reasons it wishes to remain anonymous) encouraged its heads of department to 'work on' the business with their teams. In 1997 their teams met monthly and generated over 2,200 ideas for improving the business in line with the goal of 'becoming a serious player' in their market sector. Of these some 1,500 ideas were taken forward to projects and about 500 of these projects were completed, providing an increase in net profit of 25 per cent in a single year – profits that helped them develop a competitive edge in customer service.

Step 4 Establish key indicators to control your business

Key indicators measure and help you monitor the critical elements of your new strategy, taking the pulse on an ongoing basis. They will clearly vary according to your strategic priorities. Martin Vincent of CompuAdd uses seven key indicators to monitor the progress of his strategy:

- percentage of orders delivered on time;
- level of quality defects;
- level of repeat business;
- average order size;
- gross margin;
- level of stock;
- number of post-sale calls and other measures of customer satisfaction.

Measuring and monitoring the indicators daily, weekly or in some cases monthly helped Martin control the successful implementation of his new strategy. While he clearly monitored other business measures, he felt that these seven indicators gave him control of the things that really mattered in his business.

A broader analysis of key indicators in 25 companies highlighted those that the most successful business leaders seem to focus upon:

- delivery on time;
- market share;
- source of new leads;
- level of repeat business;
- average order size;
- gross margin;
- return on capital;
- customer satisfaction level;
- management development – capability of existing team;
- stock levels;
- cash flows.

These are fairly traditional business indicators but they hardly give a full view of the company as it might be seen from another perspective. So you should use some of the following indicators to help you to see the 'pig' differently:

- Share of customer spend (measures how well you are really delighting customers).
- Effectiveness of cross-selling.
- Percentage of new business from recommendations.
- Throughput efficiency (ie effective use of planning lead time). Throughput efficiency measures the amount of time you add value or cost to a product from receipt of order to delivery to the customer. For example, products stuck waiting for the next process are adding cost. The aim is to get products as quickly as possible through your system from order to the customer.
- System consistency (percentage of systems used effectively). This can be calculated by listing all the key systems in the business and then calculating how many are being used effectively in practice.
- Percentage of profit from products/services launched in the past 12 months.
- Commitment (measure this by calculating the percentage of actions agreed at meetings that are actually completed successfully). These actions are often taken between monthly meetings.
- Leadership (measure this by calculating the percentage of people producing results beyond expectations). These are the people who surprise you with the quality and often speed of getting things done. These are the change champions who make things happen. They have the 'can do' mentality and also deliver on their promises and objectives.
- People development (measure this by calculating the percentage of

jobs filled by excellent internal candidates). These people are the natural candidates for bigger jobs. These are ready to take on more responsibilities and are much stronger than any external candidate.

■ Stakeholder balance (list the benefits to customers, employees and innovators and take action to see that they balance).

You can work out the six or seven key indicators for your business; they may include some of the above. This will give you real control of what really matters in your business.

If you then trend the indicators monthly on graphs and make this available to everyone in your business via their computer terminals, this ensures everybody is aware of and focused upon your recipe for success. They can then be proactive and take remedial actions quickly where necessary. Bill Gates calls this the digital nervous system in his book *Business @ the Speed of Thought*. Your business 'network system' is similar to your body's nervous system, which enables you to react instantly to threats and opportunities.

If you want to get right to the edge in this area you should ask your IT people to use linear regression to put trend lines through your monthly figures. This calculates the long-term trend up or down in your figures and stops any short-term knee-jerk reaction to monthly blips in your figures. This is how the big boys like Hanson – a company famed for their systems and controls – keep a tight hold on their business performance.

Step 5 Develop the customer service towards customer delight

The creation of customer delight is described in some detail on page 78.

When entrepreneurs start their business they are normally obsessed with serving their customers but as the business develops this obsession wanes and customer service often settles down to 'acceptable' industry norms. This general malaise and indifference presents an opportunity for entrepreneurs to create competitive advantage by stealing a march on their competitors and delighting their customers.

My definition of delighting customers is *doing that bit extra which creates real feel-good factors within the customer*.

This leads to three business benefits:

■ High levels of repeat business (remember the advantages of gardening over hunting).
■ Most new business coming directly from recommendations from delighted customers – cutting down on marketing and advertising costs.
■ Price is no longer the only ground on which the business is competing –

again see the example of Triple A (page 78) – meaning that margins can be increased.

Most business people think of delighting customers as simply giving that bit extra beyond the norm, but the best customer delight is produced when there is an added personal touch, accompanied by something entirely un-expected. A speedy response to a customer enquiry is another cheap way of delivering it – often produced simply by sharpening up procedures and in-volving the staff in the process.

Here is an example from my own experience.

Delighting customers at Bonar Flotex

Bonar Flotex is a firm that manufactures carpet tiles in Derbyshire.

When I arranged to visit the factory some 20 years ago, I was sent a per-sonalized road map, which took me from my office all the way to their front door. This was easily read and did not have any of those annoying illegible scribbles that often pass for guidance on 'how to find us'.

When I arrived at the gate the security guard greeted me by my name (how did they know it was me when I had never been there before?) and told me to park my car next to reception. I was surprised to see my name on a board reserving the place especially for me. At reception I was again greeted by my name (how did they do that?), and handed a security badge and very politely asked to be seated. Within a nano-second a young man delivered me coffee and biscuits, just how I liked it without asking me (how do they do that?) and told me that Mr X would be with me in two minutes (I know it's hard to believe). The man in question greeted me on the stroke of the ap-pointed time with a warm smile and made me feel really very welcome.

I came away feeling very important and wanting to do business with them and I haven't stopped telling people about my experience ever since. Without realizing it I had become an unpaid salesperson for the firm.

That is one example of customer delight. How did they do it?

I found out later that when anyone books an appointment, the secretary calls your office and takes note of your car make and number and how you take your tea or coffee. This is written in a book and there's a system to make sure your visit will be made as enjoyable as possible. Things may have changed at Bonar Flotex, but I hope they are still delighting their customers.

The question is: How does your business compare to this?

Step 6 Provide development opportunities for individuals and teams

Just as start-up entrepreneurs cannot grow a business by themselves, so too the mature business depends on having the right people, committed to the project. This means staff development needs to be given a high priority.

Mary Conneely, who runs a nursing home in Yorkshire, explained:

> We had to be professional about the whole business. I knew I needed total commitment from my staff and giving them all off-the-job skills training was the key to getting them all to really understand their role.

The training took place at all levels of the business. Mary and her assistant Lisa, key players in the exercise, put themselves down for an NVQ course in business. It had surprising benefits:

> Lisa and I went on the course together for eight weeks and as a result we got to know each other a lot better and it developed my confidence in her, and her own confidence. I feel now I can delegate parts of my role to her without a second thought, and the bank are very happy to deal with her, when in the past they wanted me to give personal attention to it. It has freed me up to concentrate on the leadership role.

The idea that the firm will help develop talent goes all the way down to staff who have problems with the most basic skills:

> Some of our staff found it hard to read and write so we helped them with this without patronizing them. One particularly successful idea was to offer them all free driving lessons when they reached 18. Now they go off and drive and find their independence. After that they often achieve things they never thought possible.

Many business people hold back from this full-hearted commitment to staff development. After all, won't the staff go off and work for other people, taking their new-found skills with them? This has not been the experience. Mary told me:

> We helped a lady who could not read or write to get a law degree and she still comes back and works for us in the summer holidays, as many others do. When she is finished I hope to have her back again. Generally we encourage people to go off and do things, but we also encourage them to come back and show us what they have achieved. That way I get up-to-date people who bring their commitment and energy and their new ideas back into the business again.

Mary's attitude is refreshingly different from some of the myopic views some employers seem to have towards developing their people, and it makes business sense. Motivated, qualified staff ensures customers are delighted which leads to better returns for the shareholders, creating a virtuous cycle.

However, there is a need to see beyond just individual personal development through training. A training plan needs to consider the development of the whole organization, in line with the agreed strategic priorities.

Take another example that illustrates this truth beautifully. CompuAdd is a firm that makes computers and is based in Bristol. The managing director, Martin Vincent, first decided his strategic priorities and then organized appropriate development for his team to deliver the strategic objectives:

Strategic need	*Development need*
Better control of the customer service process from order to post sale service	Specific supervisory skills and confidence for department heads to enable them to control the service system effectively
Selling larger order sizes to targeted customers, including a move from telesales to personal selling	Negotiating skills for some sales people and questioning and objection handling skills for others
Improve communication and reduce cross-departments rivalry	Running more effective team meetings; particularly setting cross-functional objectives
Change the culture from blame laying to problem solving	Working 'on' the business in cross-functional teams

Training which does not address a clearly identified strategic need can often waste a great deal of money, a fault that is found in some of the fashionable UK 'Investors in People' (IIP) initiatives. Another common pitfall is for firms to fall for the high-powered sales talk offered by some training consultants along the lines of 'We have the answer: now what is your problem?'

All too often training becomes an end in itself and we find the company becoming hide-bound by 'training course syndrome' – when the staff spend much of their time off the job on vaguely worthy training. Most managers leap to their external training courses directory on being told the company needs training, when company-based training almost always makes more business sense. Be warned, however: some public sector institutions in the UK have even created a whole training industry within the organization. One civil servant proudly showed me their training industry directory, which was 3 inches thick and contained over 100 courses that managers and staff could attend. Many of them carried qualifications but no one seemed to have asked if they helped to meet the strategic objectives of the organization.

What's wrong with external training courses?

External courses appear to be an easy solution to a training problem but they are often the most expensive way of training people and, in practice, often turn out to be the least effective training method.

Management training in particular often proves to be poor value for money because:

- The courses are too general and often only small parts of the course relate to the context within which individuals operate.
- They assume that everybody is at the same level when this is not normally the case. Sales courses are a good example here. Sales people are taken through the full sale process yet they may already be skilled in asking questions and presenting a sales pitch. They may only need help with handling objections.
- The courses often do not give enough opportunity to practise and most courses finish with 'action plans' taken seriously by very few course members.
- Often the tutors confuse people by introducing unnecessary jargon. This may help trainers understand things better but it is a foreign language to most course participants.
- Courses work well for a limited type of skills training but they do not really help people develop. How often do you notice that entrepreneurs who do attend training courses often say the most beneficial thing was meeting other entrepreneurs in the bar and sharing experiences?

The new approaches to training and development

In larger, more successful, businesses the management training and development process has changed over the past five years and is much more likely now to include:

Mentoring	This is a form of on-the-job training where people are supported and helped by a selected coach or mentor.
Career management	This approach aims to provide individuals with opportunities to broaden their skills in different roles within the business on a planned basis.
Project working	People are encouraged to take on projects within the business designed to develop their skills and broaden their perspective.
Action learning	Here small groups of managers work together on developing their collective skills in line with the business

	needs. Through taking action and reflecting on the outcome they accelerate their learning.
Tailored in-company development programmes	These are training programmes specifically designed to address a clearly strategic priority. This might include culture change.
EntreNet	The EntreNet is a programme for helping entrepreneurs to help each other solve their problems by sharing their collective wisdom and experiences.

These new approaches to management training and development are being developed in response to the criticism of off-the-job training programmes and are often much more effective and less expensive than traditional formal training courses.

Step 7 Providing the leadership to make it all happen

Entrepreneurial leadership was described in some detail on page 187. It is just as important in transforming the mature company into a dynamic growth-orientated business. Many entrepreneurs find it difficult to become the sort of leaders that successful business requires because they are often too egocentric and prone to wanting everyone to do as they are told. Successful business leadership is about improving the business through motivating and supporting other people: in many cases this means a change in entrepreneurial behaviour. The best leaders are coaches, facilitators and role models, not control freaks.

A recent US research study showed that 80 per cent of business development initiatives fail because the entrepreneur or CEO fails to practise what they preach. They don't 'walk the talk'.

Let me end with an example of what I mean. I recently visited an entrepreneurial MD who had been trying to improve customer service but found it difficult. When in front of his sales team I asked him when he had last personally visited and spoken with customers, he coughed nervously and muttered something under his breath. 'Sorry, I didn't quite get that,' I said. He had to admit it was more than two years ago.

The message he delivered to his team was 'Don't watch my lips, watch my feet.'

So business leaders have to ask themselves what message the staff are picking up from the deeds of top management in relation to any particular business priority. Providing the right role model is vitally important.

In summary, if you seriously want to develop and grow your business then learn the lessons from our successful entrepreneurs. Those who have engaged seriously in total business development, people like Terry Bramall, Dick Watson, David Sheepshanks, Martin Vincent, Mareena

Purslow, William Mow, David Latham, Peter Saunders, Joe Mogodi, Tom Potter, Phil Crane, Mary Conneely, Simon Keats and Tom Hunter, are now leaders in their respective business sectors.

These are the entrepreneurial heroes. I hope that now you have read this book you are ready to become part of their 'company of heroes'.

thirteen

survival

- The case of Mr George
- Causes of company failure
- Symptoms of decline
- A survival plan
- Personal survival

It might come as a surprise to some that it is possible to be entrepreneurial even in survival. If entrepreneurship is about building long-term value, then keeping the business on track is a key part of that task. When the going gets tough, entrepreneurs need to get going.

Every business enjoys periods of success and difficulty; that is just the way it is, so entrepreneurs need not feel ashamed about it. The trick is to spot the signs that you might be getting into difficulty early enough for you to manage your way through it.

That's the good news. The bad news is that if you don't then your business is almost certainly doomed to failure.

This broad picture can be applied to almost any industry you can think of. Whatever happened to John Brown's shipyard, William Morris's Nuffield Motors or, for that matter, Pan American Airlines? Incidentally, for those interested in a little nostalgia a good pub game is to reflect upon: 'I wonder what happened to…?'

Very few companies last more than 50 years. They end up being smothered beneath the weight of 'company men' and the committees and systems they love to construct. The exceptions are the companies that invariably have found some way to keep the original entrepreneurial spirit alive or managed to rekindle it before it is too late.

Put it another way. A firm that fails to promote entrepreneurial behaviour among its own staff, giving entrepreneurial talent recognition and scope, is doomed.

Since Chapter 11 we've been considering how best mature (or maturing) firms can encourage and mobilize entrepreneurial skills from within. In this chapter we look at how they can help failing firms survive and turn around their fortunes.

The case of Mr George

Let's begin by looking at a real-life horror story I came across in the late 1980s. To save embarrassment I have changed a few names.

The firm made soft furnishings and had a turnover of £10 million a year. It wasn't a classic case of industrial maturity in that the firm had lost the entrepreneurial drive it started with without as yet creating top-heavy systems. But there are lessons enough here for everyone.

Mr George was the chairman of this English family business. He insisted on everyone calling him by his first name, in a time-hallowed tradition. Previous generations of the family had built up the firm until it had become a reasonably big player. It had made good profits in its heyday, but these had now evaporated and the overdraft climbed steadily year by year. In fact, when I was called in, the total indebtedness of the company had reached £4 million.

The trouble was that Mr George was an eternal optimist and, with many of the symptoms of failure staring him in the face, chose to put the blame on the bank for refusing to extend his overdraft by another £1 million.

When I arrived, a quick look at the books made it clear that this was a company heading for the rocks. So overtime was stopped and salaries were cut by 10 per cent. (I never believe in hiding problems like this from the staff – the cut in wages and salaries made them appreciate the company was in trouble – something they would never have guessed from Mr George's hitherto cheerful demeanour.) We blocked all expenditure and started to try to uncover the true causes of the problems.

One was the message conveyed by the behaviour of the family. On the very same day the salary cuts were announced Mr George took delivery of a brand new Jaguar. Then his son, not an employee of the company, turned up at the company petrol pump and began to fill up his flash sports car. It transpired that the son and daughter regularly dipped into the petty cash tin in the office to meet their own personal expenses. This was a family who fiddled while Rome burned.

While Mr George subjected the traditional cloth-making business to benign neglect, he was spending company money to buy into businesses he knew little or nothing about. He proudly told me also that he was about to start a property development business. All this with the bank at the door panicking about its £4 million of unsecured loans and overdrafts.

The business was saved in the end, by selling off the Jaguar and the new acquisitions and by bringing in some new entrepreneurial talent to breathe new life into the dying business.

What were the lessons of the affair?

Mr George illustrates a common problem with family-owned firms. He had none of the entrepreneurial talent of the founder, but on top of that he was also bored with the company's core business, and thought that buying up other businesses was more fun because they were new and different.

This was disastrous because the core business in fact was generating positive cash flow whilst all the new non-core activities were losing money hand over fist. One result of being distracted by 'more exciting' opportunities was that the core business had gone into rapid decline and the positive cash flows had started to dry up, just when they were needed most to pay for the investment in the new companies. It is dangerous, but very common, for entrepreneurs to try to diversify away from core business problems, a policy that rarely works.

As we all know, simply investing money in an idea doesn't necessarily lead to success. You need the entrepreneurial flair and commitment to make a go of it, an element that was distinctly missing in the company.

Such talent that Mr George might lay his hands on should have been concentrated in the core business which was facing tough competition from cheap foreign imports. There was very little sign of any enthusiasm for the fight among the existing workforce and no overriding vision of what had to be done next. The sales and marketing department had cut back spending to save money and had effectively gone to sleep.

The sickness extended right through the company. The finance director was approaching retirement and preferred a quiet life to challenging Mr George. Although there was good financial information available it was to all intents and purposes being ignored.

Mr George's style – fiercely autocratic – discouraged fresh thinking and demotivated the few people in management who could see what the problems were and might do something about them.

Something was achieved. The old sales and marketing director was asked to leave, the non-core businesses were sold off and the debts reduced. A new designer was brought in to improve the appeal of the product in the marketplace, with some success. But restoring that original spirit of enterprise proved to be impossible. The firm survived but hardly prospered.

The story of Mr George I have told in some detail in the hope that some readers will recognize that their company is inflicted by a similar disease and start to do something about it while there is still time.

My belief is that the companies like Mr George's can be turned around by applying the methods used by the entrepreneurs we have met in the first half of the book, by getting back to fundamentals.

Causes of company failure

My view gets some support from the work of Stuart Slatter who examined 40 companies faced with crisis and identified the most common causes of failure in his excellent book *Corporate Recovery*, which was written in 1984.

His research, over several years, confirms much of my work with entrepreneurs in crisis:

Cause of company failure

Poor management	One-man rule, weak boards, undeveloped management
Inadequate financial controls	Cash, costs or budgets
Increasing competition	Price or product
High cost structures	Compared to competitors
Changes in market demand	Unseen and undetected
Adverse movements in commodity prices	Oil, gas or raw materials
Lack of marketing effort	Poor sales, weak marketing
'Big' projects	That go wrong and consume masses of cash and resources
Acquisitions	Attempting to diversify away from problems

His original work has just been updated and republished in 1999 as *Corporate Turnaround* and 15 years on the causes of company failure are still largely the same.

> Once we started to update the book we realized that the basic concepts and causes are as appropriate today as they were fifteen years ago.

Clearly no single cause totally explains failure; it is usually much more complicated than that. What is cause and what is effect? It can be like the chicken and the egg. However, some of these factors are normally present in most company failure situations.

Of his sample size of 40 companies, 30 successfully recovered and 10 failed. In manufacturing in 1999 we would need to add adverse exchange rates to this list of causes of company failure. Slatter found that there are normally six or seven of these factors present in crisis situations and twice as many present in crisis to non-crisis situations. This empirical work fits very much with my personal experiences.

So here is a tip that might save your business. *Get somebody you trust to look objectively at your business. If you have more than three-quarters of the symptoms outlined, call a company doctor in yesterday!* Once the business goes into decline I would also add that crisis denial in the early stage is a major cause of company failure.

Many of these causes could be prevented if entrepreneurs completed some of the tasks outlined in this book so far.

It is obviously much better to prevent problems rather than try to recover from them.

The way to help entrepreneurs to recognize and accept that they need to act to save the business is to present their current situation to them in the language they understand – bottom-line profit (or lack of it). Presenting their current reality in financial terms often leads to the acceptance of the need to take action. The only problem is that the traditional accounting tools of profit and loss, balance sheet and cash flow forecast are of limited help because they do not monitor some of the symptoms of failure, ie weak marketing or poor management.

Some of the strategies for helping entrepreneurs see the reality of their situation are outlined in the next section.

Clearly some of the measures to prevent companies getting into a crisis as outlined in this book will help prevent these problems:

Poor management	Picking the right people.
	Building a team.
	Dealing with underperformers – particularly family members.
Inadequate financial control	Four key financial control indicators.
	Monitoring your recipe.
	Hiring an accountant.
High cost structure	Cost reduction. System slippage.
	Working on the business. Redo strategy.
Changes in market demand	Removing blind spots. Redo your strategy.
Lack of marketing effort	Delighting customers. Recreating competitive advantage.
Big projects that consume cash and resources	Redoing strategy.
Competitive weaknesses	Cost reduction. Redo strategy.

Symptoms of decline

In order to help entrepreneurial businesses to survive it is important to recognize the difference between causes and symptoms of failure. Symptoms are the tell-tale signs that all might not be well, but they do not provide guidelines for the entrepreneur to take corrective actions. To do this it is necessary to identify the causes of the problem. For example, a frequent symptom of impending problems is a lack of cash. The cause could be a number of things, from simple overspending to a poor credit control system or simply lax management.

Symptoms of decline are often easier to detect than the true causes. Some of the symptoms of imminent problems which entrepreneurs should look out for include:

Increase in debt	An increase in the firms borrowing reflected in the gearing ratio. Owners/Borrowed funds is a widely recognized symptom of impending trouble.
Decrease in liquidity	Businesses fail because they simply run out of cash.
Decrease in profitability	Profits before tax showing a downward trend over time. It is helpful to calculate the profits as a percentage of sales.
Reduction in customer enquiries	Enquiry levels are declining over a period of time.
Sales conversion rates decrease	Conversion rates from quotes to customer order decline.
Customer complaints increase	Levels of customer complaints increase significantly over time.
Decreasing sales	Sales are decreasing over a period of time.
High staff turnover	People leaving regularly, particularly in the financial department, is often a sign of impending problems. It is not unusual for receivers to find unopened bills and warning letters stuffed into office filing cabinets.

Have you noticed any of these symptoms in your business?

The important thing to notice is the trends over time. This means you need to be realistic and not naïvely optimistic (like Mr George).

The famous company 'doctor' Sir Kenneth Cork once said that he had noticed several indicators in failing companies:

- A fountain in reception at head office.
- The chairman has been appointed to yet another industry advisory committee.
- Personalized number plates on directors' cars.
- The company announces a new 'world beating' product launch.
- The entrepreneur is spending most of the time improving his or her golf handicap or at the new villa in Majorca.

■ All expenditure, particularly personal and private, is charged to directors' expense accounts.

Clearly these symptoms are tongue in cheek, but they do remind us of the perils of taking the eye off the ball and living beyond the company's means.

Keeping the finger on the pulse of the business and reading the signs does not downgrade the art of entrepreneurship to that of a bureaucrat. A medical doctor routinely tests patients for pulse rate, blood, and other things dependent on the symptoms presented. Entrepreneurs do not need complicated or sophisticated control systems, but they do need to monitor their vital signs and act quickly.

When the entrepreneur notices some of the symptoms of decline, the whole business seems to go through a series of steps:

Stages of crisis	*Typical response*
1. Crisis observed through symptoms	'It's a short term blip.'
2. Crisis denial	'This is not really happening.'
3. Panic and fear	'How the hell do we get out of this?'
4. Remedial actions attempted	'Wish we had acted sooner.' Company either survives or fails.

The difficulty for entrepreneurs is that it is often difficult to trace the true causes of problems from the symptoms, for several reasons:

■ They are personally too close to the problem.
■ They are personally in denial.
■ It's hard to be objective in a crisis.
■ The problem can have multiple causes.

A survival plan

Here is an outline survival plan I use to help companies survive.

Essential ingredients of a survival plan

1. Get control of the situation:

- Conserve all cash.
- Stop expenditures.
- Cut costs (not paper clips).
- Ensure the bank is on side.

2. Get support from key parties:

- staff;
- bank;
- customers;
- suppliers.

3. Redo the strategy:

- Cut out loss makers.
- Outsource non-core activities.
- Focus on core strengths.
- Redo product/market focus.

4. Improve existing processes:

- systems;
- quality;
- efficiency;
- customer service.

5. Financial management

- Ensure finance available.
- Reduce fixed costs/assets.

Personal survival

When the going gets really tough, you need to maintain your focus and resilience more than ever. Family and friends provide entrepreneurs with their comfort zones. Taking my children out for a day or simply having a long slow family meal on a Sunday afternoon helped me to keep things in perspective, when the going got tough for me.

My youngest daughter Penny talking excitedly of her adventures at her new school, with a beaming smile on her face, never fails to renew my spirit.

Heart-to-heart talks with my partner always seemed to help me in some of the darkest hours of my entrepreneurial career.

Other entrepreneurs engage in physical sports or take long walks. Make sure you maintain your physical and mental health during the stressful periods of survival. We all need to develop our own personal survival strategies to help us cope with trying to survive in business.

If you want to work at improving your confidence in sorting out difficult survival problems, here is an approach known as brief therapy.

Brief therapy is based on the assumptions that whatever may have caused your problem, you are the one who has its solution. It sidesteps the issue of what caused the problem. It seeks a shortcut that leads directly to a solution.

It does this by trying to help you identify hints of the solution in what you already do and know and then build up your confidence to put them into practice.

At the heart of the brief therapy's strategy are two questions. They are known as 'the miracle question' and 'scaling'.

It goes like this: 'Imagine that while you are asleep one night a miracle happens and your problem disappears; when you wake up, what will be the signs that a miracle has happened?'

The miracle question helps you identify parts of the solution to your problem; the scale question helps you to put them into practice. The scale question has two parts. First you have to say how bad your problem is on a scale from 0 to 10. Zero is the worst it has ever been, and 10 is the morning after the miracle. Scaling is used to help you identify the things that keep you off the bottom of the scale and things you could try to do to move yourself up the scale – even if only by half a point.

By identifying what you can do yourself, you get a double benefit. You get better but you also get more confident because you have made the improvements yourself and you can work out how to bring about further improvements. This makes progress very rapid.

Have a go; it certainly worked for other entrepreneurs I know and for me personally.

in **the company of heroes**

In the Company of Heroes started with the premise that entrepreneurship is vital for the future health of any economy, that too little is known about how entrepreneurs operate, and that individuals, organizations and maybe even society as a whole would benefit from understanding how the best entrepreneurs go about building and sustaining a business.

I also wanted to challenge public perceptions about entrepreneurs. The common equation of entrepreneurs with spivs and racketeers means that in the UK at least entrepreneurs often feel like second-class citizens – villains, not heroes. By now you will know that the opposite is actually true. Entrepreneurs are people who take risks in the pursuit of a dream and by doing so create wealth for society and jobs for those who need work. Astonishingly they often build this wealth from practically nothing. Despite this, they do not seek accolades; they simply want to be treated with dignity and given a little respect.

Of course, they are not all saints, but that is true of any professional group, be they doctors, lawyers, teachers, bankers, or even politicians!

By encouraging them to tell their stories and share their wisdom, this book will have done much to correct any public misconceptions about what entrepreneurs actually do, and what motivates them. I hope it will also have provided real insights into the art of entrepreneurship.

In Chapter 1 we summarized the entrepreneurial process into three key processes, which continue throughout the entire life cycle of the business (Figure 14.1).

I hesitate to use the word 'process' in describing the business behaviour of entrepreneurs, because it summons up an image of the sort of business organization you read about in the traditional business book – one built around 'business plans' and 'business processes'. In fact, as we have seen, entrepreneurs do not behave in the way described by such books – their behaviour can only be properly described by creating a new vocabulary incorporating terms such as 'roughing it at the start', 'beg, borrow and befriend' and 'backfilling'.

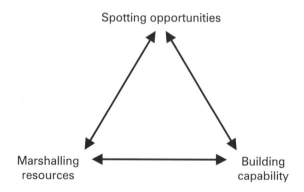

Figure 14.1 *The entrepreneurial process*

Entrepreneurs (with a few notable exceptions) are not products of an MBA course; instead they are mavericks and warriors who use their creative energies to build valued businesses, often from practically nothing.

Entrepreneurship is a natural process at the start-up and growth stages of any successful business. At this point there is lots of drive and energy. However, as we saw, it gets much more difficult to remain entrepreneurial through the mature stage of the business life cycle, and the failure to keep the entrepreneurial spirit alive results in eventual decline and failure. The encouraging message of this book is that entrepreneurial processes *can* be reintroduced into mature businesses, enabling them to revitalize and reinvent themselves, and even turn themselves around. Ailing businesses can be made healthy again using the same entrepreneurial approach displayed in the early days, but now spread much more widely throughout the company.

If entrepreneurship is truly a human creative act requiring vision, passion and obsessive commitment, there seems little point in finishing this book with checklists, models or even an elegant conclusion.

Instead, as this is a book for entrepreneurs by entrepreneurs, I think it best to end with three entrepreneurial stories. For me they capture the spirit and possibilities of entrepreneurship at the individual, organizational and societal level:

- Chris Keating is an enterprising individual from Scunthorpe.
- Leo DeGroot, Managing Director of Westernport Coolstores Pty Ltd of Victoria, Australia, used his entrepreneurial skills to transform the fortunes of his apple-growing business.
- Muhammad Yunus is an exceptional entrepreneur who helps millions of people daily in Bangladesh.

Chris Keating, C J Scanners

Chris Keating's business card reads 'Christopher Keating, boss of C J Scanners'.
When Chris started his business in 1998, his dream was to offer a service with a difference. He wanted to offer a very personal design and printing service for individuals and organizations that wanted their own high-quality stationery. All the design work he does himself. In fact the same is true of the printing side and the company administration, because C J Scanners is a one-person business.

Chris has designed and produced his own colour catalogue, which he uses to reach potential customers and convince them of the value for money he offers. You might think there is nothing remarkable about Chris, so here is a copy of a quotation he sent to my 11-year-old daughter Penny:

Dear Miss P Hall,

I am writing to you with a quote for the 30 colour letterheads which comes to £5.00. I hope you find it quite reasonable. You will also find enclosed all the types of paper you can have for the letterheads at no extra cost.

To see the designs arrange to meet Chris in the form room at dinner.

Yours sincerely

Chris Keating

You see, Chris is just 11 years old. He has launched his business while still at school, and is deadly serious about it. But how did he get started? Like many successful entrepreneurs he started in a small way:

I saved up £70 from Christmas and my birthday and I used this to buy a scanner. I then started to do scanning jobs for people. Before long people started to ask me if I could design and produce letterheads, business cards and leaflets, something I could do on my home computer, and they seemed to like what I produced. It just expanded from there.

Now he carries his sales brochure, order pad and samples around the school:

I go round the dining room showing people my stuff and taking orders.

His business is not confined to the school dining hall. He has won a contract to publish the local church magazine and is making modest profits. He already has plans to use them to develop the business.

> I am going to reinvest them in better equipment and a new computer, so I can take the next step forward and offer my customers a better service.

One thing is clear: this is not a schoolboy doing favours for his friends or running a hobby. Chris is so serious about building his business professionally that he booked himself on a one-day small business start-up programme with adults being run on the day after he broke up for the summer holidays. To look the part among the other businesspeople on the course he insisted his grandmother had his suit cleaned and pressed.

And Chris has already mastered some of the basic entrepreneurial skills. When my daughter offered to help him with his administration, he declined, saying:

> This is a one-person business at present, I need to keep my costs under control, but can I interest you in some birthday invitation cards designed specially for you?

Chris reminds me of another school-boy entrepreneur, who established a well-known business – Virgin.

Leo DeGroot, Westernport Coolstores Pty Ltd

Traditional food producers are under pressure in Australia. Here, as elsewhere, the cities and towns have seen a proliferation of popular fast food chains, while supermarket shelves are crammed with prepackaged snacks. As in most developed countries, there are worries about the long-term health implications of diets over-rich in fat, sugar and salt.

In the shorter-term it is the farmers and the fruit-growers who have most to worry about. To make matters worse for them there has been a steady increase in imported produce from neighbouring developing countries, amid accusations that these countries are 'dumping' surplus fruit and vegetables onto the Australian market.

In light of these two issues, Westernport Coolstores Pty Ltd, a quality apple-growing and marketing company based in up-country Victoria, has embarked on some very innovative research and development, seeking to go with the grain of market trends towards snack foods, rather than hoping there will be a spontaneous swing back to traditional fresh foods.

The company began by posing internally a number of questions:

- If fresh fruit could be packaged like lollies (sweets in the UK, candy in the US), would more children eat it?

■ If such a product were achievable, could it be commercialized?
■ Would such a product attract markets overseas?

Answering these questions – all in the positive – has led to the development of a fresh fruit snack product, which they have named 'Snack Apple'. Basically, the apples are peeled, cut into chunks, and then coated with a novel preservative coating, made of entirely natural vegetable gum, which gives the fruit snack a shelf life of 14 days. These coated apple chunks are then packaged to appeal not only to the fast food customer but also to the school-age market.

Further market research found that the idea of fresh food which stays fresh, married to attractive packaging, would also appeal to many potential customers in the adjacent Asia Pacific region, particularly Japan. So Westernport is now developing a potentially lucrative outlet in these countries.

The man behind this entrepreneurial response to a potentially fatal shift in the market is Leo DeGroot, the Managing Director of Westernport. In February 1999 he estimated that in its first year, 'Snack Apple' would generate sales of A$600,000 in Australia and New Zealand, and up to A$400,000 in exports. In all it is good news for a rural area of Victoria plagued by job scarcity and unemployment – and without the entrepreneurial flair of Leo DeGroot and his colleagues it would never have happened.

Muhammad Yunus, The Bank of Grameen

There are many ways to die, but somehow dying of starvation is the most unacceptable of all. This is certainly the view of Muhammad Yunus, who used to teach economics to students in Bangladesh until one day he asked himself what good elegant theories were, when people were dying on the streets outside. He decided to become a student again, not by going back to college but by turning the streets themselves into his university.

He came across one near-destitute woman making bamboo stools, sitting in the dirt while her children ran naked in the yard. When he asked her how she paid for the bamboo canes that were her main business cost, she unveiled the source of her poverty. She depended on local moneylenders who charged her a staggering 10 per cent *per day* in interest. As a result she made one penny on every stool she produced, while the moneylenders made themselves rich. A little more research uncovered 42 other desperate families in the area, all in debt to the moneylenders. Between them they owed just £17. All this misery for £17!

Yunus concluded that there was a need for a bank prepared to lend to these small producers at a rate of interest equivalent to that enjoyed by established big businesses. At a stroke poverty would be relieved and the poor given a decent chance to climb out of the trap they found themselves in. The problem was that Yunus knew nothing about running a bank. Undeterred, he decided he would simply have to learn as he went along.

The bank he founded operated on revolutionary principles. His clients – the poor and dying – were required to show how poor they were, not how rich, in order to qualify for a loan. There was a risk involved in this approach and conventional banks would certainly not have taken it.

But in practice Yunus found he had stumbled onto a formula which made eminent business sense. To his amazement and surprise he found that repayments by people without collateral were much better than those whose borrowings were secured by enormous assets. Over a period of 12 months 98 per cent of all loans to the poor were repaid, way above the average for bank loans. Apparently the poor knew this was the only opportunity they might have to break out of their cycle of poverty and were all the more punctilious in repaying the debts on time and in full.

Yunus began his work in Bangladesh 30 years ago. His bank, the Bank of Grameen (Grameen means village in the local language), now has 12,000 employees and 1,112 branches in Bangladesh. The staff still go out to meet the customers, and encounter 2,300,000 face-to-face on their own doorsteps.

Most of the customers are women, because they are more in need but also because they prove more dependable. The bank argues that this is not simply because they are closer to the children. Despite the fact that many of these women cannot read and write, the bank believes they have the vision to see further than the men, and are willing to work harder to achieve their goal.

Ammajan Amina provides a good example of the grit displayed by these women and of the role 'micro-credit' has played in changing lives. Before the bank came along she was a street beggar. Her husband had fallen ill and all the family's money had been spent trying to find a cure, without success.

When he died she was reduced to begging, a humiliation for a proud woman. Then more disaster struck. Her house was destroyed by the monsoon and she found her eldest child dead under the rubble.

She knew that no moneylender would give her credit and without some capital she had no chance of setting up any enterprise, no matter how small. When the Bank of Grameen opened up she presented herself as one of the first customers, secured a small loan and started making baskets. That gave her the means to provide for her children and help rebuild her life.

Ammajan remained a bank customer all the way through to her death last year. Now her daughter continues to come to Grameen for help and support.

In setting up the Bank of Grameen Muhammad Yunus has created something of value, an institution that really helps people stand on their own two feet, and he did it starting with practically nothing himself, an example of true entrepreneurship in practice. The story suggests that developing countries suffering from terrible poverty can begin to create the wealth they need without massive injections of capital from western banks and institutions. Which means – like the clients of the Bank of Grameen – they can avoid shackling themselves with massive debt. The lesson seems to be that entrepreneurial ingenuity can in itself turn poor societies around.

These three stories show why I consider entrepreneurs to be 'heroes'. They capture the true nature of entrepreneurship much more elegantly than I ever could.

If you are planning to join them, then the very best of luck and good fortune. If you are already an entrepreneur and were seeking new inspiration from this book then I sincerely hope you found it.

May the entrepreneurial force be with you.

references

Preface

Hall, D (1997) Recognizing, Understanding and Supporting Entrepreneurs, Scottish Enterprise, Glasgow. The original entrepreneurial models were first developed in a research project with successful Scottish growth companies sponsored by Dr Brian McVey of Scottish Enterprise.

The research was repeated with South Yorkshire companies one year later, sponsored by Christopher Duff of Rotherham Chamber of Commerce Training and Enterprise.

Chapter 3

Case, N (1989) The origins of entrepreneurship, *Inc. Magazine,* June. Sources of new opportunities were taken from this article, which was based on a study of 500 fast-growth companies.

Chapter 5

Hall, D (1992) *The Hallmarks for Successful Business*, Mercury Books (now Management Books 2000), London. This was my first attempt at trying to capture and understand how UK businesses developed.

Stanley, T J and Danko, W D (1996) *The Millionaires Next Door*, Longstreet Press, Marietta, USA. This book provides fascinating insights into how American entrepreneurs create valued businesses by being frugal.

Chapter 6

Warnes, B (1992) *The Genghis Khan Guide to Business*, Osmosis Press, London. This is an inspiring guide to controlling a business and is recommended reading for any entrepreneurs wanting to sleep easier in their beds.

Chapter 7

De Gaus, A (1997) *The Living Company*, Nicholas Brealey, London. This book won the Financial Times Booz Allen and Hamilton Global Business Book Award for the most insightful management book in 1997. It is an excellent introduction to how large companies survive in the long term by remaining entrepreneurial.

Chapter 9

Hall, D (1997) *Innovation in Export*, Development Board for Rural Wales, Newtown, Wales. My research into the success patterns of Welsh exporters identifies some of the key lessons learned by successful export entrepreneurs.

Chapter 10

Egan, G (1993) *Adding Value*, Jossey-Bass, San Francisco. Professor Egan's book outlines many of the key issues in managing a business and coping with change, based on his experiences working with some of the world's largest and most successful businesses.

Mazzarol, T (1999) *Case Studies of Small Business Success*, Curtin Business School, Perth, Australia. Dr Tim Mazzarol, of Curtin Business School, uses the Hallmarks models to identify key success factors in Australian growth businesses.

Chapter 12

Gates, B (1999) *Business @ the Speed of Thought*, Penguin Books, London. Bill Gates' latest book tells how businesses use a digital nervous system to unite all systems and processes under one common infrastructure, allowing companies to make quantum leaps in efficiency, growth and profits.

Kotter, J P and Heskett, J C (1992) *Corporate Culture and Performance*, The Free Press, New York. This book identifies the key factors for success and failure in businesses. It relates corporate culture to the performance of the business.

Chapter 13

Slatter, S (1984) *Corporate Recovery*, Penguin, Harmondsworth. This excellent book identifies successful turnaround strategies in failing businesses. Stuart Slatter has updated his earlier work and written *Corporate Turnaround* (1999, Penguin, Harmondsworth) with David Lovett which reviews how entrepreneurs manage companies in distress.

talk **with the author**

You are invited to contact the author David Hall direct via e-mail if you:

- have any questions you want to put to him directly about anything in this book;
- want to share any of your personal entrepreneurial experiences that mirror this book's content;
- require any further information about any of the processes presented.

David can be contacted at: Davidhall.uk@btinternet.com

index